Tuskegee Airmen

1941-1945

Produced by
The Chicago "DODO"
Chapter

Life To Legacy, LLC

Tuskegee Airmen 1941-1945
by: the Chicago "DODO Chapter"
Copyright © 2013 (revision)

ISBN 13: 978-0-939654-05-2
IBSN 10: 193965405X

Printed in the United States
10 9 8 7 6 5 4 3 2 1

Cover reproduction by:
Jennifer LuVert,
Forerunners Ink LLC
forerunnersink.com

Edited by: Shelby Westbrook

Reproduced version published 2013 by:
Life To Legacy, LLC
P.O. Box 1239
Matteson, IL 60443
(877) 267-7477
www.Life2Legacy.com

DEDICATION

To the men and women who worked so hard to make the Tuskegee experience a success. Those of us who were a part of this great effort, it will renew old memories. To those who were unaware of this large group of Black men and women who served in the military, this book will give further knowledge of Black History.

The following named individuals are to be thanked for their encouragement and their financial assistance:

Robert Martin	Carl Ellis
George Taylor	Lyman Webber
Richard Highbaugh	Ralphy Orduna
Harold Hurd	Henry Hervey
Quentin Smith	Felix Kirkpatrick
Shelby Westbrook	William Farley
William Dean	Leon Bowden
Roy Chappell	Laverne Shelton
Bill Blinkley	Frank Banks
Jesean Phillips	Joseph Merton

Robert L Martin
100th FS Itay 44 '45

Edited By
Shelby Westbrook

Published By:
Tuskegee Airmen Inc.   Chicago (Do Do's) Chapter
P.O. Box 19063   Chicago, Illinois 60619

On the Cover:
Standing: Ace Lawson, Charles Hall, Howard Baugh, Graham Smith, George Bolling, Price D. Rice
Kneeling: John Rodgers, John Gibson, Elwood Driver

General Daniel (Chappie) James, Jr., is Commander in Chief, North American Air Defense Command (NORAD), a bi-national military command consisting of United States and Canadian air defense forces. He also serves as Commander in Chief, United States Air Force Aerospace Defense Command (ADCOM), the United States element of NORAD.

FROM THESE ROOTS

From the ideology of Freedom of Worship in the American Revolution through the shattering social catharsis of Viet Nam, the story of the Black American in the Military has been compelling. Perhaps in no other world society has a color-coded citizen been forced to wage such an intensive, relentless and continuing battle simply for the right to fight for his birthright!

TUSKEGEE'S AIRMEN ultimately waged their military battles in the newest dimension of warfare — in the air. We thereby wrote our own unique chapters in Black Military History. A continuum. We were, in this respect, falling in behind the honored Cavalry and Infantry units of our forefathers. The storied 9th and 10th Cavalry, famed as the Buffalo Soldiers. In the Infantry, the 24th and 25th Regiments, and precedent to the Black Soldier in an integrated military who would yet find no surcease to being FROM THESE ROOTS. Some ramifications are found in but a few vignettes.

John Steward Sloan — Shelby Westbrook

BLACKS IN THE ARMY AIR FORCES DURING WORLD WAR II, a well documented 1977 publication of the Office of Air Force History, refers extensively to a study of Blacks in World War I by the Army War College. A landmark conclusion in this study was that Blacks did not develop leadership abilities because "Blacks evolved from mediocre African ancestors (and) coupled with the slavery experience, did not have the mentality to compete with Whites." This 1925 revelation fostered an obvious policy position within the military, that the Black man needed White leadership in order to succeed as members of the armed forces.

Studies and conclusions such as these are considered as deliberate attempts to discredit the Black man as a potential leader. It followed that Black officers demonstrating leadership abilities in the military might well intensify America's social problems. Their status and influence would contrast dramatically with the country's contemporary civilian racial patterns. In 1925, domination of the military establishment by Southern Whites was almost total. It was imperative that they extend and solidfy the prevailing view that Black people were mentally inferior to Whites and incapable of military leadership. Much actual military history aside.

One very interesting "aside" is found in the 1972 ARMY LINEAGE SERIES, INFANTRY—PART I (Office of the Chief of Military History). This publication records the regimental units in number sequence from the 1st through the 23rd THEN SKIPS TO THE 26th which was activated in 1905. Somehow omitted in this "historical lineage" are the 24th and 25th, Black regiments activated in 1867! These stellar Black units served through the Indian wars, the Spanish-American conflict, saw duty in the Phillipines. In Korea, 1950-51, the 24th's Sgt. C. H. Carleton and Pfc. Wm. Thompson were awarded the Congressional Medal posthumously.

The Spanish-American War provided other examples of Black participation and leadership somehow minimized by some official historians. In Cuba, four Black regular Army regiments were comanded by White Officers. Additionally, there were four regiments of Black volunteers with a majority of Black Officers. The 8th Illinois Infantry regiment was commanded by Black Col. John R. Marshall with no Whites of rank in the unit. In WW I, the 8th became the 370th regiment of the 93rd Division. This totally Black outfit was well decorated when returning from France led by Col. Franklin Denison. For the DSC there were 21 recipients, another 68 soldiers wore the Croix de Guerre. The 93rd Division had the unique distinction of seeing ALL FOUR of its regiments awarded this distinctive French decoration.

In 1940, with WW II just over the horizon, the War Department was once again confronted with the demand that Blacks be accepted for training and equal assignment opportunities in all branches of the military. Ultimately the Black community responded as one voice attacking the military's final bastion reserved "for Whites only," the Army Air Force. Leading the attack was the NAACP, plotting the strategies, recruiting the media and organizational "support troops" determined that the Air Force walls of racial exclusion would come tumbling down! TUSKEGEE AIRMEN know from personal, often bitter experience, the obstacles confronted as we met the challenge. As had others in the other branches of the service, teh Black Airmen succeeded against almost impossible odds; the military establishment's racism, the demanding skills of combat flying, the enemy — in White communities stateside — in the air over Africa, Italy, and Europe. Some 450 Black pilots saw combat duty in WW II with some 150 earning the highest award of the Air Force, the DISTINGUISHED FLYING CROSS.

Black leadership in the Air Force was outstanding with Generals B. O. Davis, Jr., and the late Daniel (Chappie) James, Jr., the epitome. Gen. James scaled the heights in Command while Gen. Davis fought unheralded battles in confrontation with the Washington military/political establishment. Gen. Noel Parrish, one time CO at TUSKEGEE, best represents those Whites who were sensitive to the struggle. Speaking of the 99th Fighter Squadron, the 332nd Fighter Group and the 477th Bomber Group, Gen. Parrish stated:

> ". . . considering all circumstances I thought they did better than anyone had a right to expect."

A true recording of history is both revealing and effectively conclusive. The racist arguments of Black inferiority are destroyed. But detractors persist and in the 70's, some are advancing a racial Sickle Cell trait as the new device to limit duty assignments and advancement of Blacks in the military. It's reported that the Air Force and some airliens are currently disqualifying Blacks from flight duty when testing reveals the sickle cell trait. Once again our "roots" command a response, this time from Sr. Flight Surgeon, Col. Vance Marchbanks, Ret. Col. Marchbanks has initiated and conducted a broad study of more than 1,300 Black Air Force flying officers together with members of the TUSKEGEE AIRMEN. The resultant medically supported conclusion is that a sickle cell trait SHOULD NOT BE DECISIVE in disqualifying Blacks from flight duty.

Individual and social sentiments regarding the country's military policy will vary with time and circumstance. Remaining steadfast is the Black American's determination to continue the fight for Freedom and Equality, whenever the time, whatever the circumstance.

BENJAMIN O. DAVIS, JR.
Lieutenant General, USAF (Retired)

General Davis was born 18 December 1912 in Washington, D.C. He graduated from Central High School in Cleveland, Ohio, and later the University of Chicago.

He entered the U.S. Military Academy in July 1932. Graduated from the U.S. Military Academy (1936) and commissioned a Second Lieutenant of Infantry.

Assignments: In June 1937, after a year as Commander of a Fort Benning, Georgia, Infantry Company, he enrolled as a student at the Infantry School there, graduated a year later and assumed duties as professor of Military Science at Tuskegee Institute, Tuskegee, Alabama. In May 1941, he entered Advanced Flying School at nearby Tuskegee Army Air Base and received his wings in March 1942. He transferred to Army Air Corps in May 1942. As Commander of the 99th Fighter Squadron At Tuskegee Army Air Base, he moved with his unit to North Africa in April 1943, and later to Sicily. In October 1943, he returned stateside to assume command of the 332nd Fighter Group at Selfridge Field, Michigan and returned to Italy with the organization two months later.

From June 1945 to the following March, he commanded the 477th Composite Group at Godman Field, Kentucky, later assuming command of the field. In March 1946, he performed double duty as Commander of the 332nd Fighter Wing and Base Commander at Lockbourne Army Air Base, Ohio.

After attending Air War College in 1949 - 50, he was assigned to Deputy Chief of Staff for Operations, Headquarters, USAF, Washington, D.C. He served in various capacities until July 1953. He completed the Advanced Jet Fighter Gunnery School at Nellis Air Force Base, Nevada in November prior to assuming new duties as Commander, 51st Fighter-Interceptor Wing, Far East Air Forces (FEAF), Korea.

He served as Director of Operations and Training at FEAF Headquarters, Tokyo, Japan, from 1954 until 1955. He assumed the position of Vice Commander, 13th Air Force with additional duty as Commander, Air Task Force 13 (Provisional), Taipei, Formosa.

In April 1957, he arrived at Ramstein, Germany, as Chief of Staff, 12th Air Force, USAFE. With the transfer of the 12th Air Force to Waco, Texas, in December 1957, he assumed new duties as Deputy Chief of Staff for Operations, Headquarters, USAFE, Wiesbaden, Germany, until July 1961 when he became Director of Manpower and Organization, Deputy Chief of Staff for Programs and Requirements, Headquarters, USAF in February 1965 and remained in that position until his assignment as Chief of Staff, United Nations Command and U.S. Forces in Korea, in April 1965. In August 1967, General Davis assumed command of the 13th Air Force at Clark Air Base in the Republic of the Philippines.

In August 1968,, He became Deputy Commander in Chief, U.S. Strike Force Command, Mac Dill Air Force Base, Florida.

Decorations: USAF Distinguished Service Medal; U.S. Army Distinguished Service Medal Silver Star; Legion of Merit with two Oak Leaf Clusters; Distinguished Flying Cross; Air Medal 2/4 Oak Leaf Clusters; Air Force Commendation with two Oak Leaf Clusters; European-African-Middle Eastern Campaign Medal with 8 Bronze Service Stars; World War II Victory Medal; Korean Service Medal; Air Force Longevity Service Award with one silver and one bronze Oak Leaf Cluster; United Nations Service Medal; Republic of the Philippines Legion of Honor.

DEPARTMENT OF TRANSPORTATION
FEDERAL AVIATION ADMINISTRATION
AVIATION EDUCATION STAFF

NEGRO FLIERS

In 1939 the Civilian Pilot Training Program opened the field of aviation to the Negro. In the 36 years which had passed since Kitty Hawk, individual blacks had learned to fly, but in common with all pioneer pilots, except those in the services, they logged their hours the hard way, and when certificated, found no welcome in the career field. The hope was that now they might.

For example, in 1928, Mr. Charles Alfred Anderson of Bryn Mawr, Pa., bought an airplane for $3,000 and took instruction at an airport near his home, paying $10.00 an hour for his flying time. Four years later, in 1932, he acquired his commercial pilot's certificate—undoubtedly the first of his race to do so, although there is no official record—and he estimated that the small piece of paper had cost him more than $6,000. (This included the price of a second airplane.)

In 1932, of course, aviation was probably at the lowest ebb in its existence and the picture was bleak indeed—no jobs and no future for anybody—let alone an ambitious young Negro. However, Mr. Anderson managed to stay with it and by 1939[1] was in business. He and a partner were operating a Piper Cub mounted on floats from a seaplane base at the foot of Second Street, S.W. and the Potomac River in Washington, D.C., and a WACO cabin plane from Beacon Field in nearby Virginia, when the CPTP was announced. Later he was able to put his knowledge and experience to good use helping to get the Program started at Howard University and became a flight instructor there. Mr. Anderson has continued to stay with aviation and today is one of the Regional Directors of Negro Airmen International, an organization of professional fliers.

Howard was one of the six Negro colleges which took an active part in the CPTP. The others were:

Tuskegee Institute, Tuskegee, Ala.
Delaware State College, Dover, Del.
Hampton Institute, Hampton, Va.
North Carolina Agricultural and Technical State University, Greensboro, N.C.
West Virginia State College, Institute, W. Va.

There was a scattering of Negroes in many other schools throughout the country[2] and two Negro non-college units in the Chicago area, one of them

---

[1] In 1939, according to the Bureau of the Census, eight Negro pilots held Commercial ratings.

[2] Out of a class of 50 at the University of Minnesota, the first student to solo was a Negro. At Joliet Ill., in a non-college unit, the student to make the highest grade was a Negro, Earl Franklin.

operated by a young woman, Miss Willa Brown. This was the Coffey School of Aeronautics, located at the Harlem Airport, Oak Lawn, Illinois, named for Miss Brown's husband, Cornelius Coffey, one of the nation's earliest certificated flight instructors who, additionally, held the airplane and engine mechanic's certificate. The Coffey School offered the full range of CPTP and War Training Service courses, and was the hub of Negro Civil Air Patrol activity after that program was conceived in 1941.

Photo courtesy Edward A. Gibbs

Miss Willa Brown and some of her students. Miss Brown owned and operated the Coffey School of Aeronautics and carried out the full range of CPTP and War Training Service courses.

Tuskegee Institute, largest of the group, became one of the CAA's most important contractors. In the early days of the Program when 400 colleges were offering primary flying, advanced work was restricted to some 60 Centers, most of them long established in the business. Though a late comer on the horizon, Tuskegee was given Center status in 1940, and was one of the few educational institutions to provide flight as well as ground instruction at that time.

By 1941 the Institute had five flight instructors, one of them the aforementioned Charles Alfred Anderson, who was recruited by CAA and sent to Chicago in the summer of 1940 to qualify for the secondary rating. That summer the Institute had a total of 12 airplanes—eight Piper Cubs for the elementary classes and four WACOs for the advanced. The next year, Stinson, Howard, and Piper cabin aircraft were added for the commercial pilot courses.

After a year and a half the primary classes were enlarged from 15 students each to three annual groups of 30. With one exception the secondary quota began and remained at 10 students per session, spring, summer and fall. This quota was much too small and operated to the disadvantage of the CPTP'ers, many of whom were drafted by the Army before an opening was available in the advanced groups. This also proved to the disadvantage of the Air Force when larger numbers of cadets who had completed CAA secondary were needed.

The one exception was a special class of 30 convened in early 1941. At that time the Army planned, rather than set up a primary flying school exclusively for Negroes, to draw upon Tuskegee's CAA secondary graduates for cadet material, and provided the Institute with aircraft for this purpose. The 30 men chosen represented a cross-section of students from Hampton Institute, West Virginia State College, North Carolina Agricultural and Technical College and from Howard University as well as Tuskegee. Their physical examinations were given at Maxwell Field, Alabama, requirements being the same as for all aviation cadets.

Before this class was finished, however, the Air Force changed its mind and plans were announced to establish a military flight program at Tuskegee Institute, the candidates to be selected from men who had completed CPTP's secondary course of instruction. For some reason, however, only one of the 30 special students was included in the original class, but before the year was out they were all drawn in and became part of the 99th Pursuit Squadron, the first all Negro combat unit.

Ironically, Tuskegee almost didn't get into the Program at first because there was no airport within the requisite 10 miles. However, the Institute's President, Dr. Fred L. Patterson, and the Director of Mechanical Industries, George L. Washington, were resolved that their students should not be denied the opportunity to fly because of this technicality. With characteristic determination, Mr. Washington traveled to Washington and presented his case with such force and logic that an exception was made and on October 15, 1939, Mr. Hinckley notified Dr. Patterson that Tuskegee's flight training was approved for the Montgomery Airport, 40 miles away. For several months in early 1940, the trainees made the 80-mile trip almost every day, even though it took too much time from their other studies and was far too expensive for everybody. However, by March 1, at what seemed the point of no return, through the "never say quit" attitudes of Messrs. Patterson and Washington, a lease was seured on a tract of land about five miles from the campus. This was known as Kennedy Field.

From the very beginning those two gentlemen had made up their minds that the Institute should have an airport closer to its own grounds and began working toward that end. (Eventually they were successful, but it took some doing, and is a story in itself.) They started an alumni drive to raise the needed funds, but the money—$5,000—went toward the improvement of the Kennedy acreage which, between the alumni contributions, the students' own hard labor—they helped clear brush, cut down trees, fill holes, put up markers, lay out runways and build a two-plane hangar—and the whole-hearted cooperation of the CAA's Atlanta office, was finally made into an adequate flying field.

As soon as possible thereafter the commuting ended. Operations were transferred to the new site and in May the first class received their private certificates and were happily flying. However, the size of the Tuskegee program increased so rapidly that for a while secondary students had to use a field at Alabama Polytechnical Institute at Auburn, Ala., 20 miles away, driving back and forth in a station wagon. This was almost as unsatisfactory as the Montgomery arrangement but there was no alternative until Kennedy underwent further enlargement and all CAA training could carry on from that point.

Eventually Tuskegee was to operate three airports. The elementary field, Kennedy, which became known as No. 1, and was referred to frequently as the "mother field." Airport No 2, about four miles away, built with money borrowed by the Institute from the Julius Rosenwald Fund through the help of Mrs. Eleanor Roosevelt who was a member of the Board of Trustees. This was restricted to Army primary trainig of all Negro cadets under a contract with the War Department which stipulated that Tuskegee would provide instructors, aircraft and other facilities.

Airport No. 3 was all-military, built with appropriated funds and officially designated the Tuskegee Army Air Field (TAAF). Here it was that the new pilots learned combat techniques and received their wings and commissions.[1]

Tuskegee Institute participated in all the CAA-sponsored pilot training courses, beginning with the first CPTP session in 1939 - 40 until that Program's termination after Pearl Harbor, and on through the War Training Service which succeeded it and came to an end in late 1944.

Institute authorities estimate that about 400 students successfully complated CAA elementary, secondary, instructor, cross-country, instrument and flight officer courses; that under CAA War Training, approximately 500 enlisted student reservists were given ten (10) hours of dual flight indoctrination in light aircraft, and that 2,411 aviation cadets from all sources were sent to the Army Primary Flying School at Airport No. 2. All of this was carried on under contracts with the Civil Aeronautics Administration and the War Department.

In its initial course, the Institute set a record in the Southeast by passing 20 out of 20 students in ground school, all with exceptionally high grades, and then sending the same 20 through the flight tests to receive their private pilot certificates. Two of these were girls, Miss Mildred Hansen and Miss Mildred Hemmons, both residents of Tuskegee.

The excellent records made by these students on the written examination was attributed by the CAA to the strong teaching staff under the direction of Mr. Washington. Two of his students scored among the highest grades achieved in the entire 1939 - 1940 group of 10,000 in Civil Air Regulations, Meterology and Navigation. They were Alexander Anderson, who scored 100 on the CARs and 92 in the remaining subjects, and Charles Foxx[2] who averaged 97 per cent in each. Subsequent classes retained these high standards.

---

[1] A complete account of the activity at Tuskegee, the struggles and triumphs of the Negro flying men and their subsequent war records is given by Charles E. Francis in his book *THE TUSKEGEE AIRMEN*, published in 1955 by Bruce Humphries, Inc., Boston, Mass.

[2] Foxx became a career commercial pilot and at one time ran a fixed base operation at Glen Rock airport near Norfolk, Va., one of a small group of Negro pilots who were able to go into business for themselves as a result of their CPTP training.

Hampton Institute's advanced instructor contingent at Tuskegee in 1942.

The other Negro colleges, being smaller than Tuskegee were not equipped to operate on a similar scale. However, all of the CPTP courses at Tuskegee were available to elementary graduates of these schools.

Information supplied by their various Departments of Educaton show that;

between 1939 and 1942, a total of 197 men were certificated at Hampton Institute and more than half of them went on to Tuskegee where 20 became instructors in the advanced courses. Additionally, Hampton graduates comprised some two-thirds of the instructor force at the Institute's Army Primary Flying School.

Delaware State College, which took part in the CPTP for three years, has figures for only the first two; these show that 10 students were certificated the first year and 20 the second. The number who went into secondary training is not available.

North Carolina Agricultural and Technical State University had an enrollment of 60 between 1939 and 1942 and certificated all but 10. Many of its graduates took the advanced military training, were commissioned, and saw service both in Europe and the Pacific. Complete records on the accomplishments of these men are not available; something is known about the following three:

Lieutenant Calvin Harris, after service during the war, retired and became a civilian flight instructor.

Lieutenant Sam Bruce, one of the best known pilots in the group, was killed in action in Italy preparing for the American landing at Anzio Beach.

Lieutenant Theodore Wilson remained in the service. Immediately after the war an Air Force ROTC was established at the College and continues to this day, graduating annually about 25 officers. By 1960, Lieutenant Wilson had become Lieutenant Col. Wilson and was assigned to A&T as Professor of Air Science.

Howard University, In Washington, D.C. had a 1939 - 40 quota of 11 primary students, and a 1940-41 quota of 10. From the initial class, who were all certificated, three went into the advanced classes at Tuskegee; and an equal number from the second group followed the next year. By the time the third program was being organized, the country was at war and for many reasons, among them a lack of qualified applicants, the CPTP at that University came to an end.

Miss Dorothy Layne, student at West Virginia State College.

West Virginia State College, located at Institute, West Virginia, is a small school and in its CPTP years, 1939 through 1942, graduated 70 primary students, but what it lacked in numbers it made up for in achievements. It has the distinction of being the first Negro college to win CPTP approval. Credit for this goes to the school's President, John W. Davis who, always on alert for new opportunities for his students, sent Mr. James C. Evans, Director of Trade and Technical Education, and Mr. Joseph Grider, a faculty member, to Washington armed with a complete plan endorsed by state aviation officials. They presented it to the CAA and in record time the contract was in their hands.

West Virginia State enrolled a number of white trainees in its 1940 summer unit, which undoubtedly made it the first educational institution in West Virginia to integrate its classes.

Two young ladies, Miss Rose Agnes Rolls and Miss Mary L. Parker, were also enrolled that summer and both became qualified pilots.

West Virginia State had the only Negro CPTP Seaplane Unit, based in the nearby Kanawha River, and was the first Negro college to place its CPTP pilots — one man and one woman — in an established wing of the Civil Air Patrol.

It may also be said of West Virginia State that it helped integrate the Air Force. One of its CPTP students, George Spencer Roberts, after completing advanced work at Tuskegee in 1941, was the first Negro from his home State to be examined and accepted into the Air Force. He became a member of the famous 99th Pursuit Squadron and remained on active duty until retiring recently with the rank of Colonel.

It was on January 17, 1941, when the War department announced that Negroes would henceforth be accepted into the Air Force and trained in combat flying at Tuskegee Institute, and on March 19, 1941, the 99th Pursuit Squadron was activated officially. However, it was April 2, 1943, before the 99th boarded the evacuation train enroute to overseas duty. Its complement was 33 officer pilots (half of them CPTP graduates), a ground force of 400 officers and enlisted men, and 33 aircraft. In command was Lt. Col. Benjamin O. Davis, Jr., a West Point graduate who went through primary, basic and advanced military pilot training at the TAAF, Field No. 3.

In February 1944 the squadron became part of the 33d Fighter group, also in command of Colonel Davis, and began operations in Italy with the Twelfth Air Force, using P-40s to escort convoys, protect harbors and fly armed reconnaissance missions. In all its 200 escort missions the Group lost not a single bomber to enemy fighters. Later, the Group converted to faster planes — P-47s and P-51s, and operated with the Fifteenth Air Force from May 1944 to April 1945, protecting bombers that struck such objectives as oil refineries, factories, airfields, and marshalling yards in Italy, France, Germany, Poland, Czechoslovakia, Austria, Hungary, Yugoslavia, Roumania, Bulgaria and Greece. Also they made strafing attacks on airdromes, railroads, highways, bridges, river traffic, troop concentrations, radar facilities, power-stations and other targets.

The Group received a Distinguished Unit Citation for a mission made on March 24, 1945, when it escorted B-17s during a raid on a factory at Berlin, fought the interceptors that attacked the formation, and strafed transportation facilities while flying safely back to the base in Italy.

It was returned to the United States in October 1945 and inactivated the same month, having campaigned in Northern France, Southern France, the Appenines, the Po Valley, the Rhineland, Central Europe, Rome-Arno, and Normandy.[1]

In 1959, Col. Davis was made a Brigadier General, the first Negro to achieve that rank in the Air Force. In 1965 he was promoted to three-star rank, setting another precedent for the Negro in the military. Lieut. Gen. Davis retired from the service on February 1, 1970. After a series of sky-

[1]From The Air Force Historian and Air Force Combat Units of World War II.

jackings, holding of hostages and destruction of aircraft, President Nixon, the following September, appointed General Davis Director of Civil Aviation Security for the Department of Transportation.

Air Force Brigadier General Daniel James, Jr., Deputy Assistant Secretary of Defense for Public Affairs. General James learned to fly in the Civilian Pilot Training Program at Tuskegee Institute, completing all its courses. Later as a civilian flight instructor he taught Army Air Corps cadets, also at Tuskegee, until he became one himself. Commissioned a Second Lieutenant in July, 1943, General James was confirmed in his present rank on March 31, 1970.

On December 29, 1969, President Nixon nominated Colonel Daniel James, Jr., of Pensacola, Fla., a member of the 99th and 33d for the rank of Brigadier General and he was confirmed on March 31, 1970. General James, familiarly known as "Chappie" got his early flight training in the CPTP at Tuskegee, one of the many notable pilots who "first saw and put their hands on" airplanes as a result of that Program. His World War II record was outstanding, as was his record in Korea where, as a Command Pilot, he completed more than 100 combat missions. General James is presently on duty in the Pentagon, as Deputy Secretary of Defense for Public Affairs.

Commenting on Negro participation in the CPTP and the WTS, the distinguished educator George L. Washington, who directed the CAA Programs at Tuskegee Institute, and was in a position to oversee the military training, has this to say:

> We, at Tuskegee Institute, were much concerned to see that Negro college students, in the South particularly, be given the opportunity to take both the elementary and advanced flying courses offered by the Civil Aeronautics Authority.
>
> While in parts of the Nation, where segregation of the Negro was not legal, a few students might have gotten this training, nonetheless had Tuskegee not gone all out for aviation, I doubt that many would have become flight instructors or commercial pilots. I have serious doubts that were it not for the Civilian Pilot Training Program that there would have been a 99th Pursuit Squadron or a 33d Fighter Group.
>
> Tuskegee's efforts might well now be referred to as encouraging segregation because of the radical change in thinking today on civil rights. As a matter of fact, Negroes were split on Tuskegee's endorsement of and participating in the separate military pilot training operation, particularly in view of the NAACP's unsuccessful efforts to crack open Air Corps training at established military flying training bases. This was a hot issue in 1940. But so far as I and other officials at Tuskegee are concerned (as well as the Negro colleges which sent boys to Tuskegee for training) if we had to do it over again we would do the same thing — insist on separate training centers in order to insure that Negro students got a fair opportunity to demonstrate their ability as pilots. The few Negroes who would have been taken into the established units (at that time) would have been lost and few would have gotten through because of psychological deterrents and real obstacles set up for them.
>
> As I look back, any criticism of the Civil Aeronautics Administration that I might have would be that it did not grant programs to a greater number of Negro colleges, and increase the individual quotas. for despite the number of students turned out at Tuskegee, and the other Negro colleges, the draft board got too many qualified elementary fliers because of the limited number of advanced slots at Tuskegee.
>
> However, I feel that some consideration must be given to the fact that the CPTP and the WTS were really war programs, which meant that the CAA was not free to do what it might have done had the circumstances been different. Normally CAA was most cooperative in the development of the flight programs for our young Negro men at Tuskegee and, I understand, at the other colleges where the Program was instituted.

Reflections on the Tuskegee Experiment

An Interview with
Brig. Gen. Noel F. Parrish, USAF (Ret.)

by James C. Hasdorff

In the summer of 1941, Capt. Noel Francis Parrish was sent to Maxwell Field, Alabama, to plan for the opening of the Tuskegee Flying School for blacks. Thus the future general was launched into a long and challenging assignment, oftentimes marked by frustration and bureaucratic inconsistency, which nonetheless proved rewarding in the end. This article is based on an official USAF Oral History Interview that was conducted by the author in June 1974 at Trinity University in San Antonio, Texas.

A S so often happens, there are any number of cases where a quirk of fate casts a person into a prominent role in history. Undeniably, this occurred when Noel F. Parrish became a principal figure in the aviation training of blacks during World War II. Parrish himself noted that this was an accident that did not have anything to do with faith, attitude, or background, contrary to what many people assume.

Although he had an interest in the matter, he did not ask for the assignment. Instead, it was more or less an evolutionary process in which he initially gave support to a civilian pilot training school for blacks at the Chicago Municipal Airport while serving as an assistant supervisor at another civilian training school for air cadets at nearby Glenview, Illinois. A number of civilian flying schools had been set up in various areas of the country, mostly at colleges, and the school at Chicago and another at Tuskegee, Alabama, were appendant training areas established exclusively for blacks. This training arrange-

ment enabled the Air Corps to build a base for expansion without pulling a large number of pilots from tactical units to make them instructors.

Not only was it happenstance that Noel Parrish became a renowned instructor and leader of blacks, but also his being in the military was somewhat of a phenomenon in itself. Being the son of a Disciples of Christ minister, he had an aversion to war and considered himself a pacifist. In fact, while

Col. Noel F. Parrish, Commanding Officer, at his desk, 1943.

in Houston, Texas, he organized a Christian Endeavor Society in the church he attended and attempted to get the congregation to express its disapproval of war and segregation. On top of this, Parrish had been "very frightened" of airplanes and recalled how appalled he became when hearing of deaths associated with aircraft accidents.

But little did the idealistic young man realize at the time what fate had in store for him. Shortly after graduating from Rice Institute at 18, the Depression of 1929 drastically altered his lifestyle by forcing him out of jobs that he held in the Houston area. In order to avoid further the embarrassment of not having employment, young Parrish headed west to San Francisco to try his luck there. To his dismay, conditions were even worse, and the only source of salvation appeared in the form of an Army recruiter who would tell him each time he passed on the street that, "Son, we need you in the Army." After several days this finally affected the dispirited and unemployed young man, and he enlisted. He chose the Eleventh Cavalry at Monterey because it was the busiest and toughest outfit around, and he felt that this would improve his poor physical condition. Within eight months this proved true, and his weight rose from a puny 120 to a muscular 165 pounds.

Because of his improved physical condition and because life in the cavalry was "a rather monotonous existence," Parrish applied for the aviation cadet program. He still considered airplanes "suicidal instruments," but the pay was better as were prospects for the future.

15

Everything about it was a lot better than that $21 a month on a horse, which I found out could kill you also if you weren't reasonably lucky. I just went into it scared to death, but by that time it didn't matter that much. I would rather have a short life and an interesting one than a dull existence in a very routine occupation.

So the youthful-looking former cavalryman embarked on an aviation career, although he was almost eliminated during primary training. Following flying school he was commissioned a reserve second lieutenant and served a year at Fort Crockett, Texas. Afterwards, he was discharged in 1933, during the height of the Depression, and because job prospects were bleak, he decided to reenlist. Fortunately, Parrish was allowed to fly as an enlisted man, and he ferried aircraft and delivered engines for repair depots.

Finally, in 1935 Parrish was offered a regular commission, which he was somewhat reluctant to accept because he "did not have the tremendous admiration for all officers that most officers assumed enlisted men had," and because he greatly enjoyed flying everywhere without any additional responsibilities. An old master sergeant, however, took him aside and urged him to take it, as the opportunity might not again present itself. He accepted the sergeant's advice and resumed his flying position as a career regular officer. Then in 1938, when the Air Corps was undergoing some expansion, Parrish was picked out of a tactical squadron at Barksdale Field, Louisiana, and sent to

Randolph Field, Texas, to serve as a flying instructor. This seemingly insignificant event was ultimately to lead him to the training assignment at Tuskegee.

With the buildup of the civilian flying schools around the country, Parrish was moved over to Glenview, Illinois, where he gave his support to the black training effort at the Chicago Municipal Airport. He noted that the Air Corps ordered the Glenview facility to advise and assist this effort, but there were no specific instructions other than to take an interest in the endeavor. Moreover, his commander at Glenview "had no interest in the project whatever," and turned the matter entirely over to him. Although Public Law 18, approved 3 April 1939, stipulated that at least one of the civilian primary flying training schools would be designated for the training of blacks, the USAAC was very reluctant to train them because "it might result in political pressure being directed against the Secretary of War to admit Negroes into the Air Corps."[1]

Parrish went over to the airport to talk to the two black instructors and was very much impressed with them. He found that they were hardworking and sincere, but a bit puzzled as to what they were supposed to do for the Air Corps.

Parrish and the two instructors soon learned that the arrangement as it then existed was not going to satisfy the requirements of the law, and plans were soon made to open at least one installation that was strictly a black military primary flying school. This, of course, left important questions that needed to be answered. First,

where was the school to be placed? Second, where were the graduates to operate once they completed their training? In reality it became a matter of setting up a new air training force within the present white air force structure. It was to be a separate training unit and eventually a separate combat unit, all of which was so complex that Parrish often wondered whether it was ever to work at all.

In due time Parrish became involved in selecting a site for the black training unit and flew around the country looking for a flat spot near a city that would be suitable for an airfield. Finding an adequate geographical site was not the real problem, however, as Parrish soon found out. For example, while checking out possible locations near Chicago, he queried the Joliet Chamber of Commerce about locating the black installation near their city. He was informed in no uncertain terms that Joliet already had a prison in the area and that they did not need a black training base to further compound their problems. Finally, it was decided that the school at Tuskegee Institute would be developed into a location for Air Corps black cadets.

The original idea was to put the black installation in Chicago, probably because the only black congressman at that time was from the area. Because war was becoming imminent and because Washington did not want to become involved in Chicago politics, the decision was made to place it in the South. The real reason why it was not placed in Chicago, Parrish asserted, was that Washington feared that black "agitators" would interfere with the operation of the school. This was considered less likely to happen in the South, although it was admitted that troubles might arise with the Southern whites.[2]

BECAUSE Noel Parrish was the only Air Corps officer who had direct contact with the blacks, it was logical that he was selected as the supervisor of the black primary flying school at Tuskegee. At the time this was being constructed, work also had started on a basic and advanced school in the same area. Because the initial effort began at Tuskegee and because not too many people were seeking this type of work, it was decided to place the entire operation there. This turned out to be quite a burden on both the town and the Tuskegee Institute once the war started and once the training effort began to expand.

The complexity of this situation certainly could have been alleviated had integrated flying training been established from the beginning, and this was strongly advocated by influential blacks such as Judge William H. Hastie as well as the NAACP and black newspapers like *The Pittsburgh Courier* and *The Chicago Defender*. Although inte-

CLASS 44-B

Twin-engine training section, Tuskegee Army Air Field, 1944.

gration would have seemed easier and a more natural step, Parrish learned that few people in the Air Corps or out supported it at that particular time. Moreover, Southern senators and congressmen had seniority in nearly all committees, particularly in those dealing with the military, and could have thwarted any attempt at integration.[3]

Initially, Parrish was told that he would not be saddled with such a difficult non-combat task for the duration of the war, and that if he stuck with it, he would be given a P-51 squadron in Europe in a year or two. Although he felt these assurances were sincere, they never worked out. He was told to stay at Tuskegee.

As time went on, there were so many things done wrong, and it became necessary to know and to understand so much about the feelings and attitudes of individuals involved, both civilian and military at higher levels, and to know how to get decisions and to influence opinion, that I couldn't honestly say that I thought the thing would run properly after I got out. It was one of those syndromes where you get to thinking that you are the indispensable man.

During the critical part of the war when flying casualties were especially high, Parrish's distance from the scene of combat bothered him quite a bit; but as conditions improved and more pilots became available, he did not feel as much needed in combat as before. At any rate, he was generally too busy to think about it much.

As noted earlier, Parrish's initial assignment at Tuskegee was supervisor of the primary school, and he was soon moved over as director of training at a large military base that was being built nearby for black basic and advanced trainees. His transfer coincided with the movement of the first primary class to the basic training section of the new base, which was under the command of Maj. James A. Ellison. Ellison was burdened with increasingly difficult problems and was replaced by Col. (later Gen.) Frederick von H. Kimble who had been an aide and personal pilot to Gen. Douglas MacArthur. Parrish observed that Kimble also faced unresolved dilemmas.

He seemed to want to do his duty as a military man but wasn't quite clear in his mind as to whether his duty consisted of trying to make this thing a success, and thereby to saddle the Air Force with a problem as to what to do with the graduates, or whether he should inconspicuously allow it not to succeed, and thereby do everybody a favor.

Kimble, Parrish noted, tended to be hesitant, as were many base commanders, in enforcing new rules for integrated facilities on all bases. He was encouraged to think this way by many senior officers as well as political people. Because this was the South, it was deemed wise not to enforce integration too strictly and thereby incur the wrath of the natives. Segregated signs on restrooms and restaurant facilities were first taken down by base personnel and then ordered replaced on several occasions. This culminated in a difficult situation for the commander. Furthermore, when Secretary of War Henry L. Stimson and his deputy, Robert A. Lovett, had made an inspection tour of the facility at Tuskegee, Kimble voiced little hope for the success of the black training effort. He had not flown with them and did not in fact know much about their abilities, so that his opinions were "always guarded and vague" but not encouraging.

Because Parrish was included in some of the talks held with Stimson and Lovett, he soon learned that the two officials had a plan to send the first 35 or so black graduates, enough to comprise a squadron, to Liberia to fly sumbarine patrol along the African coast. This was not a very inspiring prospect for either the black pilots or for black people in general. It brought criticism from the black press and the NAACP once it became known. They felt it was merely an effort to shunt the black unit aside to insure that they would not receive credit for anything, all of which was considered to be almost an insult.

When the North African invasion began, the plan was changed to move into that area instead of Liberia. However, the Thirteenth Squadron did join other USAAF squadrons in North Africa, participated in the attack on Pantelleria Island, and then moved on into Italy. Evenutally, their numbers grew to a total of four squadrons, which at that time formed a group but later became a wing. All was under the command of Col. Benjamin O. Davis, who later in his career was to rise to the rank of lieutenant general.

Prior to the black squadron's move to North Africa, however, no thought was given to committing them directly into combat. Secretary Stimson, for example, informed Kimble that Washington considered Liberia to be a "quiet area," and that they hoped it would continue to remain that way. Parrish found Stimson to have a "highly paternalistic" attitude toward the blacks and other minority groups, and he simply considered them people toward whom any gentleman would take a patient and hopeful approach.

At the time, I suppose that was rather liberal in its way, but if you were working directly with people as individuals this kind of group thinking was disturbing. It was disturbing to me, and yet it did show that he meant and expected us to go on patiently working, and even failure wouldn't be surprising. We weren't to be too upset by it; just be patient. That was the way it was and continued to be for some time. Later, when we began to have some success, the attitude changed. But at that time, we hadn't proved anything.

Stimson, undoubtedly, was no sincere friend of minorities, as he was a principal figure in making a national issue of placing the Japanese-Americans in detention camps at the beginning of World War II.[4] Likewise, Morison noted that when Stimson learned Archibald MacLeish of the Office of Facts and Figures was going to give a speech on the alleged discrimination against Negroes in the Army, he spent an hour with him "pointing out" how "this crime of our forefathers had produced a problem which was almost impossible of solution in this country and that I myself could see no theoretical or logical solution for it at war times like these...."[5]

On the other hand, Parrish was impressed with Secretary Lovett, who seemed much more alert and understanding of what the realities were, and was "less inclined to pontificate on the whole thing." Because Parrish had been working with the black cadets, Lovett wanted to know what he thought of them, and Parrish replied that they were individuals and they varied as individuals. Other than some percentage basis, he stated that it was impossible to generalize about them in any way that was reliable, and that it was too early to draw any conclusions. Some, he pointed out, were highly competent and showed great promise whereas others were incompetent; however, the same thing was true for their white counterparts. At any rate, Par-

rish stated that there were enough competent black pilots available to form a black unit; but at the time this did not solve the more basic problem of just how the new outfit was to be utilized in the future.

ONCE the black squadrons had moved into Italy and proved their ability to handle a combat situation, a new problem arose back at Tuskegee. Both the black press and the NAACP were expressing dissatisfaction with the fact that no black pilots were being trained in multi-engined aircraft, and because they were not getting experience in flying the larger types, they would be unable to qualify for jobs with the airlines when the war was over. Because their future was limited for this reason, there was a demand for the formation of a multi-engine unit, and again the most logical place to form this was at Tuskegee. This further added to the training complexities there, but an entire new wing of B-25 pilots was trained. According to Osur, the AAF was slow to move from single-engine to twin-engine training for the blacks because they did not have "the necessary background." Moreover, "they were never permitted to train in four-engine bombers" during the war.[6]

After these B-25 pilots were trained, however, there was no place to send them. Initially, they were kept in the area flying training missions, but with a P-40 program already on the base, it became difficult to house and keep them busy. There were not sufficient aircraft to retain the increasing number of graduates, and it appeared ridiculous not to use a combat-trained unit with a war going on. Yet Parrish could get no indication from Washington as to how this steadily increasing number of black pilots was to be utilized. After a few trips to the Pentagon and checking with the training personnel for whom he worked, he learned that there were neither plans nor a date for their deployment. The Secretary of the Air Staff did tell Parrish that a plan was being worked on, but there was no indication as to when it would be completed.

Finally, Parrish took it upon himself to visit Secretary Lovett, whom he had earlier met at Tuskegee, and explain the impasse. Lovett was rather amused at the brashness of this young officer, but also was sympathetic and told him to tell the training staff that they did have a plan. Parrish repeated that they did not, but the Secretary insisted that he "go and tell them that I told you to tell them they had a plan." This he did, and the Secretary of the Air Staff in-

★ ★ PERSONALITIES ★ ★

Lieutenant Colonel Benjamin O. Davis, Jr., a Tuskegee graduate, and the highest-ranking colored flying officer in the armed forces.

Commander of All-Negro Fighter Group in Italy Receives DFC From Father

ROME, Sept. 11. (AP)—Col. Benjamin Davis Jr. of New York, commander of the all-negro 332nd Fighter Group in the United States 15th Air Force, received the Distinguished Flying Cross today from his father, Brig. Gen. Davis of the inspector general's department.

The elder Davis is the first negro to hold general rank.

His son was cited for brilliant leadership over Northern Italy on May 9 when he led a group attacking over 100 enemy fighters which were attempting to intercept bombers.

Propeller class at Tuskegee Army Air Field, 1944.

formed him that one would be drawn up. Within a few weeks a movement plan to the Pacific area was received.

Still another problem arose of where to obtain combat-experienced pilots to form the nucleus of the B-25 group. The only black pilots available were those who had flown 50 missions or so in P-51s or P-40s in Italy, and the Air Staff directed Parrish to inform these men that it was their duty to become twin-engine pilots to furnish leadership in the newly emerging group. Parrish remarked that they surely were not going to appreciate being sent out in bombers right after a full tour as fighter pilots. And this is precisely what occurred when it was taken up with the returnees. They felt that the whole proposition was unattractive as well as unfair. In combat duty, they had risen rapidly from exclusion to double inclusion. Eventually, some veterans did volunteer, but before the B-25 unit was deployed overseas, the war was over and there was no further need for them.

Another recurring problem that vexed the training effort at Tuskegee was the Army Air Forces' policy of pulling personnel out of the Training Command and shipping them overseas where they were needed in combat areas. In one instance, orders were received to send immediately all six of the black propeller specialists to Italy, although their absence would have immobilized the training effort altogether. These were the only black propeller specialists in the U.S. With great difficulty, Parrish was finally able to find someone at USAAF headquarters who was sympathetic enough to partially countermand the

order. Three of the specialists were eventually sent overseas and three others were, in time, acquired to replace them. This kind of thing was always on the verge of happening, and it illustrated the

> many impossible and terribly expensive, disturbing aspects of trying to operate an air force within an air force with a separate personnel system, a separate training system, a separate everything. I figured the expense made it cost several times what it would have cost to have integrated forces and not have to depend on these separate procedures for which exceptions always had to be made.

General Parrish did note, nonetheless, that although it was easy to amplify the prejudices and the smugness of people that existed during these times, it is equally easy to overlook the many officials who were patient and willing to do additional work and to take risks to keep the effort going, when they easily could have sabotaged the entire thing by merely sticking to the rules. Parrish felt very gratified that there were some people in high places in the USAAF who were sympathetic enough, despite the inconvenience to themselves, to lend a hand and help make the endeavor work.

Of course, the effort had its detractors in the Pentagon who more or less looked upon the Tuskegee program as a nuisance factor. An example of this was one halfhearted suggestion to assign Martin B-26s to the Tuskegee school. The early models of this aircraft had a short wing and a high

wing loading characteristic that caused them to spin in if proper airspeed was not maintained on the landing approach. A few trainees had been killed in the aircraft, and it had become unpopular. Thus it was suggested that these planes be sent to Tuskegee, and not only would the USAAF be relieved of this albatross, but a few more accidents at Tuskegee might cause the demise of another thorn in the side as well.

General Parrish recalled that he had treated this suggestion as consciously silly, although it was not altogether so, and he did recognize that the Pentagon people were confronted with what appeared to be two insolvable problems, and they might have imagined that something could be solved by combining the two. Parrish reminded the officials that he was working with these people as individuals and could not go along with giving them an unusually dangerous airplane. He then received the retort that "Somebody has to get it," and "Why should yours be treated any different?" The Tuskegee commander told them that they could not impose upon any special group, regardless of who they were, and such a situation could cause many repercussions. The officials sheepishly admitted this, and the problem was eventually solved by initially scattering the B-26s around to various units and later putting a longer wing on them.

ALONG with the numerous problems with Washington officialdom, a more immediate issue was the tenuous situation of having a concentration of black military personnel in a highly segregated Southern town that already had a great majority of black residents. One official history noted that "The local townspeople of Tuskegee viewed the project with amusement, and suspicion, when flying first started. It was generally their opinion that Negroes would not make satisfactory Army pilots, and many felt the government was wasting money in setting up the school."[7]

The population of Tuskegee was around 4,000; 900 of these were white and ran everything.[8] A few blacks of distinction, such as professors at Tuskegee Institute, were admitted to the voting rolls, but the great mass of blacks were frozen out of any part in the governmental process by one means or another. Such a potentially volatile situation was not enhanced when the great influx of black trainees arrived on the nearby base. Many of these blacks were from the North and were quite resistant to the segregation laws,[9] and a very small number had brought white wives, which could not help but antagonize some segments of the white populace.

An Eastern Flying Command history noted:

Many Northern Negroes found it degrading to be subjected to the attitude of southerners toward colored people in general. No less detrimental were the tents, mud, and general lack of comfort at Tuskegee during the first few months. There was practically no amusement until the spring of 1942, when special services and other morale activities began to set in motion worthwhile programs.[9]

Parrish recalled:

The town's segregation laws were very strict. The movie was divided into two sides. It was even illegal to have a public meeting in which blacks and whites were present. The laws were very difficult. To try to enforce all of this they felt was necessary, because if they began not to enforce their laws there would be more defiance of the law, and they could predict anarchy. So they were very nervous about who ran the base and how it was run.

On one occasion the situation became quite precarious. A black military policeman from Brooklyn saw the two local law enforcement officers arrest a drunken black soldier, and the MP decided, on his own, that they had exceeded their authority. He drew a gun and demanded that the officers release the soldier into his custody, which he felt was a superior authority. Under these circumstances, the police did release the prisoner, but later they acquired some reinforcements and were able to slip up on the black MP; he was clubbed, disarmed, and placed in custody. Because there was no martial law in the area, the local authorities were more within the law than the black man had been. Nevertheless, the news soon spread to the base that a black had been arrested downtown, and two truckloads of armed black soldiers were soon on their way to rescue a man whom they had heard was officer of the day.

Parrish was in Tuskegee at the time but was not aware of the incident until he was notified by Benjamin O. Davis that the two trucks were on the way to town. After receiving this distressing news, he hurriedly drove toward the base and was luckily able to spot one of the trucks at Tuskegee Institute. The black soldiers had stopped to find out where to go, and Parrish was able to intercept them at this point. He told them that he appreciated their concern and patriotism, but it was not the time to become militant. The soldiers were finally talked into returning to the base until a better appraisal of the situation could be made, and Parrish then proceeded to investigate the matter.

Sure enough, I went downtown and found that whites were arriving from all over. They had a system of storing guns in the basements of stores. They

Military Police town patrol, 1943.

had built up a kind of vigilante group to move in when this thing might happen—just what was happening—to reinforce. Mostly they had shotguns, so it could have been carnage if everybody had gone into town.

Colonel Kimble, the base commander, arrived on the scene. After some discussion, the black MP was released with the commander's pledge that military discipline would be served against him.[10] Kimble then ordered that an investigation be made of the affair, and he placed Noel Parrish in charge. He was directed to interview all people involved and to make recommendations that could forestall a recurrence of such a potentially volatile affair. The black MP had to be interviewed in the hospital following the working over he had received from the local lawmen, and a meeting was called with the blacks to inform them that the military did not have jurisdiction over the town. Although a war was on, he declared, we were not at war with the state of Alabama or the town of Tuskegee, and there was no justification for taking military action.

One of the things that Parrish recommended was that the military police no longer be armed downtown, something that might have been avoided to begin with, as there was no requirement that they should be. Eventually, the affair died down, but it left a feeling of uneasiness in the town with the white vigilante organization strengthened; the barely averted confrontation with the blacks had justified their existence. Moreover, minor harassments still continued to plague the black soldiers. State and local authorities would pick the

men up for not coming to a complete stop at stop signs, following too closely behind school buses, etc., and were making things unbearable in general. After a number of conferences, the base authorities were able to get the soldiers to understand that they could not start a feud with the local enforcement officials, who in the long run could make life miserable for them. Also, compromises were worked out with the police and the sheriff as well.

When queried about the over-all effect that this segregationist attitude had on the patriotism of the blacks, General Parrish replied that it was discouraging to them from a standpoint of national ideals and idealism. He noted that it gave those who were looking for an excuse, such as there are in any group of people, "not to make sacrifices and not to seek opportunities for service," as they would have a valid reason for not being "enthusiastically patriotic." In some cases it led to resentment against the black press whom they felt was trying to shove them into battle "to save their reputations and improve their political statures." This resentment was especially apparent when the 99th Squadron was first being sent overseas.

They had been expecting and waiting for this, and they weren't too happy about it. You see, they didn't have much confidence in leadership; very few of them had confidence that they would be treated fairly. They had a feeling they might be either shunted aside, which would make them feel useless, or be pushed into some unusually dangerous situation which would test them too severely in order to make them fail.

20

The kind of confidence that you have in your leadership is a very important element of morale. While they may have been satisfied with their flying instructors, a few of us who were there at the base, at least reasonably so, they didn't know what they would face in a combat situation. I would say it took an extra amount of dedication and idealism to really stick to it and not cop out as any group of people is tempted to do at times, that is, individuals in any group.

In assessing the black pilots' over-all performance in combat, Parrish pointed out that it was a difficult thing to judge, but at any rate, they did much better than anyone had a right to expect, including those who worked with them.[11] For political reasons, some senior commanders would publicly exaggerate their accomplishments and then criticize them in private, and it was difficult to draw any valid conclusions from this. At the same time, a study Parrish had seen indicated that the black airmen had an above average court-martial rate in Europe, and their maintenance record was below average in Italy. Also, the study showed a lower than average percentage of kills of enemy aircraft; and while this may have gratified some people, the general felt that this was misleading because it was Colonel Davis' declared policy to stick with the bombers and not go chasing off after enemy fighters. The black leader felt that if he took one chance leading his group into bad weather, which happened sometimes with others, and lost part of it because of a misjudgment on his part, it would be cited as an indication of failure for the whole black program. "Being conservative and conscientiously so by nature," Parrish observed, "he followed a conservative attitude about their performance." In fact, Davis' unit was commended by some bomber-stream commanders for being the most faithful in sticking by them during bombing missions.[12]

The entire matter of objectively judging their performance, therefore, was extremely complicated, and it involved more than simply lining up units and rating them from "best to worst." There were too many factors to take into consideration, and no unit would be on the bottom in everything or on the top in all respects. At the same time, however, General Parrish estimated that they were certainly not the "worst squadron in Europe," nor for that matter were they the "best." Where they fit in, he could not positively say.

I don't see how they could possibly have been an outstanding unit, because we had in the beginning almost nobody to draw from. There were very few black automobile mechanics; there were very few

WILBUR I. GEORGE

CHARLES A. HILL

4 4 - F

Lena Horne visits Tuskegee, 1944.

black specialists of all types. There were of course almost no black professional pilots, maybe a half dozen or a dozen. None of them had family background, tradition, or even close friends in aviation.

Unlike the ground Army, the Army Air Force had no black units when the war began. The Army not only had black officers, but also a number of white officers who had worked with blacks. On the other hand, the AAF had almost no officers with such experience, and, therefore, those who later were confronted with this task "had all sorts of right and wrong notions about them." Nevertheless, the Army's black 92nd Division fared so poorly that even some blacks felt it necessary to apologize for their performance. Much of the blame for this, Parrish averred, rested with the commander and the policies that were followed. Conversely, he never felt it necessary to apologize for the black flying unit, even though it was started from little or nothing.

Considering all of that, you have to be proud of the Air Force record. You have to be proud of the black people who really did it. It was a great achievement for the Air Force. It encouraged us, Secretary [W. Stuart] Symington and other Air Force leadership, to go ahead with integration ahead of the other services. We got

ahead not only in performance, but in policy, as a result of the success of the Tuskegee people.

Although General Parrish is proud of his past association with the blacks and found it highly rewarding, he has always been anxious to avoid their regarding him as the "Great White Father, their leader, the Moses of the blacks," and that sort of thing. This was a temptation, and some officers and politicians readily succumbed to it, oftentimes for selfish motives. The General noted that he felt more gratified by people "who didn't do too much public praise and were a little conservative in their public statements," but were sincere in their private efforts to promote the betterment of the blacks.

The General's long association with the black training program, which commenced in 1941, finally came to an end in 1946 with the closing of Tuskegee Army Air Field. He rose from the rank of captain and Director of Training to full colonel and Commander during this tenure at the installation, and then went on to serve in such important posts as Special Assistant to Chief of Staff Hoyt S. Vandenberg and Air Deputy of the NATO Defense College. His illustrious Air Force career came to a close with his retirement in 1964, but he has since gone on to earn M.A. and Ph.D. degrees in history from Rice University. Presently, he

21

teaches military history at Trinity University and is actively engaged in writing and traveling. One of his more enjoyable pastimes is to attend the periodic reunions held by the Tuskegee Army Flying School graduates. And it is only fitting that he should, as he played an important role in making black aviation history.

REFERENCES

1. Alan M. Osur, "Negroes in the Army Air Forces During World War II: The Problem of Race Relations" (Ph.D diss., University of Denver, 1974), 47.

2. Arguments regarding the placement of an Air Corps black training center, from the viewpoints of both blacks and whites, are related in Ulysses Lee, *The Employment of Negro Troops* (Washington, D.C.: United States Army, 1966), 116-119.

3. Additionally, a Special Mission report noted that "The governors of six southern states are on record as having stated their cooperation with the armed forces can be obtained only so long as the 'customs of the South' remain unmolested and 'Jim Crow' laws operate." Col. Elliot D. Cooke, "Special Mission Report for the Chief of Staff in Connection with Colored Troops" (Washington, D.C.: War Department, Office of the Inspector General, 25 June 1942), Albert F. Simpson Historical Research Center [Cited hereafter as AFSHRC].

4. Richard N. Current, *The Statecraft of Henry L. Stimson* (New Brunswick: Rutgers University Press, 1954), 197-198.

5. Elting E. Morison, *Turmoil and Tradition: A Study of the Life and Times of Henry L. Stimson* (Boston: Houghton Mifflin Co., 1960), 554-555.

6. Osur, 335.

7. History of the 66th AAF Flying Training Detachment, Moton Field, Tuskegee Institute, Alabama, Section III, 1 Jan. 1943 to 31 Jan. 1944, AFSHRC, 3.

8. The 320th history supports Parrish's figures: "There were 3,937 persons living in incorporated Tuskegee in 1940. Over two-thirds of these persons were Negroes. There were 27,103 residents of Macon County in 1930, with the Negro population of the county exceeding that of the white by a ratio of almost 5 to 1." History of 320th College Training Detachment (Aircrew), Tuskegee Institute, Alabama, March 1943 to March 1944, ARSHRC, 5.

9. History of AAF Eastern Flying Command, 7 Dec. 1941 to 1 Jan. 1943, Vol. II, AFSHRC, 1177-1178.

10. Parrish is given no credit for helping to quell the situation according to the official history which notes that "Colonel Kimble arrived on the scene early and he is given much credit by this headquarters for preventing a real crisis." History of AAF Eastern Training Command, 7 Dec. 1941 to 1 Jan. 1943, Vol. II, AFSHRC, 1178. Likewise, Ulysses Lee does not mention Parrish's involvement in the incident, except for the statement that "White officers from the post residing in the town rounded up most of the soldiers and returned them to camp, but not before soldiers on the post had become alarmed at the prospect that armed townsfolk might attack the airfield." Lee, *The Employment of Negro Troops,* 356.

11. A 66th history noted that the black training effort "achieved a degree of success which has perhaps surpassed the hopes of even its most enthusiastic supporters." History of the 66th AAF Flying Training Detachment, Moton Field, Tuskegee Institute, Alabama, Section III, 1 Jan. 1943 to 31 Jan. 1944, AFSHRC, 1.

12. Lt. Gen. Ira C. Eaker remarked after the war that "The reason, in my opinion, they did a good job is that they had an outstanding leader, Colonel Davis, a West Point graduate, at the head of that group. He is a remarkable young leader." Cited in Lee, *The Employment of Negro Troops,* 522-523.

James Curtis Hasdorff is Deputy Chief, Oral History Branch, Albert F. Simpson Historical Research Center, Maxwell AFB, Alabama. He holds a Ph.D. in history from the University of New Mexico. Since joining the Oral History Office in 1971, he has interviewed a number of eminent military and civilian figures, including Gen. Bernard A. Schriever, USAF (Ret.); Gen. James Ferguson, USAF (Ret.); Gen. Frederic H. Smith, USAF (Ret.); Gen. O. P. Weyland, USAF (Ret.); Gen. Paul D. Harkins, USA (Ret.); former Ambassador to South Vietnam Frederick E. Nolting, Jr.; former AF Under Secretary Joseph V. Charyk; and former AF Assistant Secretary for R&D, Dr. Alexander H. Flax.

ARMY AIR FORCE SERVICE DETACHMENT #99

by Elmer D. Jones, Colonel, USAF (Retired)

In the interest of providing a lost segment in the record of Black air units in the U.S. Military operations, this article is about a unique organization designated *AAF Service Detachment #99*. This small unit played an integral and essential role in the successful combat operations of the 99th Fighter Squadron. It is not well known, and hardly ever mentioned, but I am sure it will not be forgotten by the original members of the 99th who saw action in Europe.

The Detachment was activated 22 August 1942 at TAFS, and first designated, Detachment, 366th Service Squadron. It had a complement of two officers and thirty-four airmen came from the 366th Service Squadron, eleven of whom were graduates of technical schools at Chanute Field. The rest were also well trained and thoroughly dedicated. This was a "one-of-a-kind" organization conjured up by the Army Air Force to deal with one of the consequences of their racist policies. During World War II, flying units were deployed in Group strength or larger. Each Group was accompanied by and supported in the field by a service squadron which furnished aircraft supplies and higher echelons of aircraft maintenance, normally for three flying squadrons.

The Army Air Force was seriously considering deploying the 99th in isolation at some remote location like Liberia, or maybe even Ascension Island with an area of thirty-four square miles and a population of five hundred. So, to them, it appeared to pare down the TO&E of a service squadron to provide for the needs of a single fighter squadron. This is how the detachment came into existence.

After considerable political pressure to send the 99th off to combat, a sequence of revised movement orders, and having to endure alert status for eight months, we received a telegramm in late March 1943 directing us to the Port of Embarkation (POE). With the 99th on the USS Mariposa, we sailed from Camp Shanks, New York, for our overseas destination and arrived in Casablanca on 24 April 1943.

During our first seven months overseas the mission of the Detachment was somewhat elusive and we were becoming frustrated in not being able to procure the balance of our organizational equipment which was so vital to our effectiveness. At our base in Tuskegee, we had been told that we would receive our equipment at the POE. At Camp Shanks, we were told that we would receive it at the Port of Destination (POD). In the Theater of Operations we were told that they had never heard of an organization like ours. We were usually greeted with "What is your official TO&E?"

In spite of these obstacles, the Detachment went right to work for the 99th with the resources at hand. At the combat training base at Oued N'ja, French Morocco, the Detachment made the 99th's first engine change overseas. The men worked side by side with the ground crews of the 99th and started to gain field experience and build an adquate technical suply on which the squadronn could draw.

Eventually, on 1 January 1944, at a base near Termoli, Italy, we were assigned to the 315th Service Group and, from that day, we were to function and be acknowledged as the Air Force service unit for the 99th. Over the next few weeks our organizational mission became better understood and we began to receive the bulk of our organizational equipment. The 99th was heavily engaged in combat missions and the Detachment had a full schedule of providing them with vital technical supplies and repairing damaged aircraft which could not be accomplished by the squadron.

It was during this period that Master Sergeant William S. Surcey of the Detachment earned the Bronze Star Medal for exceptionally meritorious conduct. During the period 23 January to 28 February 1944, at a time when the fighting on the Cassino and Anzio sectors was especially crucial, Sergeant Surcey, Engineering Section Chief of the AAF Service Detachment #99, supervised the successful completion of third and fourth echelon repairs on seven P-47 Warhawks, and their transfer to a fighter group operating over these sectors. Under his able leadership, these tasks were efficiently performed with but a skeleton crew of men, inadequately equipped with essential material and tools, and working under most adverse conditions. In my view, this recognition of one of many instances of meritorious accomplishment exemplifies the spirit, determination, and professional skills of all the men of the detachment.

The 332nd arrived in the theater in January of 1944, and so the 366th Service Squadron, then a part of the 96th Service Group located south of Naples, was designated to service the fighter group. In March 1944, I was relieved of assignment with the Detachment and given command of the 366th, making it a 100% Black organization.

Meanwhile, Lieutenant Percy Sutton was assigned to take over the Detachment, which was then attached to the 366th. Two months later, Lieutenant Sutton was transferred to the 332nd as an intelligence officer and Lieutenants Omar Blair and Williams were transferred from the 366th to the Detachment with Lieutenant Blair in Command.

At the end of June 1944, all personnel of the Detachment were transferred to the 366th Service Squadron, which to most was like returning home, and the AAF Service Detachment #99 was deactivated, ending a proud and exemplary existence of only twenty-two months.

This Rolls Royce V-12 Merlin engine, used in the P-51 Mustang, was rebuilt by the 366th Service Squadron. Sgts. Woodson and Coombs, of the 99th Squadron, are returning the engine to its air frame.

TO INSURE THEY NEVER FAIL FOR LACK
OF TOP-FLIGHT GROUND SUPPORT

GEORGE L. WASHINGTON

ABOUT THE AUTHOR

Dr. Patterson
President of Tuskegee

Mr. Washington

Mr. Washington was greatly involved in the technical training program that produced the highly skilled man and women who made the success of the flying units possible.

In the area of civil and military aviation, Dr. Patterson, former President of Tuskegee Institute, often referred to Mr. Washington as "the daddy of aviation of Tuskegee." He was *Coordinator, Civilian Pilot Training,* an FAA war preparatory program, ini iated 1939 in 1,200 colleges and universities; *Director, FAA Advanced Flying Training Center* initiated 1940 (changed to "War Training Service" 1943); *General Manager, 66th AAF Flying Training Detachment at Tuskegee;* rendered *Consultation and Assistance* to AAF Southeast Training Command, in behalf of Tuskegee Institute designated by General Henry H. Arnold, in establishing military pilot training in Tuskegee area including program and physical establishment of Tuskegee Army Air Field, recruitment of personnel for training for TAAF, liaison services and trouble-shooting between the Southeast Command and War Department (DOD), etc.

Mr. Washington held positions at three colleges: the North Carolina A. & T. State University, Tuskegee Institute, and Howard University. In General Administration, (he was *Assistant to the President* at Tuskegee and Howard, *Business Manager* of Howard, and a part of another position was administratively responsible for *Operation and Maintenance of Physical Plant* at all three colleges, except that at Tuskegee *Design and Construction of New Facilities* was added. In Instruction he was *Dean, School of Mechanic Arts* at A. & T. College (engineering, architecture, technology), *Dean, School of Mechanical Industries* at Tuskegee (degree level curricula and vocational trades), and *Administrator (acting dean), School of Veterinary Medicine* at Tuskegee. Mr. Washington also served Tuskegee three years in Indonesia, carrying out the contract between the Republic of Indonesia and Tuskegee Institute, involving the upgrading of in-service teachers and teaching facilities. As *Chief Advisor, Tuskegee Team* he was director of the educational specialists and consultant to the Indonesia Ministry of Education. Involved were 300 public technical schools.

Mr. Washington also served Organizations Servicing Colleges. He was *Director, Special Services,* United Negro College Fund, providing oncampus assistance to officials of member colleges, and promoting activities to help members (collectively and individually) make a maximum utilization of resources already on hand. He was *Executive Director, College Service Bureau,* representing 81 black and white colleges in their federal government relations in Washington, D.C. He was *Executive Director, Alabama Center for Higher Education* on a terminal basis, to get the consortium on a going basis and help with program planning and development (involved the 8 black accredited colleges of Alabama). As *Project Director, Under Contracts* separately with the Agency for International Development and Bureau of Educational and Cultural Affairs of Department of State, researched, developed and published information on black colleges as specified.

In addition to serving colleges and organizations servicing higher eduation, Mr. Washington was *Field Coordinator* and subsequently *Deputy National Director, College Housing Loan Program,* U. S. Department of Housing and Urban Development. As *Management Consultant* he was employed to survey and recommend the reorganization of the Executive Branch of the U. S. Virgin Islands Government. As *Consultant to the Board of Education* of the Bahama Islands Government, made economic survey and recommended program of vocational education of islands.

TO INSURE THEY NEVER FAIL FOR LACK OF
TOP-FLIGHT GROUND SUPPORT

G. L. Washington

INTRODUCTION

The Greater Philadelphia Chapter of the Tuskegee Airmen is to be highly commended for the adoption of "THE GROUND SUPPORT TEAM" as the Theme and "THEY KEPT 'EM FLYING" the Slogan of the Tuskegee Airmen's 1976 National Reunion. Three decades have passed during which the general public has heard much about the black pilots of World War II, but very little of the ground forces upon whom they relied. Therefore, it is timely and appropriate that high tribute be paid the ground support team embracing the personnel of the ground services that supported the Fighter and Bombardment units activated at Tuskegee, including the 366th Service Group because of the maintenance service it provided at the depot level.

Top-flight ground services related to combat, as well as pilots, are a must for an effective combat unit. Therefore, every effort was put forth by all concerned to insure that the 99th Fighter Squadron's ground support would be beyond reproach and second to none. No matter how good the pilots, their full combat potential might never be attained without this kind of backstopping. Further, the future of blacks in military aviation would depend upon the performance of the 99th. The birth and training of this ground support is featured in this article.

The Army once wrote "No other ground crew in America has had more favorable publicity than the men of the fighting 99th . . . These men know their job and have the confidence of the men who fly the ships they service." (1942) And in the Citation of the 332nd Fighter Group "for outstanding performance of duty in armed conflict with the enemy" due recognition was given the ground support team as follows: (Oct. 5, 1945)

". . . Realizing the strategic importance of the mission and fully cognizant of the amount of enemy resistance to be expected and long range to be covered, the ground crews worked tirelessly and with enthusiasm to have their aircraft at the peak of mechanical condition to insure the success of the operation . . ." "By the conspicuous gallantry, professional skill, and determination of the pilots, together with the outstanding technical skill and devotion to duty of the ground personnel, the 332nd Fighter Group has reflected great credit on itself and the armed forces of the United States."

The public and press are inclined to center their applause on the pilots, which I have sensed is disappointing to many of the ground support, if not the majority. One reason for this may be that the general public is unaware of the various ground services and their importance to successful combat. Another is the public has often been thrilled by war movies showing aerial combat which is indeed spectacular, glamorous and daring.

Such featuring though, did not include the ground services related to combat. Further, there is little about these services considered glamorous.

After accepting President Richardson's invitation to write this article, I found it hard to decide what to write that would be meaningful and in keeping with the Reunion Theme. Also anything I wrote should be addressed to the general public as well as Tuskegee Airmen. That is why I inserted a ground support chart to assist the layman with a conception of ground support.

And, finally, why the title, "TO INSURE THEY NEVER FAIL FOR LACK OF TOP-FLIGHT GROUND SUPPORT?" That could have been the slogan of the many fine young men in college and out who were ready to drop what they were doing and train at Chanute Field, to insure the black pilots on trial dedicated, top-flight ground support second to none.

PREFACE

Statusquo, Fall, 1940; Developments, Conflicts

• **Tuskegee Institute:** had become nationally distinguished and a leader among blacks in field of aviation training, having proven beyond a doubt before the nation the ability of blacks to excel in civil piloting; on the alert for opportunity to influence favorably fair trial of blacks in military piloting, completing two-fold purpose in aviation.

• **War Department (a projection):** Air Corps' failure to enlist blacks had brought mounting pressure upon Army, and thus War Department, to accept blacks on integrated basis, court suit thereon getting closer and closer; general resistance to integration; *strategy = plan separate training under existing "separate-but-equal" doctrine, drawing Tuskegee Institute in on the planning and announcing the program if and when suit is filed in court.

• **Equal Rights Movement:** for integration in Air Corps training, NAACP's Walter White leading attack on outside, Civilian Aid to secretary of War William H. Hastie leading attack inside the War Department; NAACP preparing to sponsor a suit, and to fight segregated training in Air Corps.

Strategy is the projection, since Tuskegee had no part in such planning. However, the Yancey Williams suit was filed early January, 1941 and the War Department announced trainig of blacks in Air Corps at Tuskegee, January 16, 1941. Projected: Tuskegee Institute participation would divide blacks and strengthen case for separate training.

GROUND SUPPORT SERVICES RELATED TO COMBAT

Aircraft Maintenance Crews - Rapair and maintain aircraft to assure maximum combat effectiveness and safety for air crews. **Specialists:** air frame and engine, propellor, hydraulics, electrical, instruments, sheet metal, paint-dope fabric machinists.

Armament Specialists - Calibrate, maintain and repair gunsights, bombsights, and gunnery cameras; store and load munitions; maintain and repair guns and bomb racks. (Ordnance personnel: receive, store, and dispatch explosive material: bombs, fuses, ammunition; overhaul weapons)

Communications Specialists - Maintain and repair aircraft radios; operate control towers; and install and operate ground radio stations and telephone systems

Link Trainer Instructors - Operates and maintains instrument trainers

Parchute Riggers - Inspect, repair and pack parachutes and survival gear, rafts, seat, dinghies, May Wests

Weather Personnel - Forecast weather conditions for mission planning; teletype repair and maintenance. Personnel: Weather forecasters, observers; teletype operators

Intelligence Personnel - Report on enemy dispositions and capabilities for mission planning and debrief combat crews on return from combat missions

Medical Personnel - Perform medical examinations and services to keep air crews physically and mentally fit for combat. Nurses, corpsmen, laboratory assistants, dental assistants, ambulance drivers

Supply Personnel - Store and issue aircraft and automotive parts, tools, fuel and oil, tents and clothing. (Also Quartermaster Supply)

Transportation Personnel - Maintain and operate all types of vehicles including wreckers and flatbeds for troop transport and hauling. (Also Quartermaster's Motor Pool)

Fire Fighting Personnel - Operates ground powered equipment. **Specialists:** generators, heaters, compressors

Administrative Personnel - Provides for payment of the troops; operates mess halls; maintains personnel records; and takes care of all other administrative functions of the organizations

Depot Level Maintenance - Aircraft, etc. - 366th Service group (96th and 97th Service Squadrons)

Tuskegee Institute's goal was a fair tryout for blacks in military piloting, especially one it could influence for the better. The matter called for a careful assessment: separate-but-equal vs. integration, in relation to existing "climate."

SEPARATE-BUT-EQUAL

(Existing Armed forces Doctrine)

a. Blacks' best chance of Air Corps training until after War

b. Most likely a better job of training black pilots could be done hereunder (largely because student likely to have less real or imagined personal problems hereunder than if a pioneer under integration)

c. A larger number of blacks likely to be assigned for pilot training, as well as a larger percentage graduated

d. Opportunity for large participation of blacks in professional and technical areas of the ground support services

e. The best opportunity blacks would have to prove themselves in combat would be in all-black units under black leadership. Would get full credit for successes and failures

INTEGRATION

(Not Armed Forces Doctrine)

a. Chance of desegrated Air Corps training of blacks not likely in view of imminence of U.S. entrance into World War II which would and possibly had already started to require total concentration on winning. War

Department won't volunteer overcoming deep rooted sociological problems involved that all three branches of Government never solved.

b. Possible mental strain, or undue distractions, added to a normally very strenuous life of a flying cadet, might mitigate against too many blacks

c. Most likely smaller numbers of blacks would be assigned, and smaller percentages graduated

d. Opportunities for fewer, if any, blacks in ground services

e. Blacks would always be the smaller number in the units, and would lose identity. Thus, it would be more difficult to prove what blacks can do

---

Taking all into consideration, separate-but-equal training seemed the most advantageous route. The rationale was defensible. Tuskegee could afford to support separate training facilities, so long as they were, in fact, equal. Long before separate training became a reality, we were encouraged by the stand taken by representatives of our leading black colleges, meeting at Tuskegee. It was in full support of Tuskegee's position, should it be called upon to endorse separate training.

The War Department & Tuskegee Institute

The War Department sought the cooperation of Tuskegee Institute in accomplishing essentials leading to the establishment of military pilot training in the Tuskegee area (November 1940). Tuskegee Institute consented and working conferences began a few days thereafter. Representing Tuskegee Institute: Dr. F.D. Patterson, President, and G.L. Washington, Dean, School of Mechanical Industries. Representing the War Department: Major General Walter R. Weaver, Commanding Officer, AAF Southeast Training Command, and Major Luke S. Smith, Director of Training, AAF Southeast Training Command (SETC).

Meetings were held mostly at SETC, Maxwell Field and Tuskegee Institute, in the field, or War Department, Washington, D.C. The Institute had direct working relations with SETC and the War Department and helpful troubleshooting between the two was occasionally done by either President Patterson or Mr. Washington or both.

The direct relationship with the War Department, and the Department's reliance on Tuskegee, continued beyond help with establishing the Tuskegee Army Air Field. The last opinion the Department sought of Tuskegee was whether to continue or close the TAAF.

War Department Announcement, January 16, 1941

While still in the early stage of planning the establishment of military pilot training, the War Department announced that blacks would be accepted into the Army Air Forces and trained as fighter pilots at Tuskegee. Negotiations with Tuskegee began for the conduct of Pre-Flight and Primary Flying Training under contract, which would be the 66th such contract in the nation and the 42nd in SETC. (Tuskegee qualified for the Army primary flying training contract because it had a CAA rated Primary and Advanced Flying Training School Certificate.

THE BIRTH AND TRAINING OF THE 99th FIGHTER SQUADRON'S GROUND SUPPORT

January 6, 1942: A working conference convened at Maxwell to consider recruitment and training of ground support personnel for the 99th Fighter Squadron.

Parenthetically, at a past meeting on another subject, General Weaver had informally and just in passing advanced the idea of putting facilities and personnel at Tuskegee Institute to train ground support personnel for the 99th. Major Smith (over 6 feet) rose to say "I beg to disagree, Sir. The Air Corps' best facility for this is Chanute Field. All of the training should be done at our best established posts." Dr. Patterson and I wanted to say amen to that. But that settled that, and at this meeting we didn't have that to contend with.

(The Chanute Field referred to was the Air Corps' School for training enlisted men in fields ranging from administrative clerks to master mechanics on the flight line. It also trained aviation cadets to become engineering officers over aircraft maintenance. The 99th Fighter Squadron's ground recruits needed comparable training in Communications and Armament. To facilitate matters and keep the group rogether, teachers and teaching equipment were transferred to Chanute from Scott (Communications) and Lowry (Armament) Fields to do the training.)

The meeting was brief. General Weaver opened with the suggestion that Tuskegee take the initiative in assisting with recruitment. Major Smith then handed me a list of 7 recruits, four to be trained as aviation cadets, and three, enlisted men. General Weaver added a flight surgeon. When I asked about qualifications, Major Smith suggested I talk with a classmate of his at the War Department in Washington, Major R.E. Nugent, a key officer in Personnel. He said he would telephone him about me and an appointment the morning of January 9, which I suggested.

Before going to Washington, I thought about nothing but personnel and recruitment for the 99th. We had already requested and been assured that Benjamin O. Davis, Jr., would be transferred in time from Fort Riley to train with the first class of flying cadets, looking to his

becoming the Commanding Officer of the 99th. He just had to fly, because it was important that a black lead the squadron in battle. The complementary must was ground support services second to none in the Nation and dedicated to insuring our pilots would never fail for lack of backstopping beyond reproach.

I concluded that ground support recruitment was a number one problem, as I saw it. Communications between Army headquarters in Washington, draft boards, and Army recruitment over the Nation were not good, to say it mildly. Policy and plans changed so that many releases were obsolete before they reached their designation. Assuming we could get top men to enlist, would they end up at Chanute or get lost? Judging from the heavy daily flow of mail to my office from all over the country from youth, confused and wanting right information, the majority would get lost.

The answer seemed to be a special recruitment and enlistment plan to propose to Major Nugent in conference in Washington for discussion, a plan that (1) would involve leaders in black colleges, particularly those having endorsed Tuskegee's military aviation approach, in carrying out an effective recruitment plan on campuses, in cities where located, and among young alumni, and (2) would by-pass regular recruitment channels in that applications (we would devise, along with complete information) for Training at Chanute Field would be forwarded to my office for review and transmittal direct to Major Smith at Maxwell, who in turn would review and route to Major Nugent in Washington to handle from there.

The conference with Major Nugent was more than expected. He understood the problem and thought well of the special recruitment and enlistment plan, which he endorsed. In addition he furnished information about all the specialties to be trained for at Chanute Field, as well

as qualifications therefore, and other information of interest to recruits. It so happened that the leading black colleges would be represented in a two-day conference at Tuskegee Institute, January 14 and 15. Major Smith spoke to the group the evening of the 15th on military pilot training, and answered many questions about the training at Tuskegee, which would be announced by the War Department the next day, January 16, 1941. It also provided an opportunity to explain the program and go over the special recruitment and enlistment plan, to facilitate their cooperation.

The recruitment-enlistment plan was a great success and enabled us to flood Maxwell Field and Washington with highly qualified aplicants in the hundreds, far more than needed fo the 99th. Since around 500 blacks were trained at Chanute back there, this may account for all-black service units that have been mentioned. The first batch of 60 applications sent to Maxwell Field comprised students recruited at Morris Brown College and Tuskegee Institute.

Trip To Inspect Training of 99th Fighter Squadron Ground Support

At the request of General Henry H. Arnold, Chief of Air Corps, arrangements were made for Dr. Patterson and me to inspect the training of the 99th Fighter Squadron's ground services at Chanute Field, June 19-20, 1941. We left Maxwell Field in a bomber the morning of the 19th and returned to Maxwell the next afternoon at 5:10. Upon landing at Chanute Field, we were welcomed by the Acting Commandant, Colonel R.E. O'Neil, Lt. Colonel A.C. Kincard, Captain Maddux and other staff officers. The officers were careful to see that our needs were attended, but refrained from such attention as might circumscribe us in our mission.

The men of the 99th Fighter Squadron had caused no problems on the post. The barracks and mess were satisfactory. The keen interest and enthusiasm regarding the training demonstrated by post officers and those in charge of instruction with respect to the general welfare, adjustment, and training of the men was gratifying, based on interviews with all of them. Cadets were in training as engineering, weather, and communications officers:

Armament - William Townes . . . . West Virginia
Engineering - Elmer D. Jones . . . . Washington, D.C.
Engineering - James L. Johnson . . . . Washington, D.C.
Communications - Nelson S. Brooks . . . Springfield, Ill.
Communications - Dudley W. Stevenson . . . .
Washington, D.C.
Armament - William R. Thompson . . . . Chicago, Ill.

The courses, duration thereof, hours of course, and enrollment in regard to the training of enlisted men were:

	Duration (weeks)	Hours	Enroll- ment
Airplane mechanics	22	770	162
Aircraft mechanics	17	595	2
Aircraft welders	14	490	2
Aircraft metal workers	14	490	2
Parachute riggers	8	280	3
Teletype operators	8	280	4
Weather observers	12	420	5
Link trainer instructors (to be entered 6/30/41)	12	420	2
Radio operators and mechanics	22	770	28
Aircraft armorers	14	560	15
Air Corps supply and technical clerks	16	640	46
Instruments (to be entered)	8	280	4
Weather forecasters (to be entered)	26	910	3
In Training			269
To be entered			9
TOTAL			278

Radio operators and mechanics were in advance of normal and ahead of schedule. Instruction eliminations were anticipated in only two or three cases. This was attributed to the fact that the individuals in question were not able to enter courses of their first choice.

During the comparatively short time at the Field, the men had taken on a soldierly bearing and deportment, we were informed, and had brought distinction and admiration from the entire post. Also they had excelled in inter-detachment athletic competition and excelled and took first place in the Chanute Field Track Meet June 18, 1941.

Lack of information on the progress and plans for pilot training of black aviation cadets was widespread among the enlisted men, cadets and the officers in charge of their training. We enlightened them on total plans to date in this regard. There was doubt in the minds of officers directly in charge of the enlisted men, as well as the men themselves as to when they would be transferred and whether to the Tuskegee Army Air Field or some other base.

Recommendations were made direct to General Arnold, copy to Army headquarters and Southeast Training Command.

At Last! At Last!

October, 1941 the initial ground crew of the 99th Fighter Squadron was transferred from Chanute Field Illinois, to the Tuskegee Army Air Field, Tuskegee, Alabama.

The Freeman Field Incident
477 Bombardment Group
The Attempt To Integrate
United States Air Corp.
April 1945
BY CORNELIUS P. GOULD

The April, 1945 incident at Freeman Air Base in southern Indiana was the culmination of a number of factors. Designated as a mutiny, it was a high point in the war within a war for equal recognition and opportunity for Black personnel. The fight by Blacks against discrimination and segregation was carried over into the military from civilian life, and in the military they found that the written and unwritten civilian laws were replaced by military directives whose interpretation or misinterpretation by senior military officers caused many of the same problems found in civilian life. The military premise that segregation was not discrimination, per se, was said to be based on civilian court findings, and therefore the military directives that said segregation would be permitted, but no discrimination, became the rule of thumb for the military. Specifically, in the Freeman Field incident, Army Regulation 210-10, Paragraph 19, and its interpretation became the focal point. Also there was the frustration felt by Black officers caused by the barriers to upward mobility in a white/black stiuation where the unwritten code said that a Black could not outrank a white in a given situation.

The fight for equal use of the officers club did not originate at Freeman Field, but rather it began at Selfridge Field in Michigan near Detroit. The 477th was moved from Selfridge Field to a southern climate to get away from the "radical elements" pressing for use of the officers club there. The large Black population in Detroit took some pressure off the issue but did not resolve it. The training program for replacements to the 332nd was moved from Selfridge for the same reasons. Moving the 477th to Godman Field in Kentucky did not lessen the demand, but there again the large Black population around Fort Knox helped the situation. Also, the white officers were permitted use of the officers club at Fort Knox, leaving the Godman club for Black officers. However, Godman Field was inadequate for the 477th because of its size (small) and poor runways not suitable for bomber use. This situation resulted in the move to freeman Field in southern Indiana near the town of Seymour. The town had a small Black population and a hostile white population which added fuel to the fire.

The question of the officers club and recreation facilities at Freeman was thought by the command to have been solved by having two "equal" facilities. This premise was based on the civilian thought the "Negroes would accept" separate facilities if they were "equal." When it became apparent that was not acceptable and that the 1940 Army Regulation 210-10 was quoted in the protests, the second idea came into being which was to be more specific in designating who would use what facility: the trainees (Black) would have one and the Base personnel (white) the other. Thus segregation would be maintained. The fallacy in this thinking became apparent when the several Black officers that were Base personnel made their intentions known. As the military command at Freeman, the First Air Corps command at Mitchell and the high command in Washington shuttled the problem back and forth, the Negro press became involved followed by the NAACP and the Urban League. Army Regulation 210-10 and its wording was the focal point and the issue became a hot potato. It should be noted here that this was not the only protest by Black military personnel against segregation and discrimination, but it was significant in that it involved over 100 Black officers.

On the evening of 5 April, 1945, the incident(s) called a mutiny began to happen. A contingent of Black officers arrived from Godman and found that the attitude of the senior officers on the questions of using the base officer club facility did not differ from previous situations. When four of the recently-arrived officers attempted to enter the club, they were told they could not enter, and they left. A short time later another group came to the club. They were confronted by the Provost Marshall. Under the threat of arrest they entered the club. The threat of arrest was carried out. Three of the officers were also charged with pushing the Provost Marshall. Off and on during the evening groups of Black officers entered the club and were put under arrest.

On 9 April, 1945, the aforementioned regulation specifically designating and classifying the clubs was issued. On that day and the following day this new regulation was read to ALL personnel after which each person was ordered to sign that he had read and understood the regulation. White personnel signed the order. More than 100 of the CCTS (Combat Crew Training Squadron) refused to sign. They were read the 64th Article of War and again given the opportunity to sign. Upon refusing, 101 Black officers were placed under arrest and shipped to Godman Field. The issue became more heated.

Between 10 April, 1945 and 20 April, communications flowed continuously between Freeman, Mitchel Field and Washington. Also during this time communication between the NAACP and Urban League were sent to Congress, Truman Gibson (civilian aide on Negro affairs to Secretary Stimson), Secretary of War Stimson and President Roosevelt. The McCloy Committee also entered the picture and following its final decision after first attempting to issue a watered-down version which was vigorously protested by Truman Gibson, published a report very distasteful to the military. Basically, the military was upset because McCloy would not undercut the decisions made concerning the officer club incidents at Selfridge, and added some recommendation to clarify the usage of facilities.

The bottom line to the whole affair was that only the three accused of forcing their way into the club were put on trial. Because two were Base personnel they were found innocent. The third was found guilty of pushing past the Provost Marshall and was fined $150. In May of 1945 all white officers in the 477th were replaced by Blacks.

Arthur L. Ward	Theodore O. Mason	Cyril P. Dyer	Haydel J. White
*James B. Williams	Donald D. Harris	Aldolphus Lewis, Jr.	Victor L. Ranson
David A. Smith	Paul L. White	Luther L. Oliver	Lloyd W. Godfrey
William C. Perkins	Charles E. Wilson	Edward E. Tillmon	Coleman A. Young
James Whyte, Jr.	John E. Wilson	Frank V. Pivalo	LeRoy F. Gillead
Stephen Hotesse	Paul W. Scott	Leonard E. Williams	Connie Nappier, Jr.
Wardell A. Polk	McCray Jenkins	Norman A. Holmes	Argonne F. Harden
Robert E. Lee	Harris H. Robnett	*Roy M. Chappell	Robert L. Hunter
George H. Kydd	Donald A. Hawkins	Leroy A. Battle	James W. Brown, Jr.
Eugene L. Woodson	Glenn W. Pulliam	Charles E. Malone	Walter R. Ray
Charles E. Darnell	Frank B. Sanders	Edward W. Woodward	Charles R. Taylor
James V. Kennedy	Walter M. Miller	John R. Perkins, Jr.	Roger Pines
Glen L. Head	Denny C. Jefferson	Alvin B. Steele	Roland A. Webber
Harry R. Dickenson	James H. Shepherd	Hiram E. Little	Samuel Colbert
*Quentin P. Smith	Edward R. Lunda	George W. Prioleau, Jr.	Rudolph A. Berthoud
Charles J. Dorkins	James E. Jones	Marcel Clyne	Clifford C. Jarrett
Maurice J. Jackson, Jr.	Sidney H. Marzette	Arthur O. Fisher	Marcus E. Clarkson
Herdon M. Cummings	Leonard A. Altemus	Charles E. Jones	LeRoy H. Freeman
Mitchel L. Higginbothan	Howard Storey	Charles S. Goldsby	George H.O. Martin
Alfred U. McKenzie	James C. Warren	Wendell T. Stokes	Melvin M. Nelson
Herbert J. Schwing	Cleophus W. Valentine	William E. Bowie, Jr.	Edward W. Watkins
Wendell G. Freeland	Ario Dixione	Bertram W. Pitts	Edward R. Tabbanor
David J. Murphy, Jr.	Robert B. Johnson	Silas M. Jenkins	Clarence C. Conway
Calvin T. Warrick	Calvin Smith	Harry S. Lum	Fredrick H. Samuels
Robert S. Payton, Jr.	Lewis C. Hubbard, Jr.	Robert T. McDaniel	Robert O'Neal
	William J. Curtis	*Edward V. Hipps, Jr.	Clarence E. Lewis

TUSKEGEE ARMY FLYING SCHOOL

TUSKEGEE, ALABAMA

NOEL F. PARRISH

Lieutenant Colonel

COMMANDING

Entered the Army as a private in Troop F of the 11th Cavalry on July 30, 1930. Was appointed flying cadet on July 1, 1931, at March Field, California. Completed primary training at that field.

Was transferred with the First Basic Class to be trained at the newly-completed Randolph Field, and finished advanced training at Kelly Field in July of 1932.

Was graduated as an attack pilot and served one year of active duty with the 13th Attack Squadron at Fort Crockett, Galveston, Texas. After completing one year of active duty as pilot, enlisted as a private in the Air Corps in September, 1933, at Chanute Field.

Was transferred to the First Provisional Transport Squadron in February, 1934, and remained on duty flying transports for this

squadron, receiving a commission as Second Lieutenant in the Regular Army in July, 1935. Upon this appointment he was again assigned to the 13th Attack Squadron, which was then located at Barksdale Field, Shreveport, La.

After serving three years for this squadron was transferred to Randolph Field, Texas, as a primary flying instructor. At the beginning of the Civilian Pilot Training Program, was transferred to the Chicago School of Aeronautics, where he was on duty until May, 1941, at which time he was transferred to the Primary Flying School at Tuskegee Institute, Alabama. Was transferred to the Tuskegee Army Flying School as Director of Training in December, 1941, and became Commanding Officer in December of 1942.

34

JOHN T. HAZARD
Lieutenant Colonel
Executive Officer

★ S T A F F ★

★

CLYDE H. BYNUM
Captain
Adjutant

WELDON O. YEAGER
Second Lieutenant
S-1

EDWARD C. AMBLER, JR.
Captain
S-2

EDWARD HENRY NORRIS
Captain
S-4

RICHARD C. CUMMING
Lieutenant Colonel
Post Surgeon

HARRY W. HECHT
Major
Post Engineer

ROBERT L. BOYD
Captain
Post Operations Officer

HERSCHEL KORNBLATT
Second Lieutenant
Acting Public Relations Officer
and Photographic Officer

JOHN G. COOKE, JR.
Captain
Commandant of Cadets

WARREN R. CRUMP
Captain
Post Quartermaster

WILLIAM J. LISKA
Captain
Post Communications Officer

FLEETWOOD M. McCOY
Captain
Trial Judge Advocate

CHARLES H. EVERETT
First Lieutenant
Post Signal Officer

DOUGLAS L. T. ROBINSON
Captain
Post Chaplain

HISTORY OF THE TUSKEGEE ARMY FLYING SCHOOL

Army Flying School Looks to Future as Noted Institute Turns Out Combat Pilots . . . School
Producing Top-Flight Pilots and Ground Forces.

The Tuskegee Army Flying School has the eyes of the world focused upon it, for here has been formed the nucleus of Negro combat pilots and skilled technicians. A little over a year ago, the first Negro cadets began their primary training at the Air Corps Training Detachment, Tuskegee Institute, under the instructions of civilian pilots with Army personnel doing the administrative work. It was during the month of August, 1941, that 12 cadets were being questioned by the nation in editorials with such questions as: Will the first class pull through? Will the program be a success or failure? etc. The initial flying class proved to the world that they, too, could become combat pilots . . . and since the first graduation, other cadets are receiving their wings monthly.

Not only is the Tuskegee Army Flying School pinning wings on Negro pilots, but it is steadily producing skilled technicians, air mechanics, photographers, radio operators, weather men, and many other technicians essential to the Army Air Forces.

The flying school is located in South Central Alabama, 13 miles from the famous Tuskegee Institute founded by one of America's foremost educators, Booker T. Washington.

THE PHYSICAL SETTING OF THE SCHOOL

To begin with, the engineers had to level several hills. One spot on the field is exactly 54 feet less in elevation than a year ago. Trees had to be uprooted and all vestiges of vegetation of every sort had to be obliterated before mile-long concrete runways could be laid down. In other words, the field now forms a big valley, a man-made valley, a beautiful rolling valley that slopes back up toward the hill. The Headquarters building and the barracks rise on the sloping hillsides, providing as fine a view as one could want to observe. The outstretched runways in the wide valley leading up to the banks of a stream that courses nearby leaves an indelible print upon all that view the site.

It is within this man-made setting that visitors to the base are able to view a modern field in every respect. Some of the largest ships of the nation have landed on the lengthy Tuskegee runways.

The Tuskegee Army Flying School was activated July, 1941. The first troops arrived during the month of October, 1941. The initial ground crew for the then so-called "99th Pursuit Squadron" was composed of men who volunteered their services to the nation, and had been trained at the famous Chanute Field, Illinois. Each man upon his arrival was eager to play his role in building up the first flying school of its kind for Negroes.

The first Commanding Officer of the field was Major James A. Ellison. He was transferred in January, 1942, and Colonel Frederick V. H. Kimble, a West Point graduate with 24 years of flying experience, was assigned as the Commanding Officer of the post. Kimble is now Commanding Officer of the 27th Training Wing and Lieutenant Colonel Noel F. Parrish is now the Commanding Officer. Assisting the Colonel are: Lieutenant Colonel B. O. Davis, Jr., highest ranking Negro officer in the Army Air Forces, is the Executive of Troops; Major Donald S. McPherson, Director of Training; Lieutenant Colonel John T. Hazard, Executive; Captain Clyde H. Bynum, Adjutant, and others. More than 60 per cent of the total quota of officers at the flying school are Negroes.

OHIOAN YOUNGEST SQUADRON COMMANDER

Second Lieutenant Mac Ross, a graduate of the initial flying class in March, 1942, is the youngest Squadron Commander on the field. He is the new C. O. of a newly activated fighter squadron.

He is a native of Dayton, Ohio, and completed his undergraduate work at West Virginia State College. He is the first American flying officer to become a member of the Caterpillar Club. As an Aviation Cadet, he achieved a high degree of efficiency as an all-around soldier. Upon becoming Commanding Officer of the 100th Fighter Squadron, he is fast proving himself to be a capable officer in every respect.

THE MEN ON THE GROUND

No other ground crew in America has had more favorable publicity than the men of the fighting 99th. In the early part of 1941, a group of high school graduates and college men volunteered their services in the Army of the United States to form the foundation crews for the present squadrons that have been activated at the Tuskegee Army Flying School. More than 500 men received training at Rantoul's Chanute Field, ranging from administrative clerks to master mechanics on the flight line. Before becoming eligible for the ground crew, the volunteers had to pass a stiff aptitude test, their results determining their training status as a soldier. Today these men are at the school that they had dreamed of for seven long months before it was constructed. They are teaching boys as eager as they were when they volunteered in the early months of 1941. The older mechanics on the line always inform the new mechanics of the significance of keeping the plane aloft in good condition, and the responsibility that rests upon the shoulder of the mechanic.

The original ground crew of the 99th can handle and service ships from trainer planes to the difficult P-40. These men know their job and have the confidence of the men who fly the ships they service. They have an exceptionally good safety record.

PHOTOGRAPHIC SECTION

Making of aerial photographs is a difficult task. However, here at the Tuskegee School of the Air, it is possible for a photograph to be made, processed and ready in less than ten minutes if the emergency demands. The post has a complete equipped laboratory with the latest equipment for developing and producing pictures.

MODERN HOSPITAL AT T.A.F.S.

The Tuskegee Army Flying School's Station Hospital, under the guidance of Lieutenant Colonel Richard C. Cummings and Major George McDonald and staff, have developed into a well coordinated phase of the Army life at the sepia school of the air. The different wards are equipped with the best modern equipment obtainable and the efficient staff through experience is capable of performing any major operations.

CLEVELAND HAS THREE FLYING OFFICERS

Leading other urban centers with flying officers Clevelanders are prominent on the flight line. Among the flying officers are Second Lieutenants Sidney Brooks, 2275 East 77th St.; Irving Lawrence, 2168 East 90th St.; and Clarence Jamison, 2252 East 85th St.

GROUND AND ADMINISTRATIVE

EMORY H. SMITH
Second Lieutenant
Assistant S-1

REGINALD B. MUNSON
First Lieutenant
Assistant S-2

MOSES W. JONES
Second Lieutenant
Assistant S-3

PHILANDER W. JOHNSON
First Lieutenant
Assistant S-3

★

WILLIAM B. EDELIN
Captain
Assistant S-4

LOUIS H. KLAER
Captain
Ordnance Officer

HAROLD D. MARTIN
Captain
Post Exchange Officer

★

THOMAS S. BURMAN
Captain
Assistant Quartermaster and
Property Officer

JOHN C. YOUNG
Second Lieutenant
Salvage Officer

THOMAS J. COLLINS
Second Lieutenant
Adjutant and Tactical Officer,
Cadet Detachment

STEVE J. DAY
Second Lieutenant
Salvage Officer

CARL O. HOLMBERG
Second Lieutenant
Tactical Officer, Cadet
Detachment

VERNON B. LINCOLN
Second Lieutenant
Assistant Post Exchange
Officer

WALTER E. MOORE
Lieutenant
Assistant Director of
Ground School

EMMETT J. RICE
Second Lieutenant
Statistical Officer

CHARLES S. TRAYLOR
First Lieutenant
Post Statistical Officer

HENRY MOORE
Chief Warrant Officer
Motor Transportation
Officer

DONALD G. McPHERSON
Major
Director of Fighter Training

ROBERT M. LONG
Captain
Director of Advanced
Training

GABE C. HAWKINS
Captain
Director of Basic Training

FLYING OFFICERS

ROBERT L. DUNHAM
Captain

WILLIAM H. GEORGE
Captain

WILLIAM C. BOYD
First Lieutenant

GEORGE L. KNOX
First Lieutenant

JAMES L. WRATHALL, II
First Lieutenant

MAC ROSS
First Lieutenant

HOWARD LEE BAUGH
Second Lieutenant

SAMUEL M. BRUCE
Second Lieutenant

MARSHALL S. CABINESS
Second Lieutenant

RICHARD C. CAESAR
Second Lieutenant

CHARLES H. DeBOW
Second Lieutenant

ELWOOD T. DRIVER
Second Lieutenant

ROBERT W. DEIZ
Second Lieutenant

TERRY J. CHARLTON
Second Lieutenant

FLYING OFFICERS

JEROME T. EDWARDS
Second Lieutenant

JOSEPH D. ELLSBERRY
Second Lieutenant

JOHN A. GIBSON
Second Lieutenant

EDWARD C. GLEED
Second Lieutenant

MILTON T. HALL
Second Lieutenant

NATHANIEL M. HILL
Second Lieutenant

MELVIN T. JACKSON
Second Lieutenant

HERMAN A. LAWSON
Second Lieutenant

WILMORE B. LEONARD
Second Lieutenant

ANDREW MAPLES, JR.
Second Lieutenant

WILLIAM T. MATTISON
Second Lieutenant

GEORGE T. McCRUMBY
Second Lieutenant

JAMES L. McCULLIN
Second Lieutenant

ARMOUR G. McDANIEL
Second Lieutenant

FLYING OFFICERS

CLINTON B. MILLS
Second Lieutenant

JOHN H. MORGAN
Second Lieutenant

CORNELIUS F. NICKOLS
Second Lieutenant

HENRY B. PERRY
Second Lieutenant

WENDELL O. PRUITT
Second Lieutenant

RICHARD C. PULLAM
Second Lieutenant

PRICE D. RICE
Second Lieutenant

CHARLES R. STANTON
Second Lieutenant

EDWARD L. TOPPINS
Second Lieutenant

ANDREW D. TURNER
Second Lieutenant

PETER C. VERWAYNE
Second Lieutenant

QUITMAN C. WALKER
Second Lieutenant

WILLIAM H. WALKER
Second Lieutenant

ROMEO M. WILLIAMS
Second Lieutenant

41

SUB-DEPOT

★

W. G. WILLIAMS
Major
Commanding Sub-Depot

EUGENE H. GRANGNARD
Second Lieutenant
Assistant Engineering Officer

JAMES L. RICHARDSON
First Lieutenant
Supply Officer

WILLIAM D. WILLIAMS
Second Lieutenant
Assistant Supply Officer

★

CHEMICAL WARFARE SERVICE

★

LOTT S. CARTER
Second Lieutenant
Property Officer

HUEY E. CHARLTON
Second Lieutenant
Instructor

★

WARRANT OFFICERS

RICHARD B. RUTLEDGE
Warrant Officer, J. G.
Headquarters Personnel

ROBERT R. SNEAD
Warrant Officer
Photo Section

EDWARD A. EDGHILL
Warrant Officer, J. G.
Engineering

GLENN L. HEAD
Warrant Officer
Armament

HOLLIS T. ARNOLD
Warrant Officer, J. G.
Officers' Pay Section

★

★

KENNETH C. PRINCE
Second Lieutenant
Commanding

RICHARD C. ALLEN
Second Lieutenant
Signal Officer

WILLIAM H. BAILOUS
Second Lieutenant
Personnel Officer

CHARLES H. BELL
Second Lieutenant
Signal Officer

717TH SIGNAL AIRCRAFT WARNING COMPANY

CHARLES A. BOWERS
Second Lieutenant
Signal Officer

ROBERT E. CAMPBELL
Second Lieutenant
Platoon Leader

REVELLE W. CROCKETT
Second Lieutenant
Signal Officer

WHITTIE ENGLISH
Second Lieutenant
Platoon Leader

JAMES D. FRANKLIN
Second Lieutenant
Assistant Personnel Officer

HOSEA HAYES, JR.
Second Lieutenant
Signal Officer

WALTER HIGHT
Second Lieutenant
Signal Officer

JAMES P. JONAS
Second Lieutenant
Signal Officer

ROBERT L. KING
Second Lieutenant
Assistant S-4

ROBERT W. LAWRENCE
Second Lieutenant
Signal Officer

43

GEORGE M. LOWTHER Second Lieutenant Signal Officer	DEAN B. MOHR Second Lieutenant S-3	JAMES D. MORRIS Second Lieutenant Signal Officer	WILLIAM WESLEY MOULDEN Second Lieutenant Signal Officer	ARTHUR B. POLITE, JR. Second Lieutenant Signal Officer

717TH SIGNAL AIRCRAFT WARNING COMPANY

FRANCIS W. POTTER Second Lieutenant Signal Officer	JAMES F. REYNOLDS Second Lieutenant Signal Officer	ROY L. RICHARDSON Second Lieutenant Recreation Officer	WILLIAM ROBERTS Second Lieutenant Supply and Mess Officer	GEORGE E. SMITH Second Lieutenant Signal Officer

DUDLEY V. SIMMS Second Lieutenant Signal Officer	ELNEE U. TIMMONS Second Lieutenant Platoon Leader	ALEXANDER W. WASHINGTON Second Lieutenant Radio Communications Expert	FREDERICK E. WHITE Second Lieutenant Signal Officer	WALDO E. WILLIAMS Second Lieutenant Radio Officer

BENJAMIN O. DAVIS
Lieutenant Colonel

BATES L. SCOGGINS
Major

TACTICAL OFFICERS

★

NELSON S. BROOKS
Captain

HAYDEN C. JOHNSON
Captain

MAURICE E. JOHNSON
Captain

ELMER D. JONES, JR.
Captain

PERCY L. JONES
Captain

LLOYD M. SPARKS
Captain

SIDNEY P. BROOKS
First Lieutenant

CHARLES W. DRYDEN
First Lieutenant

LAWRENCE H. DYRAD
First Lieutenant

CHARLES B. HALL
First Lieutenant

CLARENCE C. JAMISON
First Lieutenant

45

JAMES M. McCARTHER
First Lieutenant

GEORGE E. PETTROSS
First Lieutenant

BERNARD S. PROCTOR
First Lieutenant

THEODORE H. RANDALL
First Lieutenant

TACTICAL OFFICERS

GEORGE S. ROBERTS
First Lieutenant

CLARENCE G. SOUTHALL
First Lieutenant

WILLIAM R. THOMPSON
First Lieutenant

SHERMAN W. WHITE, JR.
First Lieutenant

BENOTE H. WIMP
First Lieutenant

WILLIE ASHLEY, JR.
Second Lieutenant

GEORGE R. BOLLING
Second Lieutenant

LEE G. BROTHERTON
Second Lieutenant

FRANK CARTER
Second Lieutenant

THOMAS M. CLARK
Second Lieutenant

WILSON H. CLEMMONS
Second Lieutenant

GEORGE R. CURRIE
Second Lieutenant

RICHARD DAVIS
Second Lieutenant

SAMUEL L. FULLER
Second Lieutenant

WILLIE H. FULLER
Second Lieutenant

REGINALD H. GEHMAN
Second Lieutenant

MORRIS M. HATCHETT
Second Lieutenant

CHARLES H. HUNTER
Second Lieutenant

TACTICAL OFFICERS

RALPH I. A. JOHNSON
Second Lieutenant

JOHN H. KRAMER
Second Lieutenant

ALLEN G. LANE
First Lieutenant

ERWIN B. LAWRENCE, JR.
First Lieutenant

THOMAS N. MALONE
Second Lieutenant

PAUL G. MITCHELL
Second Lieutenant

EUSTACE I. NAYLOR
Second Lieutenant

LOUIS R. PURNELL
Second Lieutenant

LEON C. ROBERTS
Second Lieutenant

GRAHAM SMITH
Second Lieutenant

CORNELIUS VINCENT
First Lieutenant

SPANN WATSON
Second Lieutenant

WILLIAM M. WOMACK
Second Lieutenant

MALACHI M. GIBSON
Warrant Officer

47

Colonel Noel F. Parrish, Commanding Officer, at his desk.

Captain Edward Henry Norris, S-4, and Captain Harold C. Leighton, S-3

Lieutenant W. O. Yeager, S-1.

Lieutenant Herschel Kornblatt, Acting Public Relations Officer and Photographic Officer.

★

★

48

THE BARRACKS, home sweet home for the duration, look neat under the warm Alabama sun.

ADMINISTRATION of TAFS originates in the attractive Post Headquarters building.

FIRST LT. DOUGLAS L. T. ROBINSON
Chaplain

Lyman Webber, Anyta Harris, Harold Hurd

Cadet Gleed, an advanced Tuskegee student, steps out after becoming the first colored cadet to solo a P-39 Airacobra.

★ ★ PERSONALITIES ★ ★

Lieutenant Colonel Benjamin O. Davis, Jr., a Tuskegee graduate, and the highest-ranking colored flying officer in the armed forces.

★

The puzzled expressions indicate an administration class.

The dit-da boys: a radio class in action.

CLASSES ★

Left: Complications galore for the machine medicos in engine class. Below: This is an armament class, where the hidden mysteries of war tools are carefully solved . . . blindfolded.

You can't play these instruments.

They're all in a whirl . . . a propeller class.

CADET

Plotting a flight.

Right: The "da, da, da" of the telegraphy class.

On the opposite page, Top: Ready for the final check. Below: Cadets on parade.

★

Right: Cadet stunt night at the Post Recreation Hall.

LIFE

Pinning on the bars.

Graduation Day visitors.

AVIATION CADETS

CLASS SE-43-G

Curtis M. Chears
Second Lieutenant

John Daniels
Second Lieutenant

William B. Ellis
Second Lieutenant

CLASS SE-43-B

Walter M. Downs

Claude B. Govan

William E. Griffin

James R. Polkinghorne

John H. Prowell

Roy M. Spencer

William H. Walker

CLASS SE-43-C

Clarence W. Allen

Woodrow W. Crockett

Alfonza W. Davis

Lawrence E. Dickson

Alwayne M. Dunlap

W. M. Gordon, Jr.

Walter L. McCreary

Pearlee E. Saunders

Wilmeth W. Sidat-Singh

Lloyd G. Singletary

CLASS SE-43-D

Paul Adams

Marvin T. Allen

Charles P. Bailey

John F. E. Banks

Jerry T. Bowling

James E. Brothers

James Y. Carter

AVIATION CADETS

CLASS SE-43-D

Arnold W. Cisco   Wilson V. Eagleson   Alfred T. Farrer   William J. Faulkner   Walter T. Foreman   Vernor V. Haywood   Franklin A. Hill

Heber C. Houston   Freddie E. Hutchins   Leonard M. Jackson   Sidney J. Mosley, Jr.   Quilliam A. Moore   Cecil D. Nelson   Curtis C. Robinson

Harold E. Sawyer   Lewis C. Smith   Ulysses S. Taylor, Jr.   Luke J. Weathers, Jr.   Charles I. Williams   Wendall J. Williams   Virgil J. Young

CLASS SE-43-G

Harry L. Bailey   W. R. Bartley   Eddie L. Brown   Emmett C. Burke   Lorenzo A. Carter   Lawrence O. Clark

Samuel L. Curtis   Alvin G. Daste   Frank C. Eason   George E. Greenlee   Eugene R. Henderson   James P. Howard   Daniel E. Hughes

Curtis H. Johnson   John H. Leahr   James W. Mason   Eddie A. McLaurin   William R. Melton   Aldee G. Miller   George B. Oliver

AVIATION CADETS

CLASS SE-43-G

Maurice R. Page	F. Eugene Portee	Milton B. Richardson	Edward N. Smith	Lowell C. Stewart	Matthew B. Stuart	Elmer W. Taylor
Alva N. Temple	Harold E. Ward	Walter D. Westmoreland	Robert H. Wiggins	Johnnie I. Williams	LeRoi S. Williams	Beryl Wyatt

CLASS SE-43-H

Charles W. Adams	S. E. Anderson	L. A. Archer	Alton F. Ballard	Hubron R. Blackwell	Everett P. Blake	Bruce T. Bowens
Robert F. Bowers	Edward L. Bowman	Everett A. Bratcher	Ralph H. Brown	James D. Carter	Samuel Colbert	Joe W. Connolly
Harry J. Daniels	Andrew H. Doswell	Clarence R. Dougan	Charles A. Dunne	Clarence L. Forbes	Reginald A. Freeman	Oscar C. Gadson, Jr.
George W. Giddings	LeRoy F. Gillead	Walter S. Gladding	Smith W. Green	William W. Green	Richard W. Hall	Walter D. Hall

AVIATION CADETS

CLASS SE-43-H

Seabron G. Hamilton   Thomas W. Haywood   William M. Heyward   Ernest J. Hill   William E. Hill   J. D. Holsclaw   Lawrence B. Jefferson

Samuel Jefferson   Hubert Ledyard Jones   Reuben D. Jones   William A. Kelley, Jr.   C. A. Lockett   Thomas J. Marshall   William B. McClenic

Jeremiah McCoy   M. W. Meriweather   Celestino S. Monclova   Melvin M. Nelson   Robert H. Nelson   Starling B. Penn   Driskell B. Ponder

Leon Purchase   Cornelius G. Rogers   Hefty B. Scott   Alphonso Simmons   James B. Smith   Charles W. Stephens   Norvell Stoudmire

Charles W. Tate   George A. Taylor   Arthur C. Thompson   Floyd A. Thompson   Concord W. Turner   George M. Washington   Rogers Watson

James E. Wells   Kenneth J. White   Wayne N. White   Frank E. Whitted   Fleming M. Williams   Carrol S. Woods   Willard L. Woods

Top, Left: Colonel F. V. A. Kimble at desk. Top, Right: Captain C. H. Bynum, Adjutant. Lower Left: Captain Bernie E. Compton, Investigating Officer and Civilian Personnel Officer. Lower Right: Lieutenant C. S. Traylor, Statistical Department.

Intelligence Department—Post Technical School.   Captain E. C. Ambler and Lieutenant Munson.

A few snapshots taken while strolling through the various offices and recreation rooms of the 318th Headquarters and Air Base Squadron.

Drafting Department.   Post Technical School Office.

FLOYD H. McDONALD
Captain
Commanding

NATHANIEL FREEMAN
Captain
Basic Training

318TH BASE HEADQUARTERS AND AIR BASE SQUADRON

ARTHUR P. HAYES
Captain
Recruit Training

ULYSSES G. LEE, JR.
First Lieutenant
Engineering Property Officer

JAMES A. G. GRANT, JR.
Second Lieutenant
Technical Supply Officer

KERMIT T. MELLINGER
Second Lieutenant
Assistant Special Services Officer

JOSEPH C. MILLS
Second Lieutenant
Cadet Supply Officer

HENRY MOSES
Second Lieutenant
Recruit Detachment

WILLARD B. RANSOM
First Lieutenant
Adjutant

GRANVILLE W. WARNER
Second Lieutenant
Supply Officer

DAVID WILLIAMS
Second Lieutenant
Basic Training

EUGENE P. WHITE
Second Lieutenant
Basic Training

318TH BASE HEADQUARTERS AND AIR BASE SQUADRON

(Reading from Left to Right)

First Row: Private Burton, John L.; Sergeants Childs, John A.; Dickson, William H.; Hicks, Daniel S.; Master Sergeants Collins, Edward A.; Davis, Leonard L.

Second Row: Master Sergeant Pope, Edgar A.; Technical Sergeants Donaldson, Robert E.; Ko, R. E.; McLendon, Henry T., Jr.; Prime, Norman T.

Third Row: Staff Sergeants Bell, Arthur N.; Campbell, Harvey I.; Collier, William B., Jr.; Ford, John M.; James, Voris S.; Jewett, Thurman D.

Fourth Row: Staff Sergeants Johnson, Sidney L.; Jones, Anthony C.; Mackey, Elton R.; Mathis, Raleigh; Moore, William; Mullgrav, Edgar D.

Fifth Row: Staff Sergeants Nash, Andrew; Oliver, James B.; Walker, William H.; Webber, Lyman W.; Sergeants Banks, Nathan; Boston, Leroy.

William H. Goode
Private

318TH BASE HEADQUARTERS AND AIR BASE SQUADRON

★

(Reading from Left to Right)

First Row: Sergeants Bowen, Theodore C.; Broadway, Woodrow W.; Brown, Earl C.; Chilton, Thomas A.; Dickerson, John A.; Diggs, Donald S.

Second Row: Sergeants Gumbs, Stanley E.; James, Alfred C.; Johnson, Sylvester; Jones, Solomon L.; Kelly, Robert J.; King, William H.

Third Row: Sergeants Lalande, Joseph A.; Louis, William G.; McFerren, Harold S.; Mahan, Clifton W.; Minniefield, William G.; Reid, Henry O., Jr.

Fourth Row: Sergeants Ridley, Anthony; Sablo, Rudolph; Scott, Alfred E., Jr.; Shuler, Marion M.; Taylor, James E., Jr.; Thomas, Wilbur C.

Fifth Row: Sergeants Walton, Allen W.; White, William J.; William, Green W.; Wright, Frank B.; Wright, Freeman M.; Technician Fourth Grade Sykes, Jasper C.

Sixth Row: Corporals Beams, Jacob M.; Brown, Leroy L.; Bush, James L.; Cohen, Joseph L.; Crumpton, John D.; Fletcher, Wilbert.

Seventh Row: Corporals Flowers, Harris; Freeman, Andrew B.; Fuller, Thomas; Hackett, Irvin; Harding, Hiram M.; Harrison, Timothy O.

Eighth Row: Corporals Hodge, Victor H.; Jones, John E.; Keith, Edward C.; Kirtley, Crockett H.; Mayo, Williard D.; Miller, Whitt, Jr.

Ninth Row: Corporals Osborn, Henry J.; Parrish, Leo R.; Pearson, Edward L.; Rector, Elmer R.; Reyes, Joseph; Richardson, Milton H.

Tenth Row: Corporals Roberts, Cleon B.; Robinson, Hayward N.; Shipp, Horace A.; Simmons, Clinton; Snowden, James V.; Strong, Albert L.

318TH BASE HEADQUARTERS AND AIR BASE SQUADRON

★

(Reading from Left to Right)

First Row: Corporals Swafford, Lorenzo A.; Thomas, Edward C., Jr.; Vaughn, Hiram W.; Warren, Carl; Whitaker, Hiram L.; White, James N.

Second Row: Privates First Class Badely, Milton; Branson, Lawrence D.; Buck, Clarence H., Jr.; Cooper, Bertram; Davis, Russell E.; Edwards, Carroll P.

Third Row: Privates First Class Foucher, Sherman; Gibbs, George F.; Givens, James E.; Hazly, Alton; Jackson, Julius; Jackson, Robert T.

Fourth Row: Privates First Class Jeffries, Jesse W.; Johnson, Edward; Lawson, Dennie; Nelson, B. L.; Simms, Leland B.; Taylor, Albert.

Fifth Row: Privates First Class Tucker, Stephen; Varella, Thomas J.; Way, Roosevelt; William, Reginald, Privates Alexander, Edward; Allen, Joseph S.

Sixth Row: Privates Bankston, Clifford J.; Beal, Leonard A.; Berkley, Homer A.; Bigelow, Charles D.; Blackman, Dayton S.; Boatwright, Curtis H.

Seventh Row: Privates Booker, Charles H.; Bridgeforth, Ernest H.; Buckley, Bishop A.; Bunch, Fred, Jr.; Burnam, Marshall G.; Burton, J. M.

Eighth Row: Privates Carey, Harold A.; Cartwright, Isaiah; Christopher, Vernon; Collier, Joseph M.; Cooper, Theodore B.; Crawford, William.

Ninth Row: Privates Crain, Charles A.; Cunningham, Jasper; Dabney, N. P.; Daley, James H.; Davenport, Frank E.; Deare, William A.

Tenth Row: Privates Dowell Alfonso L.; Evans, John G., Sr.; Ferguson, W. C.; Forte, Jesse A.; Fuertado, Vernon H.; Gray, William.

318TH BASE HEADQUARTERS AND AIR BASE SQUADRON

★

(Reading from Left to Right)

First Row: Privates Groce, Daniel P.; Hamilton, Clarence; Harris, Tamlin L.; Harris, Wesley C.; Harvey, Sylvester C.; Hazard, Harold A.

Second Row: Privates Hector, Francis I.; Tickerson, Robert; Hogan, Ernest; Hopkins, Mack H.; Humphrey, Benjamin A.; Irvins, Rofus S.

Third Row: Privates James, Wade E.; Jones, James L.; Jones, John G.; Jordan, Anderson A.; Law, William; Leonard, Hughey W.

Fourth Row: Privates Lewis, Napoleon B.; Logan, George W.; McAlister, Herbert R.; McIntosh, Bernard; Martin, Phil; Mattier, Ansul Q.

Fifth Row: Privates Maxwell, Thomas L.; Mitchell, Frank E.; Mitchell, William J.; Moore, Eugene; Moton, Mason, Jr.; Mundy, Earl M.

Sixth Row: Privates Parker, Carl C.; Parker, Robert E.; Rakes, John E.; Reeves, Edward M.; Rhodes, Fred; Rhodes, Joseph A.

Seventh Row: Privates Ridley, Edd; Robert, Theophilus; Rogers, Benjamin B., Jr.; Ruffins, Arthur J.; Saunders, Roosevelt D.; Shepherd, Samuel P.

Eighth Row: Privates Simms, Aaron O., Jr.; Slaughter, James; Smith, Leon E.; Smith, Stuart B.; Southerland, Ernest R., Jr.; Spight, Frank R.

Ninth Row: Privates Sport, Vernon K.; Starling, William E.; Stokes, Melvyn M.; Strothers, Edmund P.; Thomas, Robert L.; Turner, Harry.

Tenth Row: Privates Washington, Coley; White, J. D.; Williams, Charles W.; Wilson, Utha; Woodridge, Walter; Wright, Welborn L.

CLARENCE F. JONES, JR.
Captain
Commanding

DANIEL J. BAILEY
First Lieutenant

WALTER H. ENGLISH
Second Lieutenant

CASSIUS H. HARRIS, III
Second Lieutenant

889TH BASIC FLYING TRAINING SQUADRON

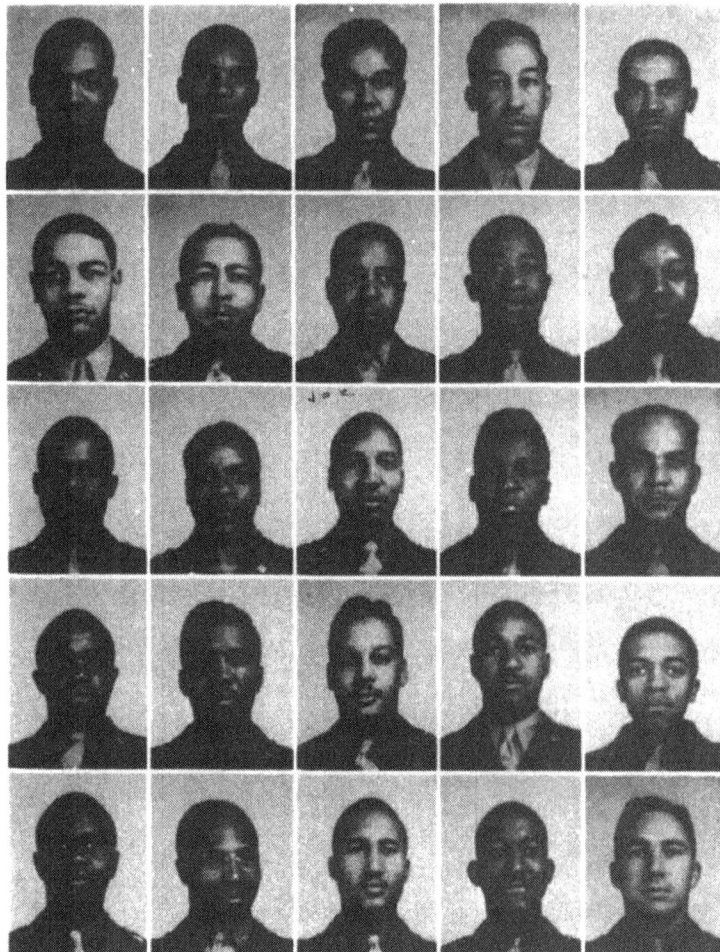

★

(Reading from Left to Right)

First Row: Master Sergeants Ausby, Earl O.; Blackstone, James; First Sergeant Dickson, William H.; Technical Sergeants Black, Bernard O.; Johnson, Duncan W.

Second Row: Technical Sergeant Marshall, Robert W.; Staff Sergeants Adams, Walter N.; Akers, O. E.; Anderson, James E.; Austin, Thomas.

Third Row: Staff Sergeants Coleman, Eugene; Dunn, Fred A.; Echols, Joseph G.; Fields, Daniel H.; Garibaldi, Harold A.

Fourth Row: Staff Sergeants Harris, Albert W.; Harris, Arthur L.; Hilton, Harold A.; Nelson, Clarence W.; Perry, Edward, Jr.

Fifth Row: Staff Sergeants Smith, Joseph N.; Spann, John C.; Tucker, Garfield; Woody, David E.; Wright, Frank N.

889TH BASIC FLYING TRAINING SQUADRON

DOUGLAS JONES
Second Lieutenant

(Reading from Left to Right)

First Row: Sergeants Bland, John; Board, George; Breeden, Dock C.; Brown, Bernard F.; Browne, Phillip C.; Bryant, William F.

Second Row: Sergeants Carr, Stanford E.; Chestnut, Harold G.; Conley, Coleman; Davis, Ralph H.; Driggriss, Harvey; Forte, Milton W.

Third Row: Sergeants Freeman, Arthur W.; George, Hunster E.; Grady, Mitchell; Green, Leslie; Griffith, Wilbur A.; Henry, George.

Fourth Row: Sergeants Hicks, Quentin E.; Hinton, David H.; Hunster, Charles; Hunt, William T.; Jones, Clellie; Jones, Millard.

Fifth Row: Sergeants Lamb, Alonzo J.; Lloyd, Frederick; Long, Judson H.; Lumsy, Dorsey; McCrary, Fred D.; Manning, Thomas.

Sixth Row: Sergeants Mitchell, Littleton; Moses, John E.; Pendleton, John H.; Rabouin, Leonace; Robins, John G.; White, John D.

Seventh Row: Sergeant Winters, Eddie L.; Corporals Alexander, Lafayette; Batchelor, Harry W.; Brown, Donald C.; Burbridge, Harry L.; Collins, Tommy J.

Eighth Row: Corporals Cook, Thomas; Cullens, Herman; Davenport, William J.; Dean, Charles A.; DeSandies, Conrad; Dillard, Richard.

Ninth Row: Corporals Dorsey, Jonathan; Gainey, Willie B.; Gillard, Edward A.; Green, Peter T.; Harris, Emmett; Height, James W.

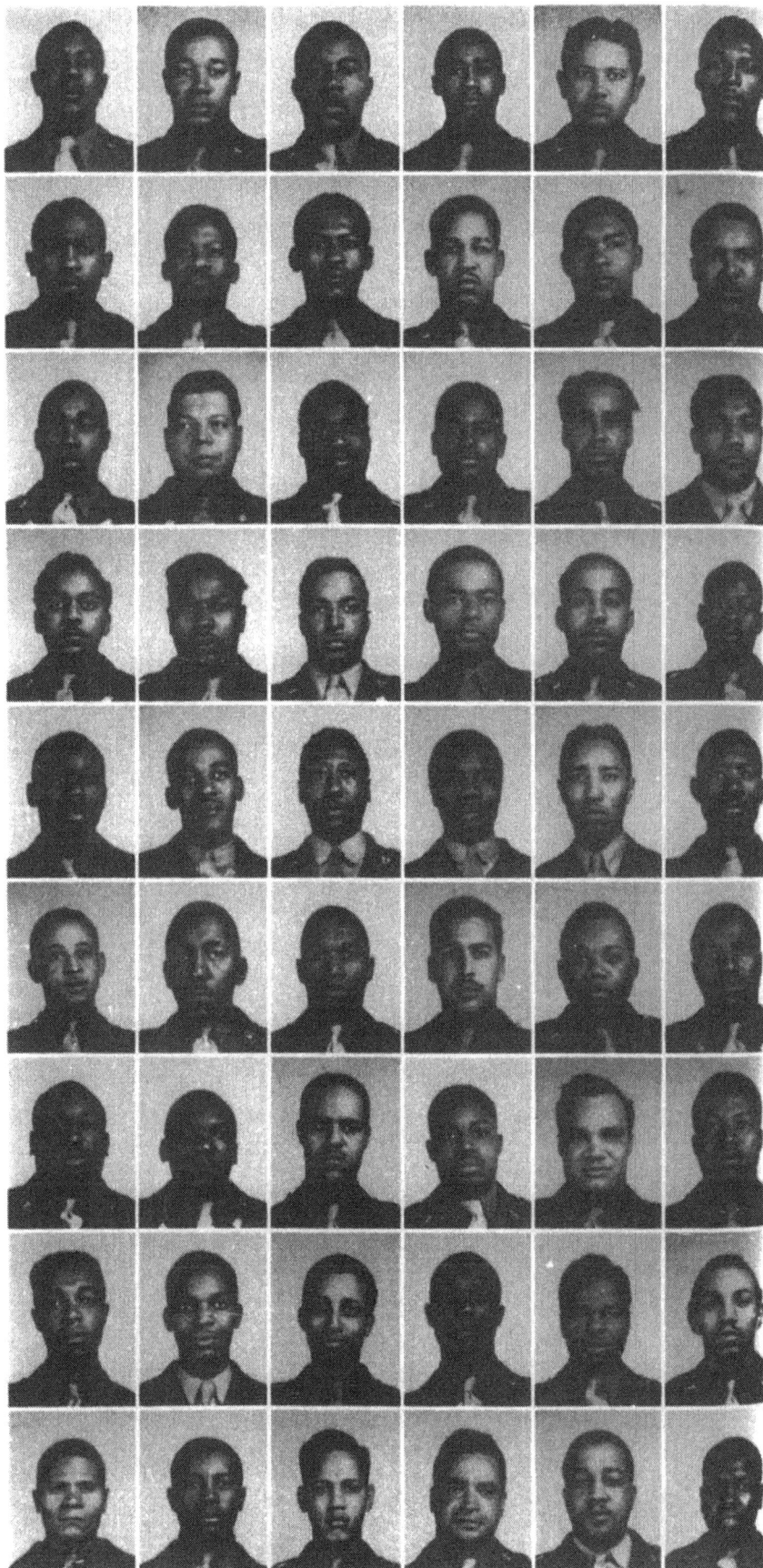

[62]

69

889TH BASIC FLYING TRAINING SQUADRON

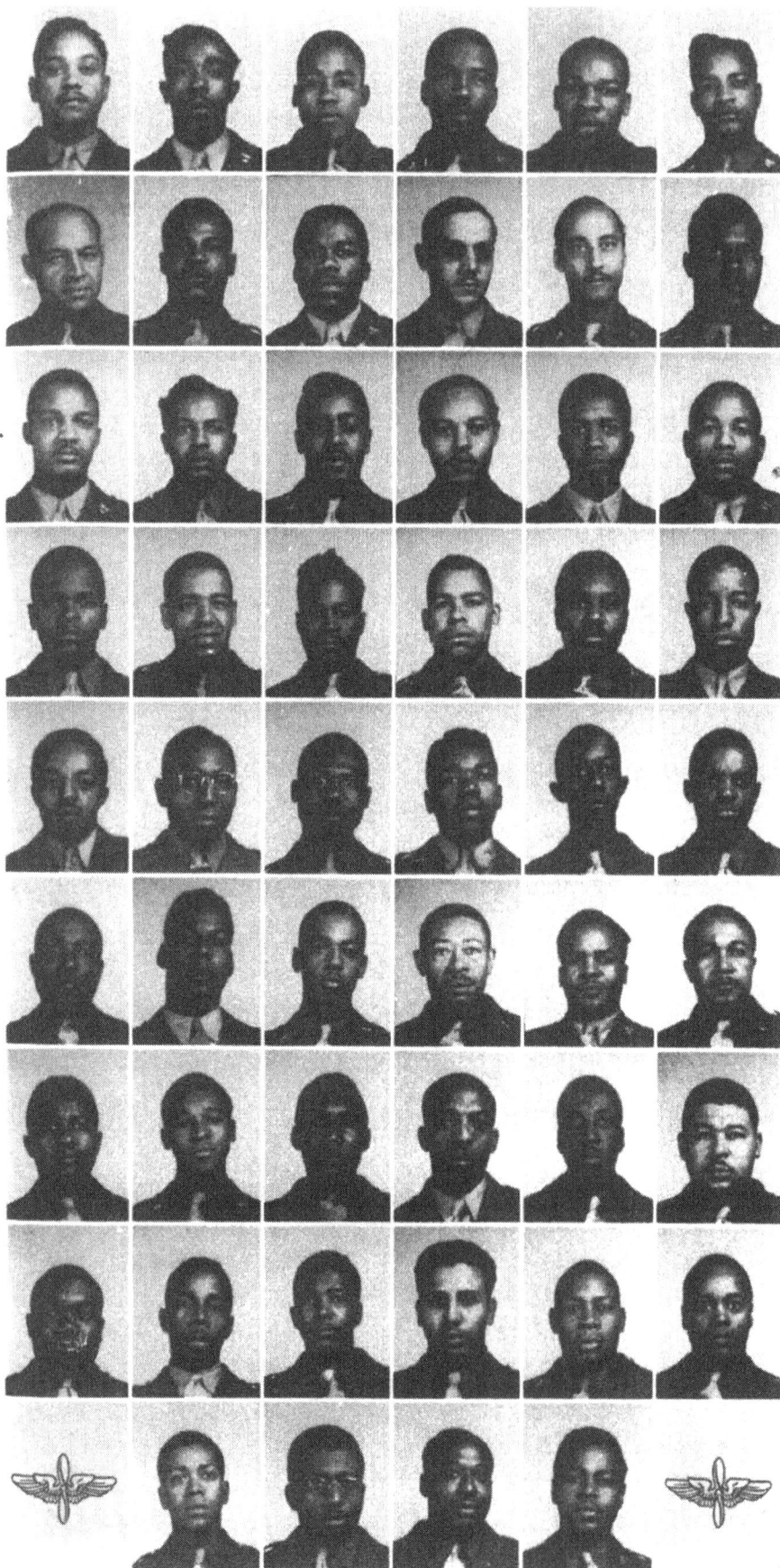

EDWARD K. NICKOLAS, JR.
Second Lieutenant

(Reading from Left to Right)

First Row: Corporals Henderson, Raymond H.; Lane, Lowell W.; Mc-Cormic, Charles; Murphy, Charles T.; Quick, William E.; Randolph, Chesteen.

Second Row: Corporals Skeete, Albert; Sykes, Booker D.; Talley, Robert; Wilson, Ralph G.; Baker, James; Private First Class Caldwell, William.

Third Row: Privates First Class Campbell, Augustus; Carroll, Augustus; Dorsey, William; Fisher, Donald B.; Flowers, Alex; Fuller, Lewis.

Fourth Row: Privates First Class Guilford, James; Higgenbotham, Aubrey; Jones, Rupert S.; Marshall, Edward S.; Matthews, John R.; Mc-Cormick, Willie L.

Fifth Row: Privates First Class Morris, Robert H.; Price, William; Robinson, Julius; Stewart, Wilbur J.; Tinsley, Leonard; Winfrey, Russell.

Sixth Row: Private First Class Young, Fred; Privates Anderson, James, Jr.; Anderson, William C.; Artis, Harry F.; Baker, Perry W.; Bridges, Jesse.

Seventh Row: Privates Bradley, Charlton W.; Booker William H.; Ford, Peter, Jr.; Foster, Ray F.; Givens, Charles; Griffin, Henry W., Jr.

Eighth Row: Privates Griffin, Walter; Hagler, Richard W.; Howell, Olden W.; Jones, James W.; Madden, Birl F.; Price, Elmer.

Ninth Row: Privates Stevens, Haywood; Whitaker, Frank; Whitaker, Roy Lee; White, William I.

99th Fighter Squadron, March, 1944
Left To Right: John S. Sloan, Albert "Bootsy" Manning

Sgt. William (Bill) Dean
301st Fighter Squadron
332nd Fighter Group

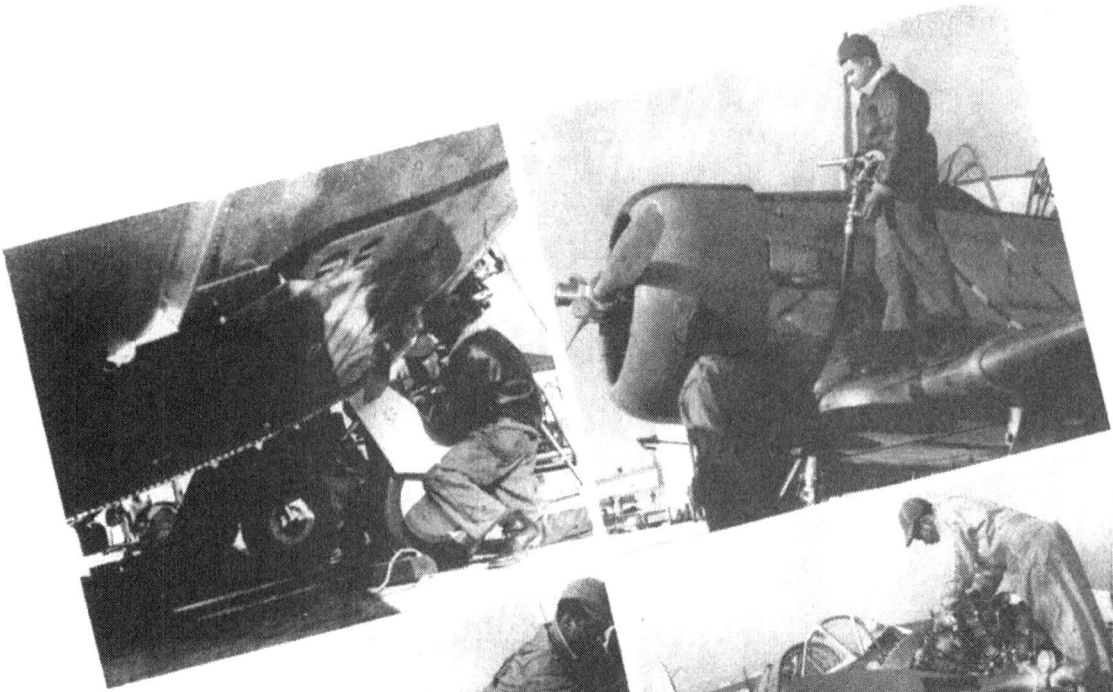

S
H
O
P

8
8
9
T
H

The 890th swings out, en route to review. Left: The Commanding Officer of the outfit, Captain Bascom F. Hodge.

890 TH

The officers and men of the 890th line up for a group shot.

Marching snappily out to "keep 'em flying."

The men work over a trainer while Captain Hodge, Lieutenant Stark, and Lieutenant Hall confer.

S ★ E ★ F ★ T ★ S

The crew chiefs.

Captain Hodge and his staff use the Technical Library.

BASCOM F. HODGE
Captain
Commanding

HOMER L STARKS
Adjutant
Second Lieutenant

CHARLES E. BELL, JR.
Second Lieutenant

DONALD M. CONKLEY
Second Lieutenant

CHARLES R. HALL
Second Lieutenant

890TH SINGLE ENGINE FLYING TRAINING SQUADRON

★

(Reading from Left to Right)

First Row: Master Sergeants Freeman, James R.; Mack, Frederick A.; First Sergeant Washington, Roscoe J.; Technical Sergeants Crenchaw, Charles M.; Cundiff, Charles W.

Second Row: Technical Sergeants Walters, William A.; Washington, Thomas L.; Young, Lee M.; Staff Sergeants Brown, Eugene L.; Champion, Jesse J., Jr.

Third Row: Staff Sergeants Chisholm, Charles S.; Draper, Quentin B.; Dudley, Herbert; Facen, Ernest E.; Fieulleteau, Ronald E.

Fourth Row: Staff Sergeants Jackson, Herbert; Lawson, George; Mayo, John R.; McCraw, Allen; McGrew, William T.

Fifth Row: Staff Sergeants Shoecraft, Robert K.; Waddell, Kermitt F.; Warren, Carl W.; Watson, Willie; Williams, Curtis O.

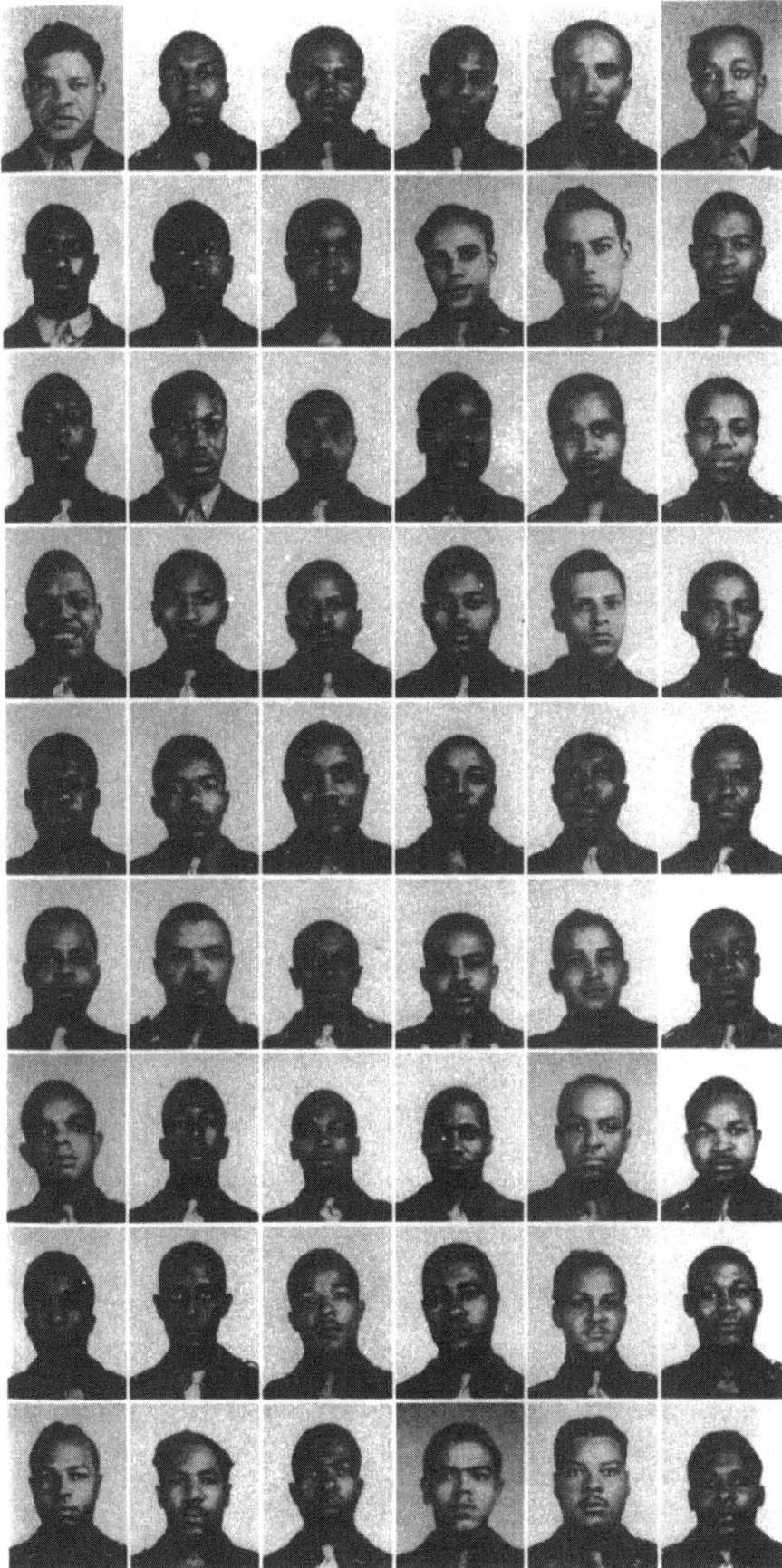

JAMES L. HORACE, JR.
Second Lieutenant

(Reading from Left to Right)

First Row: Sergeants Bailey, Henry R.; Burdine, William H.; Davis, Roy; Delbridge, Captain; Dunson, Allen; Frank, Kenneth L.

Second Row: Sergeants Gooding, Reginald A.; Grigsby, Ernest R.; Harper, Charles L. G.; Henderson, Harry V.; Jones, William P.; Kennedy, William T.

Third Row: Sergeants Lomax, James; Naylor, William A.; Parrish, Sylester; Randolph, Walter; Robinson, Asbury D.; Russell, Wheeler A.

Fourth Row: Sergeants Scott, Thomas L.; Smith, Morris L.; Waugh, Ernest R.; Williams, Spencer; Woodyear, John M.; Corporal Ailster, James W.

Fifth Row: Corporals Bolden, Isaac G.; Cochran, William H.; Colbert, Cal; Coleman, Eugene; Conley, Toy C.; Cotton, John.

Sixth Row: Corporals Davis, Alfonso J.; Durr, Marvin; Finney, Frank R.; Gaddy, Charles B.; Garnes, John R.; Harden, Joseph.

Seventh Row: Corporals Hatchette, George R.; Hausley, John R.; Henderson, Oscar W.; Hewitt, Rufus I. L.; Hubbard, William A.; Johnson, Charles I.

Eighth Row: Corporals Lawson, Clarence; Luke, William H.; Martin, Gerald F.; McCain, William; McNair, Willie L.; Mills, Perry.

Ninth Row: Corporals Moore, John L., Jr.; Morrow, Clarence E.; Nelson, Eugene L.; Peterson, Elwood F.; Pettiferde, Quentin A.; Raymond, J. R.

890TH SINGLE ENGINE TRAINING SQUADRON

★

(Reading from Left to Right)

First Row: Corporals Roberts, Delbert E.; Smith, Marvin T., Jr.; Sneed, Joseph G.; Stridiron, Clifton T.; Tanner, Cyrus S.; Watson, John M.

Second Row: Corporals White, Harold A.; Wiley, Marion L.; Williams, John C.; Wilson, Allen; Wilson, Nathan B.; Wilson, Samuel L.

Third Row: Privates First Class Ardis, Arthur; Barnes, Clarence W., Jr.; Breckenridge, Walter L.; Brewster, Walter H.; Carroll, Alonzo; Coleman, Forest E.

Fourth Row: Privates First Class Daniels, Malcolm L.; Dooley, James O. Jr.; Ector, Thomas M.; Finch, Francis; Fisher, Alexander J.; Forde, Hugo J.

Fifth Row: Privates First Class Gentry, Newton; Green, Roger E.; Hall, James E.; Hillman, John H.; Hillman, William E.; Hutchinson, Richard J.

Sixth Row: Privates First Class Jenkins, Willie E., Jr.; Johnson, Jesse L.; Johnson, Warren A.; Jones, Alfred G.; Joseph, Ronald; Lee, John.

Seventh Row: Privates First Class Lewis, F. C.; Lundy, Fred C.; Mance, Rogers; Mitchell, William A.; Moore, Noah P.; Payne, Charles F.

Eighth Row: Privates First Class Pettiford, Alexander; Priestly, Burniss, Jr.; Riddle, Thomas M.; Roy, Aricheal L.; Sisson, George B.; Taylor, Abram.

Ninth Row: Privates First Class Todd, James E., Jr.; Tutt, Charles C.; Walker, Winthrop; Washington, Buford S.; Watkins, Mannie M.; Webster, Clarence R.

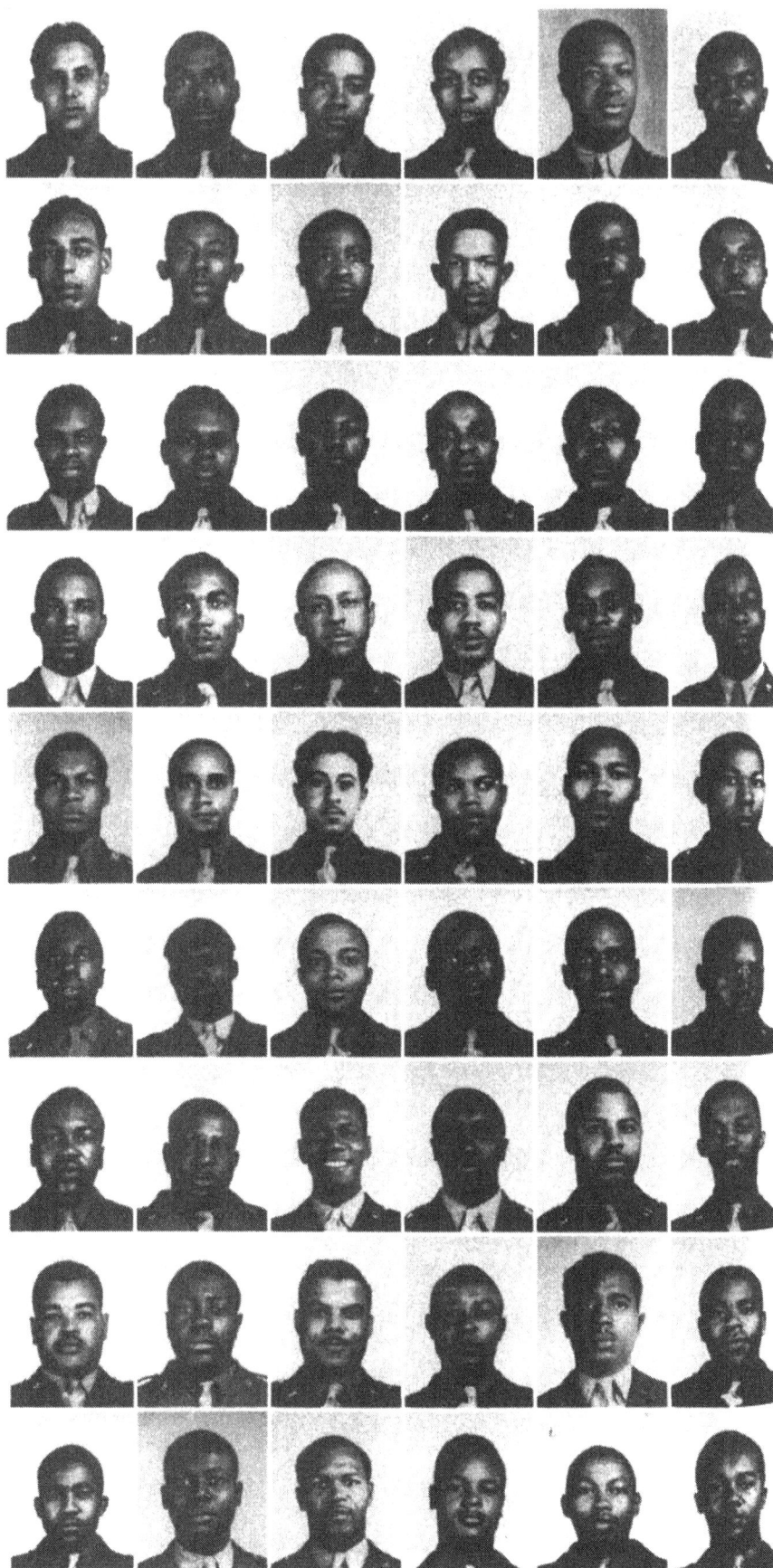

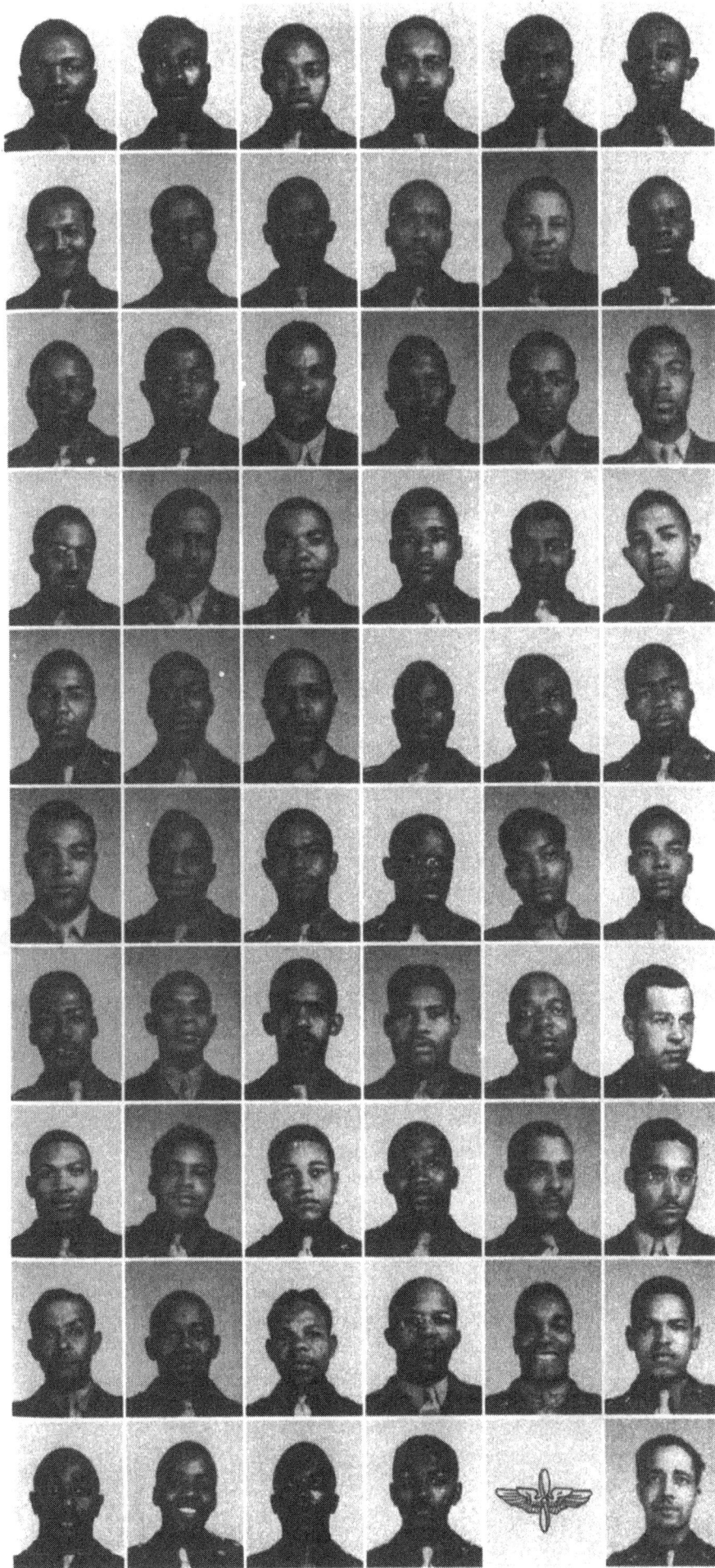

JESSIE WILLIAMS
Second Lieutenant

890TH SINGLE ENGINE TRAINING SQUADRON

(Reading from Left to Right)

First Row: Privates First Class Wesley, Howard; Whitaker, James A.; Wilson, Alonzo T.; Wood, William D., Jr.; Privates Barksdale, Arthur B.; Booker, Ralph B.

Second Row: Privates Bowman, Edward; Brown, Albert S.; Burke, Chester; Carter, Francis A.; Coleman, Charles; Collier, Matthew.

Third Row: Privates Council, Grover; Davis, Leroy H., Jr.; Dean, George P.; Dotson, Harry; Elam, Charles H.; Franklin, Benjamin K.

Fourth Row: Privates Fuller, James B.; Gaines, Thomas H.; Gee, Day; Greene, Alfred F.; Guilford, John C.; Harper, Edgar G.

Fifth Row: Privates Hawkins, Jesse N.; Henry, Thomas L.; Hicks, Fred; Hill, Leon; Howard, Charles; Howard, Ellis C.

Sixth Row: Privates Hubbard, William E.; Johnson, Joseph N.; Johnson, Mack, Jr.; Johnson, Sylvester T., Jr.; Jones, Lester; Jones, Ralph.

Seventh Row: Privates Justice, Laurence; Lake, Willie; Lyons, Joe R.; Mathews, Harold; Morris, Charles A.; Morris, Samuel O.

Eighth Row: Privates Parker, Ollie C.; Pasquet, Luke J.; Richardson, Samuel, M., Jr.; Sanders, Eugene; Sandidge, Grayson E., Jr.; Shields, Wilbur.

Ninth Row: Privates Simpson, E. L.; Smith, Elmer L.; Toney, Joseph P.; Turner, Frederick W.; Turner, William; Viverette, Thomas E.

Tenth Row: Privates Watrous, John W.; White, Ralph A.; Williams, Joseph P.; Wimberly, Charles G.

ATTACHED A. F. UNASSIGNED
Staff Sergeant Williams, Arthur F.

79

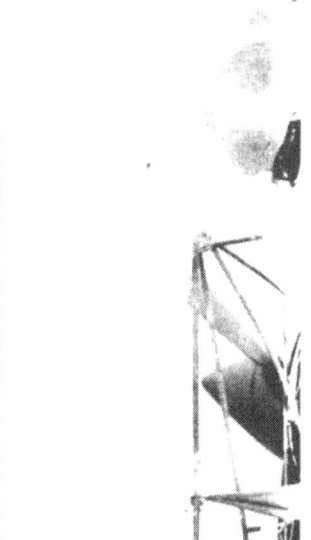

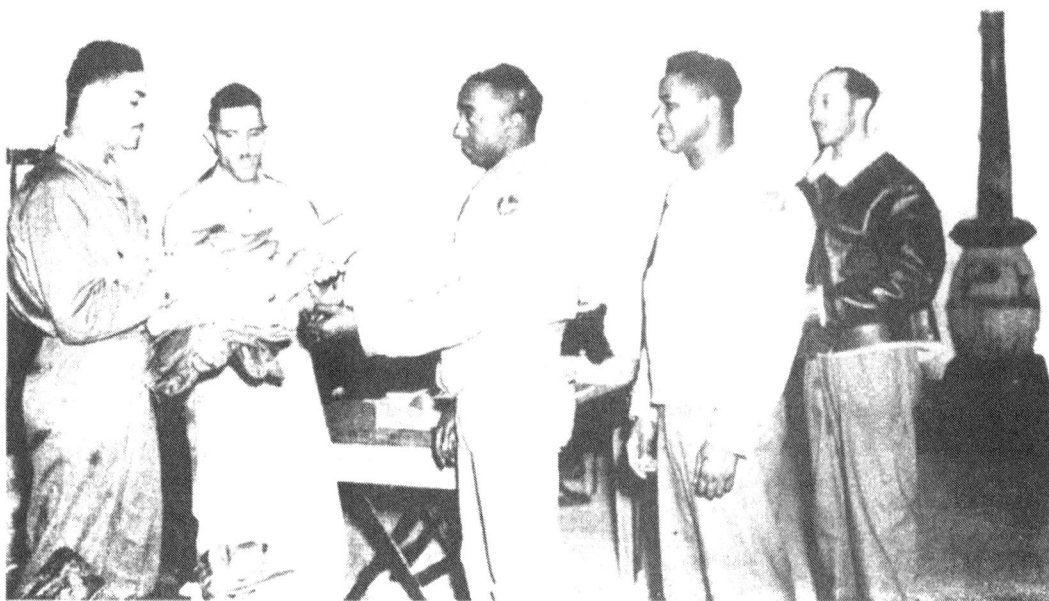

**1155TH
SEFTS**

Upper six pictures: On the line with the P-40's. Lower Left: Getting supplies. Lower Right: Sergeant Robertson and Corporal Ransom at work.

WILLIAM L. TURNER
Captain
Commanding

EDWARD B. McCARROLL
Second Lieutenant
Adjutant

JAMES PUGHSLEY
Second Lieutenant
Supply Officer

1155TH SINGLE ENGINE FLYING TRAINING SQUADRON

(Reading from Left to Right)

First Row: Staff Sergeants Brown, Robert L.: Hairston, Alonzo; Jones, Ambrose S.; Sobers, Lewis M.; Sergeants Jones, Marion R.: McIver, Alvis.

Second Row: Sergeants Mosley, Phillip; Osterhoudt, Alan L.: Pulliam, Howard D.; Smith, Earl C.; Corporals Brewster, Reginald: Brice, William A.

Third Row: Corporals Davis, Ben H.: Gordon, Willie A.; Jones, Edward L.: Kirtley, Robert; Maxwell, Charles C.; Russell, Horace M.

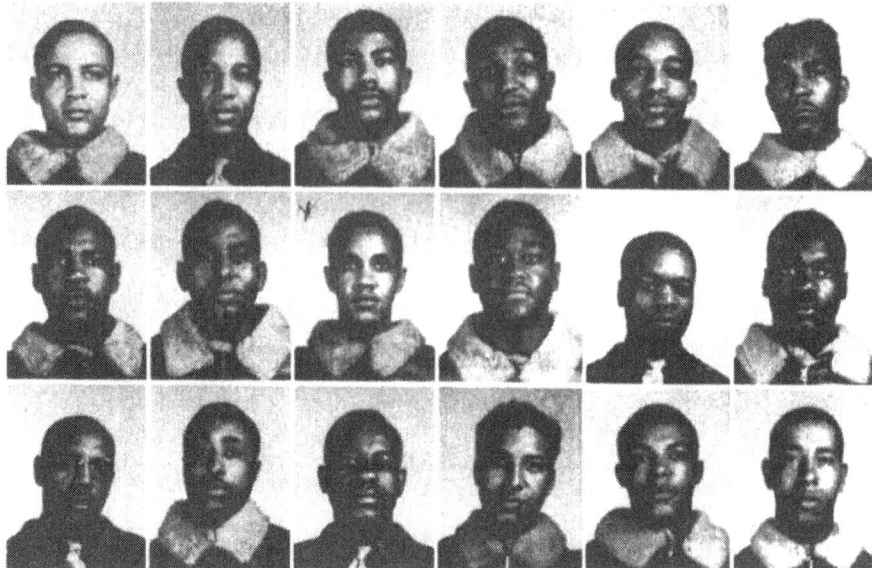

1155TH SINGLE ENGINE FLYING TRAINING SQUADRON

(Reading from Left to Right)

First Row: Corporals Stilles, Joseph; Thompson, Lester F.; Privates First Class Ball, Robert P.; DeHaven, B. B.; Galloway, Joseph.

Second Row: Privates First Class Roberts, Kenneth; Yette, Otis H.· Privates Bradshaw, Norman; Brown, George A.; Davis, Percy L.

Third Row: Privates Faggins, Willis D.; Gettys, Joseph W.; Godbee, Leonard; Harris, John; Johnson, Wilbert F.

Fourth Row: Privates Lewis, Jesse E.; Miller, Henry; Milliner, Charles; Milner, Alphonso; Parns, Milton M.

Fifth Row: Privates Pinder, William T.; Richie, William L.; Robinson, Romeo R.; Simmons, Henry L.; Washington, Nathaniel W.

Sixth Row: Privates Weeks, Vernon; Williams, John A.; Yager, Henry.

POST HOSPITAL ADMINISTRATION BUILDING

★ ★ STATION

Dental Clinic.

Laboratory.

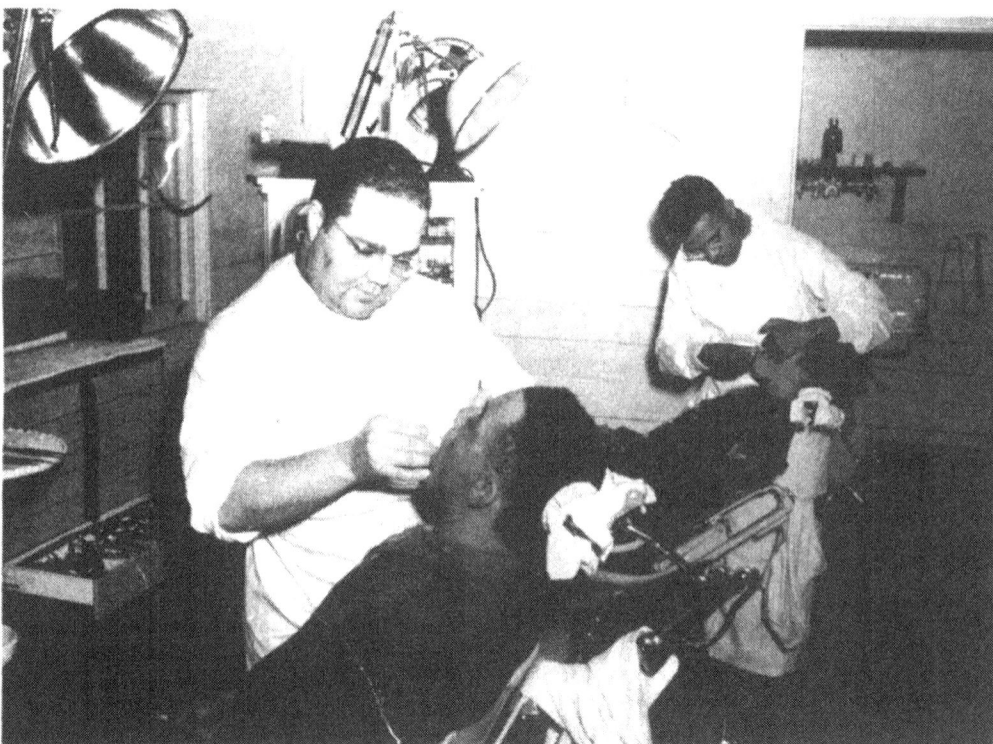

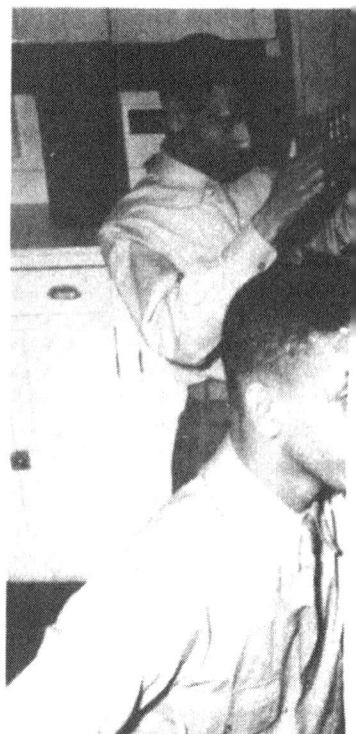

RICHARD C. CUMMING
Lieutenant Colonel
Post Surgeon

H O S P I T A L ★ ★

Laboratory.

Pharmacy Department.

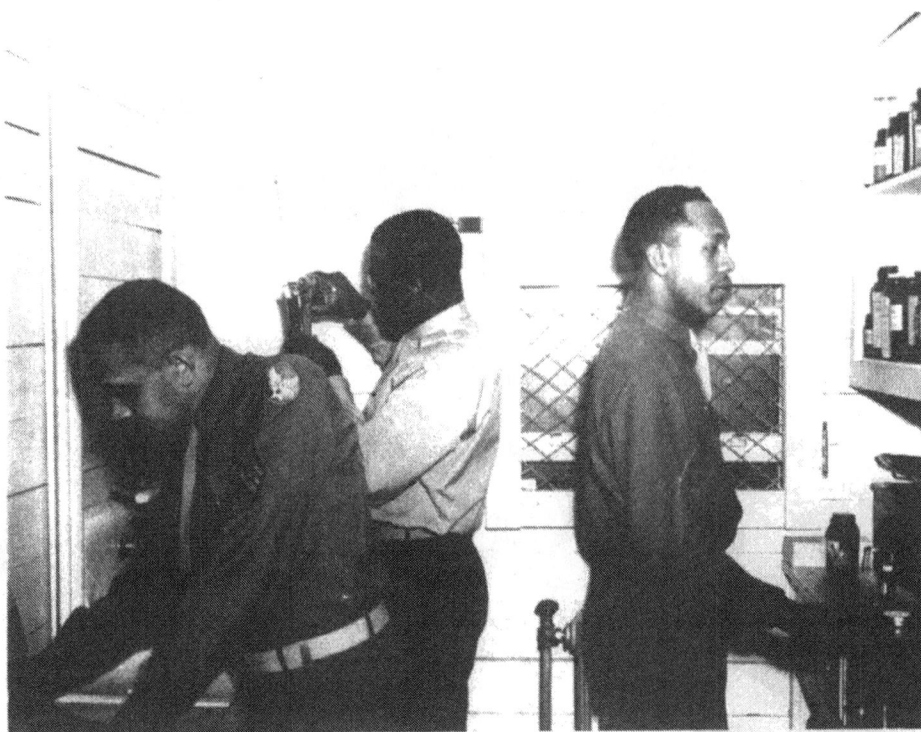

RAYMOND KING
Major
Dental Surgeon

GEORGE McDONALD
Major
Chief of Medical Services

JAMES E. FOOTE
Captain
Dental Officer

ROY C. HAIRSTON
Captain
Medical Officer

WILLIAM B. SETTLE
First Lieutenant
Medical Officer

WILLIAM K. ALLEN
First Lieutenant
Medical Officer

WILLIAM P. QUINN
Captain
Medical Officer

JAMES P. RAMSEY
Captain
Flight Examiner

HAROLD E. THORNELL
Captain
Medical Officer

FRANKLIN B. BECK
First Lieutenant
Dental Corps

R. W. DOCKERY
First Lieutenant
Medical Officer

BASCOM S. WAUGH
First Lieutenant
Medical Corps

ALOYSIUS B. CUYJET
First Lieutenant
Dental Corps

FRANK H. JORDAN, JR.
First Lieutenant
Dental Corps

ELBERT B. SINGLETON
Captain
Ward Officer

SEGINALD CHANTRELLE
First Lieutenant
Dental Corps

THOMAS H. BUSTER
First Lieutenant
Administrative Assistant

ELLIOTT J. WILLIAMS
First Lieutenant
Medical Administrative Officer

THEODORE A. HAITH
Second Lieutenant
Medical Supply Assistant

MARION MANN
Second Lieutenant
Laboratory Officer

MEDICAL DEPARTMENT

DELLA H. RANEY
First Lieutenant
Chief Nurse

DELLA J. BASSETTE
Second Lieutenant

KATHRYN Y. BAUGH
Second Lieutenant

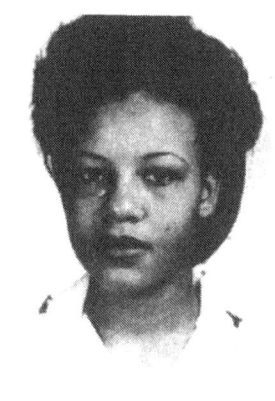

NAOMI B. BELL
Second Lieutenant

OCTAVIA M. BRIDGEWATER
Second Lieutenant

ELIZABETH T. DOZIER
Second Lieutenant

RUTH M. FAULKNER
Second Lieutenant

BEATRICE E. HILL
Second Lieutenant

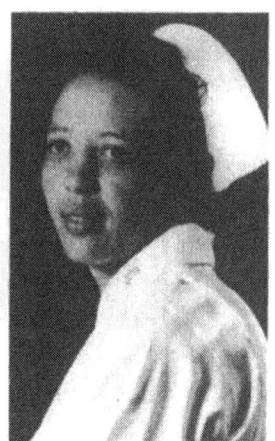

NORMA L. GREENE
Second Lieutenant

FRANCES L. McCLOUD
Second Lieutenant

RUTH C. SPEIGHT
Second Lieutenant

FATIMA DOLORES SMITH
Second Lieutenant

GERTRUDE L. SCOTT
Second Lieutenant

SARAH F. THOMAS
Second Lieutenant

MENCIE B. TROTTER
Second Lieutenant

ABBIE E. VOORHIES
Second Lieutenant

ELSIE H. WALLACE
Second Lieutenant

87

EUGENE A. SILLS
Second Lieutenant, M. A. C.
Commanding

DETACHMENT MEDICAL DEPARTMENT

(Reading from Left to Right)

First Row: Master Sergeant Hubbard, Frederick A.; First Sergeant Bush, Harry F.; Staff Sergeants Norwood, Waymon D.; Owen, Joseph M.; Parker, Perlum M.; Taylor, Robert E.

Second Row: Staff Sergeants Thompson, Roscoe B.; Weatherall, Teddy; Sergeants Jones, Ernest; Randolph, George W.; Technicians Fourth Grade Abbott, Varnice; Cleveland, Calvin.

Third Row: Technicians Fourth Grade; Lawrence, James C.; Maddox, Calvin K.; Manous, Ned; Martin, Matthew D.; Technician Fifth Grade Smith, Willie E.; Corporal Banks, James A.

Fourth Row: Corporals Birnel, Zoroastro A.; Brown, William G.; Curtis, Desabee; Groves, Berchell; Kelly, Alfonso J.; Lawton, B. T.

Fifth Row: Corporals Mills, Wellington; Phillips, Fairy; Wall, Cecil, Sr.; Technicians Fifth Grade Coates, John W.; Jenkins, Richard W.; Lawrence, Kenneth M.

DETACHMENT MEDICAL DEPARTMENT

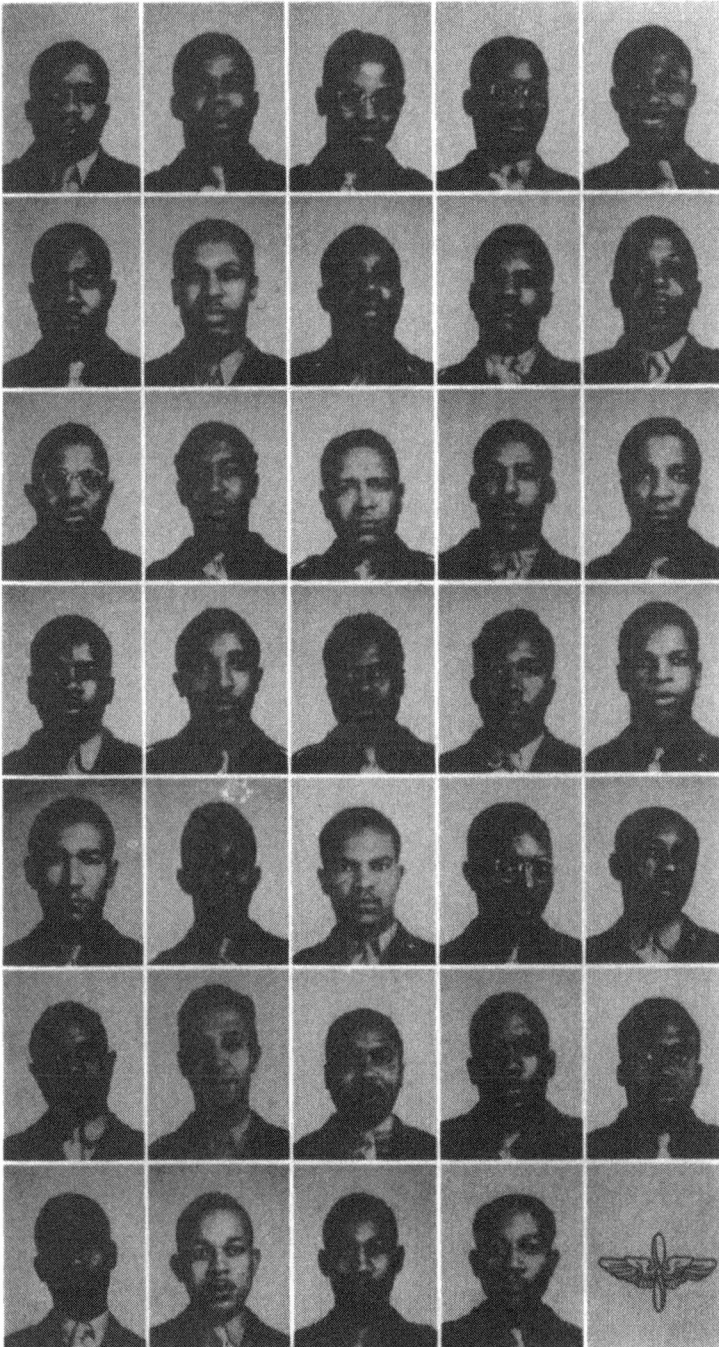

★

(Reading from Left to Right)

First Row: Technicians Fifth Grade Peterson, James; Powell, Dempsey; Smith, Bernard E.; Technician Fourth Grade Smith, William B.; Technician Fifth Grade Weston, Eric H.

Second Row: Privates First Class Anthony, Manca; Bowers, Joseph P.; Burks, Jack D.; Chatman, Dan W.; Clark, Adicus.

Third Row: Privates First Class Cook, Willie J.; Dula, Fred; Hayden, Robert L.; Herndon, Roy F.; Hill, John L.

Fourth Row: Privates First Class Jones, Lafayette; Lee, Jesse P.; Lockett, Felix; Mangum, Robert J.; Minnis, Howard J.

Fifth Row: Privates First Class Newby, George P. A.; Petaway, William; Phyfiher, Finners D.; Shannohouse, James; Smith, Clarence.

Sixth Row: Privates First Class Stephens, Elonzo E., Jr.; Wills, Richard O.; Privates Akines, J. B.; Bradley, Jesse B.; Brooks, Henry.

Seventh Row: Privates Brown, Irvin E.; Carter, Harrel C.; Cromer, John P.; Edwards, Bryant.

DETACHMENT MEDICAL DEPARTMENT

(Reading from Left to Right)

First Row: Privates Reese, Elmer E.; Green, Charley L.; Hall, Doras F.; Hall, Oliver; Harrison, Moses D.

Second Row: Privates Hitt, Clarence; Howard, Eugene; Jackson, Herman; Johnson, Thelmon; Keith, Ulysses.

Third Row: Privates Kennedy, David; Key, Raymond; Knight, Julius B.; Lambert, William B.; Lindsey, Warren.

Fourth Row: Privates Louis, Lawrence; Mackey, Henry; Madere, Cornelius; Manuel, Herman, Sr.; Mathis, L. H.

Fifth Row: Private McCall, Tuggle L.; Sergeant Mitchell, Edward E.; Privates Money, James H.; Morris, Lexadd W.; Neaves, Robert H.

Sixth Row: Privates Nichols, Virdumarus; Perkins, Henry L.; Pitts, Aaron L.; Plowden, Walter; Plummer, R. J.

Seventh Row: Privates Ruffin, Alfred; Shields, Robert F.; Smith, Abe; Vines, Simuel F.; Watts, James C.

Eighth Row: Privates White, Charles A.; Williams, S. H.; Worth, Fred, Jr.

FRANK L. DRYE
First Lieutenant
Commanding

313TH ARMY AIR FORCES BAND

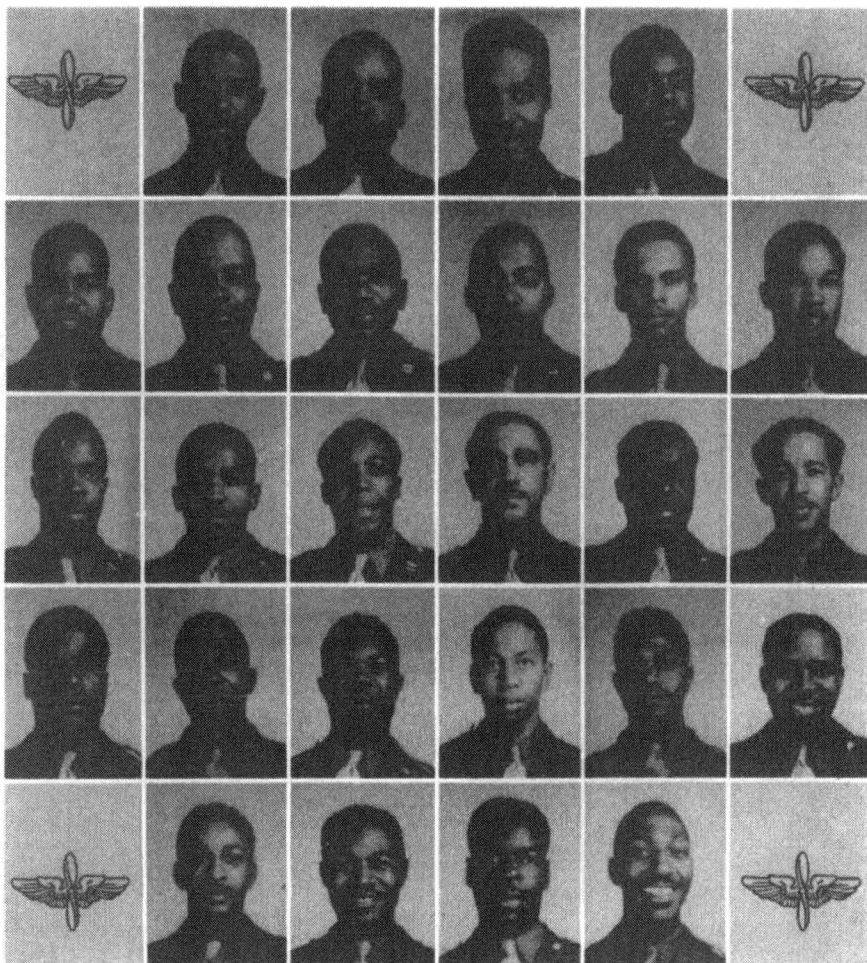

(Reading from Left to Right)

First Row: Technical Sergeant Moseley, James O. B.; Staff Sergeants Patterson, Russel L.; Thompson, George D.; Sergeant DeMond, Martin T.

Second Row: Sergeants Eaton, Robert; Morse, Newell; Corporals Baskerville, Earl Q.; Blakemore, Maurice B.; Busbv, Valentine A.; Butler, Zenas.

Third Row: Corporals Garvey, Claude E.; Holloway, Joseph P.; Pendleton, Lawrence E.; Privates First Class Brown, Edward A.; Edmondson, Clarence; Lee, Afton, Jr.

Fourth Row: Privates First Class McDonald, Alexander; McQueen, Benjamin; Maddox, James E.; Nicholson, Merle D.; Powell, Charles C.; Prather, Henry L.

Fifth Row: Privates First Class Shannon, Edmund P.; Terrell, Newman J.; Urquhart, Jesse H.; Private Chandler, Len H.

313TH A.A.F. BAND UNDER DIRECTION OF FIRST LIEUTENANT
FRANK L. DRYE

★

313TH BAND

ON REVIEW

★

The Riot Gun.

941st Guard Squadron Inspection.

Jeep Transportation.

MARCHING OF NEW GUARD

Military Police Town Patrol.

Ready for Duty.

GEORGE W. WEBB
Captain
Commanding

JOHN H. DUREN
First Lieutenant

EMMETT A. TURNER
Second Lieutenant

941ST GUARD SQUADRON

(Reading from Left to Right)

First Row: First Sergeant Woodson, Joe; Staff Sergeants Hearn, Frederick; Porter, Hayes; Sergeants Carrington, Colin; Donaldson, Livingston; Goodjoines, Clarence.

Second Row: Sergeants Hester, William; McGee, Luther; Moseley, James; Randolph, Alfred; Watson, Edmund; Corporal Alston, Wilbur.

Third Row: Corporals Bogan, William; Booker, James H.; Bouey, Nicholas; Clark, Albert; Cousins, Leo; Cummings, Charleston.

Fourth Row: Corporals Davis, Denmon; Eberhardt, John F.; Ferebee, Alphonso; Grimes, Leroy; Hill, Benjamin; Jackson, Douglas.

Fifth Row: Corporals Johnson, Andrew T.; Lee, Kelly; Pope, Clyde; Tiebout, Wilbur; Underwood, Oscar; Walls, Herbert W.

941ST GUARD SQUADRON

★

(Reading from Left to Right)

First Row: Corporals Washington, Edd A.; Watkins, Francis; Privates First Class Aitcheson, Ernest; Anderson, Frank G.; Anderson, Julius C.; Beatty, Charles.

Second Row: Privates First Class Blake, Bernard; Bradley, Sidney; Bridges, Calvin; Burns, Jake; Camphor, Jake; Charles, Wellington.

Third Row: Privates First Class Clark, Reginald; Cofield, Joseph; Cousins, Bernard; Cousins, Francis; Davis, William A.; Davis, Willie.

Fourth Row: Privates First Class Dilliard, Oscar; Gailliard, Samuel; Hall, Clyde L.; January, Charles; Jones, Allen; Lewis, Albert.

Fifth Row: Privates First Class Wesley, Paul; Orr, Broadus; Pettaway, Charles; Randall, Leon; Ricks, Caleb; Simons, Richard.

Sixth Row: Privates First Class Simpson, Rudolphus; Stoner, Walter S.; Taylor, Lee G.; Thompson, Arthur; Whitaker, Travis; Woods, Edward.

Seventh Row: Private First Class Wright, Irwin; Privates Adams, Walter C.; Allen, William S.; Andrews, Freddy F.; Bills, Dennis Sr.; Birdsong, George G.

Eighth Row: Privates Braxton James A.; Brown, Clarence; Bundy, George; Caison, C. H.; Campbell, Thomas; Carr, Marshall.

Ninth Row: Privates Clayton, William; Coleman, James A.; Collins, Tommy L.; Conwell, William; Crenshaw, Walter; Crisp, Eugene.

941ST GUARD SQUADRON

★

(Reading from Left to Right)

First Row: Privates Dabbs, Charles; Daniels, M. C.; Davenport, Earl; Davis, Jasper; Davis, Reuben; Dent, Vernon.

Second Row: Privates Dixon, Charles; Frazier, Frank C.; George, Ralph N.; Haines, Donald; Harmon, James E.; Harris, Harold.

Third Row: Privates Hawes, Phillip; Henry, Frederick L.; Holland, Alfred; Houston, George W.; Hubbard, Ben; Hughes, Rufus.

Fourth Row: Privates James, Cornelius; Jefferson, Louis T.; Johnson, Earl; Johnson, Milton E.; Jones, Felton D.; Jones, Perry J.

Fifth Row: Privates Lavender, Theodore; Lewis, Dock; Lewis, Harding; Lewis, Wilbert H.; Loggins, Aaron; Lomax, Francis.

Sixth Row: Privates Martin, Garland; Martin, Mason; Mayberry, William N.; McLemore, E. B.; Mitchell, Vincent; Moore, John L., Jr.

Seventh Row: Privates Morgan, Charles M.; Mukes, Estill L.; Owens, Lee B.; Parker, George; Patterson, William; Phillips, Josean.

Eighth Row: Privates Quarles, Forrest R.; Randolph, Philip; Rankin, William; Roberts, Percy E.; Sanders, Rufus; Smart, DeWitt.

Ninth Row: Privates Smith, Mark F.; Taylor, Preston; Thomas, Lawrence; Thornton, John; Toliver, William D.; Tuthill, Phillip.

Tenth Row: Privates Wallace, Anderson J.; Warren, Mazie; Wimbish, Maurice; Young, Edward R.

1451ST QUARTERMASTER COMPANY

JAMES L. HALL
First Lieutenant
Commanding

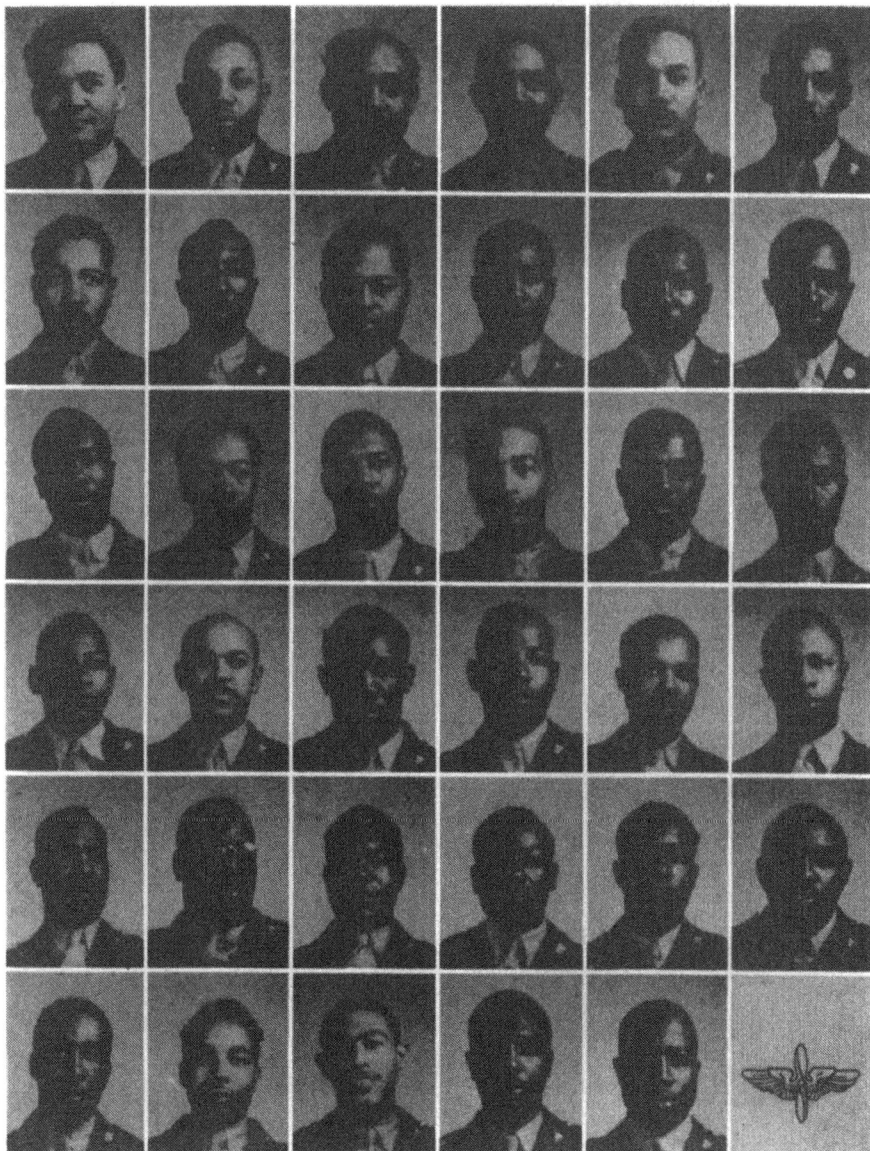

(Reading from Left to Right)

First Row: Technical Sergeant Lee, Thomas E.; Staff Sergeants Huff, Charles E.; Jones, Edward H.; Sergeants Cundiff, John A.; Farris, Leon; Plummer, Edward J.

Second Row: Technicians Fourth Grade Cobbs, John H.; Talley, Daniel W. A.; Corporal Dunlap, Walter J.; Technicians Fifth Grade Burnett, Willie J.; Carter, Agee; McDaniel, Arthur.

Third Row: Technicians Fifth Grade McDaniel, Douglas; Pelham, William E.; Privates First Class Boston, Frank D.; Clark, Albert D.; Day, Alfonza; Dowdy, Leon.

Fourth Row: Privates First Class Frayser, Latham H.; Hayden, Lucius A.; Jackson, John H.; Montgomery, Charles R.; Moore, Charlie; Neal, Rayford, Jr.

Fifth Row: Private First Class Townsend, Lewel E.; Privates Blakemon, Bryant B.; Collins, Roosevelt; Conner, Clarence J.; Crockett, George A.; Grant, Percy, Jr.

Sixth Row: Privates Jackson, Eddie; Lacey, James E.; Robert, Lucien R.; Spears, Clarence W.; Todd, David.

964TH QUARTERMASTER PLATOON

★ ★

FRED P. WRIGHT
First Lieutenant
Commanding

(Reading from Left to Right)

First Row: Technical Sergeant Watkins, Elmer; Sergeants Elleby, Rasen; Langhorn, Norwood S.; Technicians Fourth Grade Campbell, Richard A.; Curson, Leroy J.

Second Row: Corporals Daniel, King; Johnson, Gordon G.; Peterson, Willie J.; Scott, David K.; Technician Fifth Grade Beatty, Robert Z.

Third Row: Technicians Fifth Grade Booker, Phillip H.; Bradsher, John J.; Grinnage, George A.; Harris, Gabe, Jr.; Harvin, Clayburn A.

Fourth Row: Technicians Fifth Grade Marshall, Preston L.; Patterson, Raymond L.; Shults, Lloyd R.; Walker, Joseph L.; White, Lewis D.

Fifth Row: Technicians Fifth Grade Wooden, William F.; Yates, William C.; Privates First Class Barnes, Willie J.; Bennett, Woodrow.

964TH QUARTERMASTER PLATOON

★

(Reading from Left to Right)

First Row: Privates First Class Booker, Robert; Bryant, Willie R.; Dempsey, James L.; Duncan, Paul; Farve, Raphael G.

Second Row: Privates First Class Ferguson, Donald F.; Fisher, Floyd F.; Griffin, William L.; Harris, George M.; Johnson, Tilghman W.

Third Row: Privates First Class Jones, Needham; Long, Arthur J.; Otis, Roberts; Shelton, William F.; Smith, Robert D.

Fourth Row: Privates First Class Whitaker, Ralph L.; Wright, Charles R.; Privates Beasley, Floyd F.; Bugg, William P.; Cooper, Lyerly C.

Fifth Row: Privates Crawford, Lonnie; Crenshaw, Noah C.; Dempster, Rudolph H.; Deveaux, Warren S.; Hope, William.

Sixth Row: Privates Jolla, Willie B.; Knight, Leroy; Rainey, Gus; Thomas, Edgar; Washington, Jessie H.

Seventh Row: Privates Washington, Thomas J.; Webster, Alexander; Young, Wilwood T.

Washing a G. I. limousine is but one of the duties of the 964th Quartermasters.

Motor

Motor maintenance, vitally necessary to the Army, is another phase of the 964th's work.

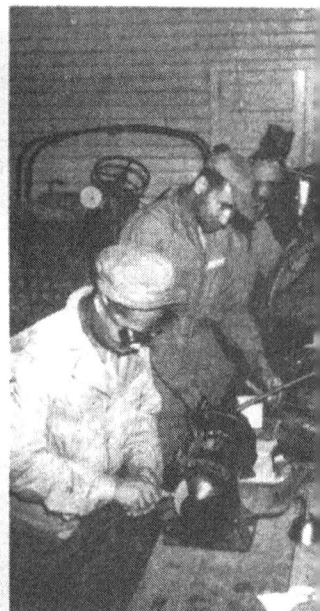

964TH ★ QUARTER

Supply quartermasters of the 1451st are shown storing their goods . . . looks like a

Besides storing supplies, these quartermasters come to the aid of men living off the post with the economical sales store.

Supply

MASTER ★ 1451ST

WILLIAM J. LISKA
Captain
Communications Officer

COMMUNICATIONS

Charging Batteries.

Using Light Gun on Tower.

Radio Repair Shop.

CHARLES H. EVERETT
First Lieutenant
Signal Officer

WEATHER, SIGNAL CORPS

Recording Winds Aloft.

W. W. TURNER
Sergeant
Chief Clerk, Signal Company
At Switch board

Taking a Balloon Run.

WALLACE P. REED
First Lieutenant

LUTHER L. BLAKENEY
Second Lieutenant

WEATHER
DETACHMENT

★

JOHN B. BRANCHE
Second Lieutenant

BENJAMIN F. BULLOCK, JR.
Second Lieutenant

PAUL F. BYRD
Second Lieutenant

ROOSEVELT RICHARDSON
Second Lieutenant

(Reading from Left to Right)

First Row: First Sergeant Mims, Arthur L.; Technical Sergeant Campbell, Vincent O.; Staff Sergeants Johnson, James G.; Mason, John L.; Sergeant Fleming, William K.

Second Row: Sergeants Forde, William G.; Jeter, Rudolph; Thomas, Harold; Corporals Pratt, Charles E.; Primus, Edward W.

Third Row: Corporals Tolbert, William J.; Woods, Carter E.; Privates First Class Ama, Charles T.; Houston, Charles A.; Phillips, William.

689TH SIGNAL AIRCRAFT WARNING COMPANY

★

HERBERT R. ORR
Captain
Commanding

EDWARD C. DeL'AIGLE
Second Lieutenant

LEWIS A. McGEE
Second Lieutenant

MAURICE I. SCOTT
Second Lieutenant

WILLIAM K. SPEARS
Second Lieutenant

LLOYD D. TYNER
Second Lieutenant

SIGNAL SERVICE DETACHMENT

Sergeant Turner, Walter W.; Corporals Lyder, John C.; Morris, James A.; Ross, Freddie; Private First Class Welsh, Noel G.

COMMUNICATIONS

(Reading from Left to Right)

First Row: First Sergeant Francois, Earl L.; Staff Sergeants Frierson, Petrow; Robinson, E. Allyn; Sergeants Cooke, Stratman; Sims, Harold W.

Second Row: Corporal Goodman, Seymour; Privates First Class Whitting, Birney; Wilcox, Herman; Young, Ervin.

JOHN F. CUYJET
Second Lieutenant

JACOB C. WOODS
Second Lieutenant

648TH ORDNANCE COMPANY

(Reading from Left to Right)

First Row: First Sergeant Bridgeforth, Cornelius V.; Staff Sergeant Jones, Simon C.; Sergeant Knox, Victor C.; Technician Fourth Grade Wright, Joe; Corporal Jackson, Willie L.

Second Row: Corporal Spencer, Jesse E.; Technicians Fifth Grade Beaty, Roy; Boyd, Adam G.; Stewart, Fred L.; Private First Class Coleman, Elijah.

Third Row: Privates First Class Davis, Lonnie L.; Ennis, Arthur; Hodsworth, Clifford B.; Horne, Thomas W.; Jones, George W.

Fourth Row: Privates First Class Latham, Y. Z.; Lawrence, Albert; Little, Willie; Mitchell, Howard; Moody, George.

Fifth Row: Privates First Class Moore, John, Jr.; Myers, Elihue; Shermon, Nelson; Tucker, Johnnie, Jr.; Watts, Eugene.

Isaac Isham

648TH ORDNANCE
COMPANY

★

(Reading from Left to Right)

First Row: Privates Battle, Lovell; Boyd, Arthur; Brown, Clement; Bullocks, Willie C. L.; Burkley, Malloy M.

Second Row: Privates Burks, Abraham; Burres, Louis, Jr.; Burton, James P.; Conyers, Hezekiah; Crandall, Howard L.

Third Row: Privates Davis, Frank; Fair, Arthur L.; Fletcher, James; Gordon, John D.; Hargro, Other E.

Fourth Row: Privates James, Leonard G.; Jarrett, William B.; King, James E.; Kinley, James H. L.; Logan, Timothy.

Fifth Row: Privates Manns, Henry; Marshall, Perry; McGill, St. Clair; Mason, Will; Miller, Elmo R.

Sixth Row: Privates Miller, James M.; Miller, Lawrence N.; Morrison, Elmer C.; Murray, Leroy; Nealey, James.

Seventh Row: Privates Newton, Waites; Parker, Frank; Randolph, James C.; Robinson, Robert; Rodgers, O. D.

Eighth Row: Privates Rucker, Willie L.; Staples, Edward R.; Stone, Walter C.; Street, Theodore R.; Tate, Alfonso N.

Ninth Row: Privates Terrell, Silas T.; Walker, Chester No. 1; Walker, Chester No. 2; Warren, Johnnie A.; Weatherspoon, Eugene.

109

T. A. F. S. FOREVER

Cadet John S. Sloan
Class SE-43-F

—I—

Here midst the halls of old Tuskegee
Deep in the heart of Alabama,
You hear the steady, pounding beat
Of Cadets marching through the street,
With heads erect and eyes afire
All with one firm and true desire;
To keep o'er the shores of our America
The cherished mantle of the free;
We learn to fly, we learn to fight,
We live for glory, Die for Right,
We'll lead our country on to victory.

—II—

After the months of toil in dusk and dew,
Our fighting soldiers fly into the blue;
The aching hearts we've left behind
Will swell with pride with passing time.
As soon the world shall come to know
Tuskegee Army Men are so
Filled with the spirit of Democracy,
Imbued with its concepts through and through,
We'll never cheer a setting sun
Until the battle has been won;
Then off, yes off again to home and you.

—III—

The years will pass as years so often do,
Still here, Tuskegee Army Flying School,
A sacred emblem to our men
Who gave their all that peace might reign;
That sons and daughters of our land
Would never live in fear again;
Still strong-hearted Cadets marching to the line
Still fly the pattern straight and true
From Army life to them has come
The meaning of a job well done,
And loyalty to our Red, White and Blue.

Men shown in this picture
Oliver O. Miller, P. W. M
Mays, B. L. Alexander, and
members of 43-E's upper
AAFFTD.

110

★

66TH AAFFTD MOTON FIELD

Tuskegee, Alabama

WILLIAM T. SMITH
Major
Commanding Officer

HAROLD C. MAGOON
Captain
Assistant Supervisor

JOHN G. PENN
Captain
Commandant of Cadets

JAMES HALE, JR.
Second Lieutenant
Adjutant

JOHN H. McBETH
First Lieutenant
Commanding Officer
Air Depot Detachment

STANLEY J. KOMIN
First Lieutenant
Assistant Supervisor

HOWARD T. FRAZIER
First Lieutenant
Intelligence Officer

VANCE H. MARCHBANKS, JR.
Captain
Flight Examiner

JOHN T. BRACKEN
Second Lieutenant
Director Physical Training

ELDRIDGE F. WILLIAMS
Second Lieutenant
Assistant Director Physical
Training

A BRIEF HISTORY OF THE 66TH AAFTD

With the Tuskegee Institute as Contractor, the 66th Army Air Forces Flying Training Detachment began operations in July of 1941, when it received its first class of Aviation Cadets. At that time, in addition to providing Primary Flying Training, the Pre-Flight School was also located at this Detachment. Although construction at the flying field had not quite been completed, student flying training commenced in the latter part of August, 1941.

The General Manager of the school from the start has been Professor G. L. Washington, head of the Department of Mechanical Industries, Division of Aeronautics, Tuskegee Institute. Professor Washington was directing the Civil Pilot Training program of the Tuskegee Institute and in addition assumed the duties of General Manager of the Army Primary Flying School. A Massachusetts Institute of Technology graduate, Professor Washington has been associated with the Tuskegee Institute for many years, and is intensely interested in the development of this school.

The first Commanding Officer was Captain (now Lieutenant Colonel) Noel F. Parrish who had, in the summer of 1939, assisted in opening the Army Primary Flying School at Glenview, Illinois, one of the original Army Civil Contract Primary Flying Schools. On December 1, 1941, Lieutenant (now Major) William T. Smith assumed command at which time Colonel Parrish was appointed Director of Training of the Tuskegee Army Flying School. Major Smith, a West Point graduate and former instructor at Randolph Field, came here after having served a year as Assistant Supervisor at the Army Primary School at Albany, Georgia. Under his supervision this flying school has expanded from a comparatively small one to its present size which is comparable to most other Army Primary Flying Schools.

Of the original staff of officers only Captain Harold C. Magoon and Captain John G. Penn are still on duty at Tuskegee. Captain Magoon, a Washington and Lee alumnus and Army rated pilot, has been Assistant Supervisor of this school since its start. Captain John G. Penn, a Virginia Military Institute graduate, likewise has been pursuing his duties as Commandant of Cadets since the school first opened.

Expansion of this school has necessitated the addition of many officers and enlisted men until now the school has a very complete Army staff.

Charles A. Anderson, pioneer Negro pilot, has been Chief Pilot since the school opened. At the start he was assisted by Milton P. Crenshaw, Charles R. Foxx and Forrest Shelton. Instructors Foxx and Crenshaw have since been promoted to Squadron Commanders.

SUPERVISORS

LEWIS A. JACKSON
Director of Training

CHARLES A. ANDERSON
Group Commander

MILTON P. CRENCHAW
Squadron Commander

CHARLES R. FOXX
Squadron Commander

FLIGHT INSTRUCTORS

★ ★

DANIEL JAMES, JR.

ROBERT TERRY

LINKWOOD WILLIAMS

PERRY H. YOUNG

FLIGHT INSTRUCTORS

GILBERT A. CARGILL

ROSCOE D. DRAPER

CHARLES H. FLOWERS

CALVIN R. HARRIS

ERNEST HENDERSON

★ **C I V I L I A N**

FLIGHT INSTRUCTORS

JAMES A. HILL

WENDELL R. LIPSCOMB

ADOLPH J. MORET

CLAUDE R. PLATT

MATHEW W. PLUMMER

FLIGHT INSTRUCTORS

SHERMAN T. ROSE

NATHAN A. SAMS

JAMES E. TAYLOR, JR.

JAMES E. WRIGHT

★

LAWRENCE E. ANDERSON, JR.
Ground School Instructor

DEPARTMENT HEADS

GEORGE L. WASHINGTON
General Manager

AUSTIN H. HUMBLES
Chief of Maintenance

GEORGE A. REED
Plant Engineer

ALICE DUNGEY GRAY
Parachute Rigger

ROBERT A. SPICELY
Director of Mess

GENERAL L. DANIELS
Custodian

P E R S O N N E L ★

Work goes on inside one of Moton Field's well-equipped hangars.

Gassing 'em up.

at WORK

The Sergeant learns
to sew.

Expert mechanics check a motor.

Covering Tips of Aeleron.

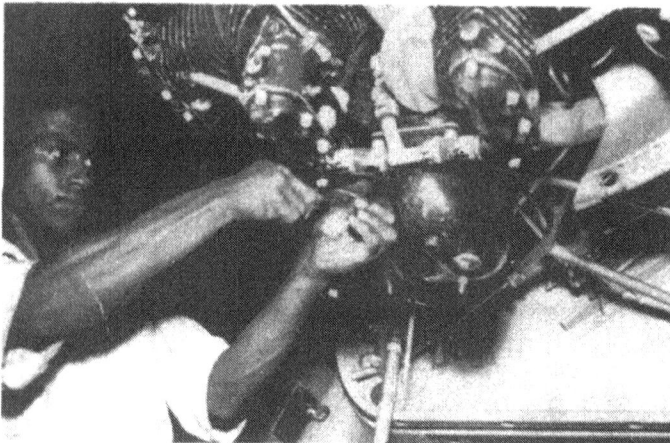

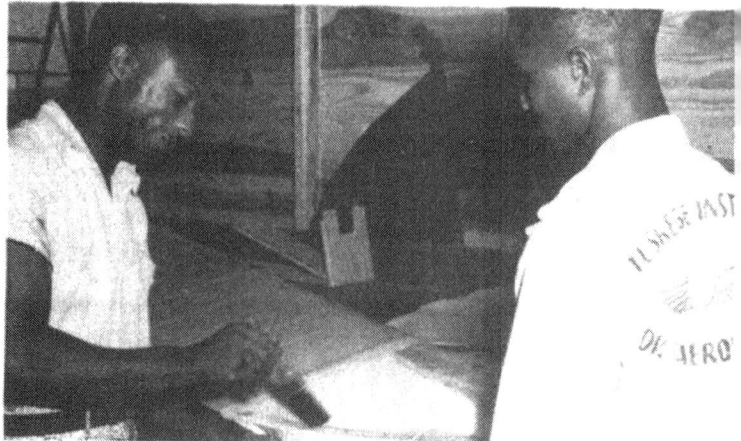

"THE IMPERIAL WINGS OF RHYTHM"

and **PLAY**

Bu!l session in the barracks.

Cade: Reading Room.

VIEWS ON THE LINE

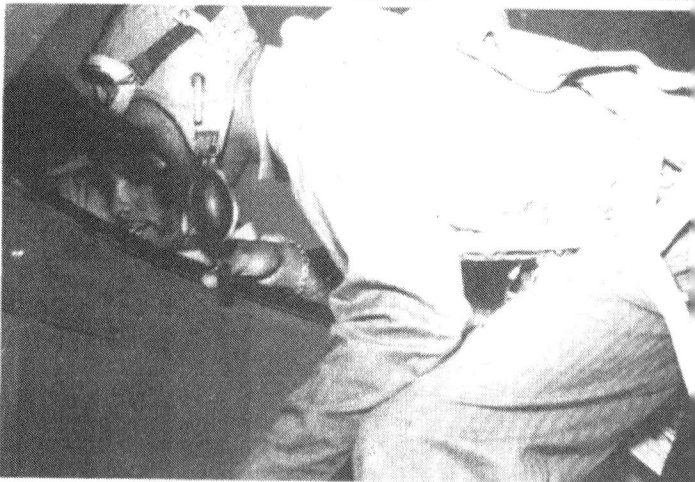

AVIATION CADETS

John L. Hamilton
Second Lieutenant

CADETS

CLASS 43-E

George B. Agard	Walter S. Beard	John F. Briggs	Milton R. Brooks	Charles M. Bussey
Spurgeon N. Ellington	Maurice V. Esters	Edward S. Flowers	Jefferson T. Friday	Clemenceau M. Givings
Joseph P. Gomer	George E. Gray	James P. Hairston	John H. Hunter, Jr.	Langdon E. Johnson

F. J. Kirkpatrick, Jr. Albert H. Manning, Jr.

Oliver O. Miller, Jr. Theopolis D. Moore Dempsey W. Morgan, Jr. Porter W. Myrick Robert L. Richardson Virgil J. Richardson Herbert M. Samuel

AVIATION CADETS

CLASS 43-E

Harry A. Sheppard   Luther H. Smith, Jr.   John J. Suggs   James A. Walker   Dudley M. Watson   Laurence D. Wilkins   Craig H. Williams

STUDENT OFFICERS
CLASS 43-F

Milton R. Henry
Second Lieutenant

Osie R. Walton
Second Lieutenant

CLASS 43-F
CADETS

R. M. Alexander, Jr.

James L. Arnold   C. C. Bivens, Jr.   Joseph M. Bloedoorn   Alexander M. Bright   Robert T. Buck   Broadus N. Butler   Charles R. Carrington

Eugene Cash, Jr.   Joseph C. Curry   Logan D. Delany   Crawford B. Dowdell   John P. Ellis   Warren H. Eusan   Terry D. Green

AVIATION CADETS

CLASS 43-F

Weldon K. Groves

L. E. Hailburton

Herbert S. Harris

Richard H. Harris, Jr.

Willie S. Hunter

Felix James

Arthur L. Johnson

Wilbert H. Johnson

Charles W. Jones

Oscar A. Kenney

Hezekiah Lacy, Jr.

Joe A. Lewis

Wayne V. Liggins

George McDonald, Jr.

Charles E. McGee

Philip E. Medley

Irving S. Moses

Guy S. Newson

Walter J. A. Palmer

Wesley S. Ratliff, Jr.

Everett E. Richardson

Eugene L. Runyon

Wylie W. Selden

James R. Simmons

John S. Sloan

Leonard F. Turner

Frank D. Walker

Johnson C. Wells

William E. Whitlow, Jr.

William G. Wilkerson

Albert P. Williams

Felix A Williams

Harrison A. Williams

William F. Williams, Jr.

Theodore A. Wilson

Single Engine Class 45E
1st Row Left to right: Marvin White, Herman Barnet, Issac Woods, Clarence Reynolds, Reginold Smith
2nd Row: Leonard Wiggins, Logan Roberts, Aaron Gaskins, Russel Collins, William Bailey
3rd Row: Wesley Hurt, Roger Duncan, Lt. Holland, Lt. McIntyre, William Fuller, Martin Saunders, Joe Scott, Eugene Williams

Twin Engine Class 45E
1st Row Left to right: Albert Whiteside, John Curry, Wm. Taylor, George Brown, W. Broadwater
2nd Row: Jerrold Griffin, Lt. Sattewhite, Lt. Choisey, Lt. Maples, Harry Ford
3rd Row: John Harris John Roach, Mexion Pruitt, Joe Bryant, Mitchel Tony, Walter O'Neal
Not Shown: Oliver Proctor

READY ROOM AND ON THE LINE

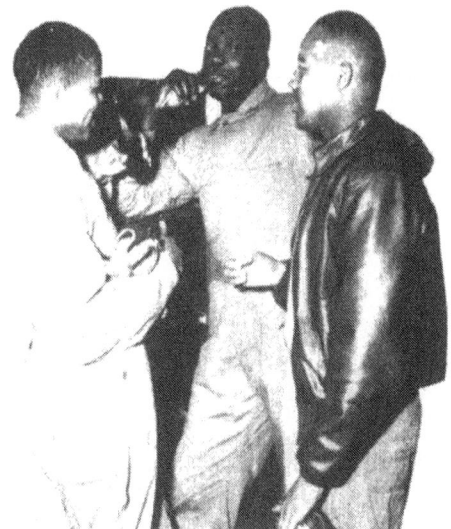

Link Trainer with Instructor.

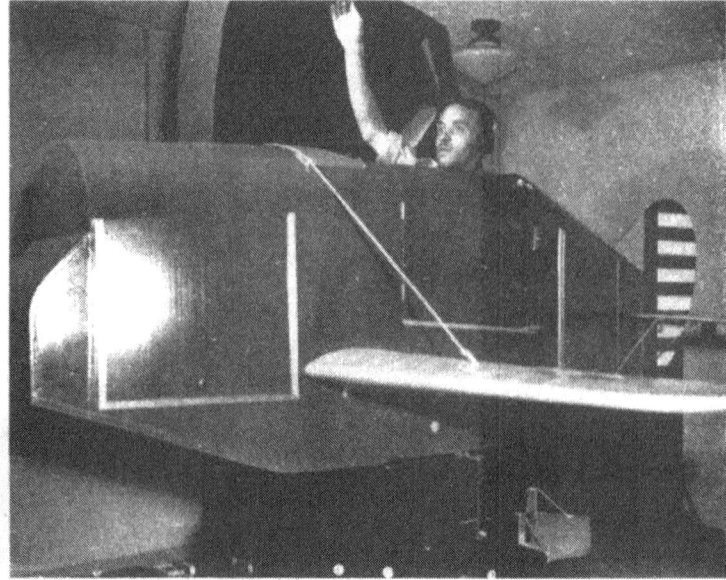
Learning with the Link.

Hangar.

Orderly Room.

Operations Office

Engineers Office

Barracks Navigating.

Explanation with model (Barracks).

Time Off · · ·
· · · Chow!

Writing the gal back home (Barracks).

Chow.

ENLISTED PERSONNEL

66TH AAFFTD

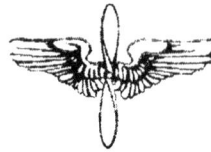

(Reading from Left to Right)

First Row: Technical Sergeant Foster, Charles V.; Staff Sergeants Cook, Robert L.; Edwards, Harry D.; Olcott, John A.; Sergeants Gann, Claude W.; Lawrence, Arthur R.

Second Row: Corporal Rosenblatt, Albert; Technician Fifth Grade Braswell, Benjamin J.; Private First Class Moore, Ernest W.; Privates Petri, Hector D.; Thomas, Elijah.

CADET ADMINISTRATION

LT. JAMES J. JOHNS
Adjutant

LT. SIDNEY S. PARKER
Tactical Officer

LT. WALTER C. DANIALS
Tactical Officer

LT. F. M. LACY
Tactical Officer

LT. BUFORD
Tactical Officer

LT. J. I. PINKETT
Tactical Officer

MRS. B. CHICHESTER
Secretary

LT. FORDE
Mess Officer
(Picture Missing)

GROUP STAFF

GEORGE H. KYDD
First Captain

HENRY R. PEOPLES
Adjutant

GEORGE J. ILLES
Executive

CADET OFFICERS
"44-D"

CELESTUS KING
Cadet Captain

WILLIAM C. COLEMAN
Cadet Adjutant

MILTON S. HAYS
Cadet Lieutenant

RAYMOND F. NOCHES
Cadet Lieutenant

CLASS 44-D

LT. V. BRASHERES

LT. A. COUSINS

HARVEY R. ALEXANDER

ROBERT D. ANDERSON

GENTRY E. BARNES

CHARLES A. BEARD

RUAL W. BELL

HAROLD H. BROWN

ROY M. CHAPPELL

JOHN H. CHAVIS

CLASS 44-D

MARTIN L. COOK

HANNIBAL M. COX

ELBERT A. CRAIG

LEWIS W. CRAIG

ALBERT R. DECATUR

EBERLE J. GUILBAUD

CHARLES L. JACKSON

WILLIAM T. JACKSON

MAJOR E. JONES

EARE R. LANE

CLASS 44-D

WALTER P. MANNING

VINCENT I. MITCHELL

PAUL L. MOODY

ROLAND W. MOODY

HAROLD M. MORRIS

FRANCIS B. PEOPLES

JAMES R. POOLE

DANIEL L. RICH

CARROLL H. ROBINSON

LLOYD R. SHULTS

CLASS 44-D

DICKERSON C. TERRY

RALPH L. TURNER

JIMMY D. WHEELER

VINCENT E. WILLIAMS

JAMES A. WILSON

MYRON WILSON

CARL J. WOODS

ALEXANDER WOOLDRIDGE

Left to Right Front: Wilburn, O'neil, Martin, Turner, Duke, Parker, Driver, Perkins, Clifton
Center: Hawkins, Harper, Jefferson, McIver, Jackson, Roberts, Bell, Hunter, Walker
Rear: Bynum, Daniels, Twine, Williams, Blue, Masciana, Rucker, Winslow, Williams

Left to Right Front: Mathews, Diggs, Farley, Hill, Hicks, Hill, Adkins
Center: Chandler, Willette, Harder, Rodgers, Braswell, Patton, Clifton, Moody, Long, White, Wise
Rear: Gorham, Gay, Westbrook, Caitor, Gordon, Macon, Williams, Gould, Audount

Left to Right Back: Ayles, W. Brown, R. Brown, Rayner, Merton, McCarroll, Hall, Rapier, Calhoune, Decator
Middle: Brewer, Young, Stigger, Williams, Haywood, Porter, Marshall, White, Whittaker
Front: Price, Hutchins, Wheeler, Rohlsan, Dean, Wilson, Unk. Nightengale

On Wing: Price
Standing: White, Porter, Whittaker, Wheeler
Kneeling: Williams, Young

CADET OFFICERS
"44-E"

HARRY J. DAVENPORT
Cadet Captain

ROBERT M. WILLIAMS
Adjutant

AARON HARRINGTON
Cadet Lieutenant

RICHARD H. BELL
Cadet Lieutenant

LT. E. CROOM

CLASS

LT. C. DIEZ

LT. LUCAS

LT. K. M. WRIGHT

EDWIN N. BARRETT

LEONELLE A. BONAM

BERTRAND G. BRAITWAITE

CHARLES V. BRANTLEY

HAROLD H. BROWN

4 4 - E

JOSEPH L. CHINEWORTH

JOHN W. DAVIS

SAMUEL J. FORMAN

LOUIS J. GRADY

JOSEPH R. GRIFFIN

LOUIS K. HARRIS

THOMAS L. HAWKINS

GEORGE K. HAYS

EARL S. HIGHBAUGH

WENDELL W. HOCKODOY

JAMES R. HURLEY

MARVIN S. JACOBS

THOMAS W. JEFFERSON

SIMON KING

JAMES LANHAM

CLARENCE A. OLPHANT

JAMES C. RAMSEY

LEROY ROBERTS

ARNETT W. SPARKS

WILLIAM C. WALKER

SAMUTL W. WATTS

BERTRAND W. WILSON

HIRAM WRIGHT

HARRY J. WILKSRSON

PHYSICAL TRAINING

LT. E. WILLIAMS
Physical Training Director

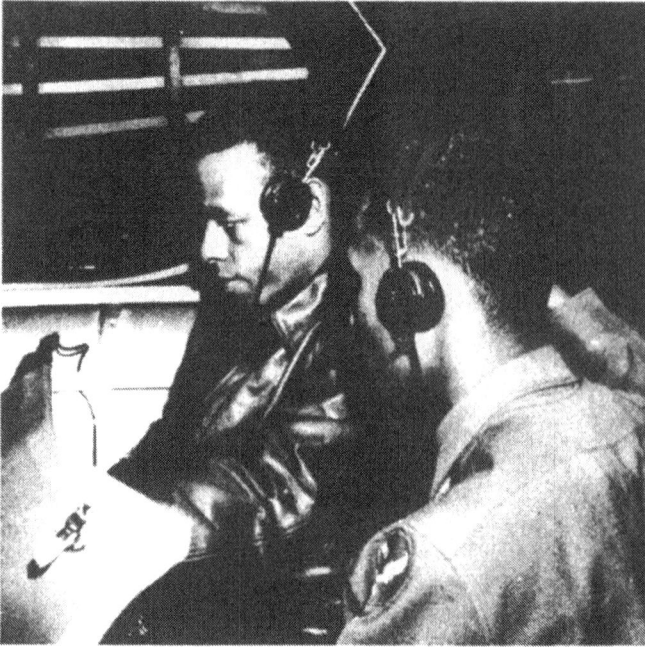

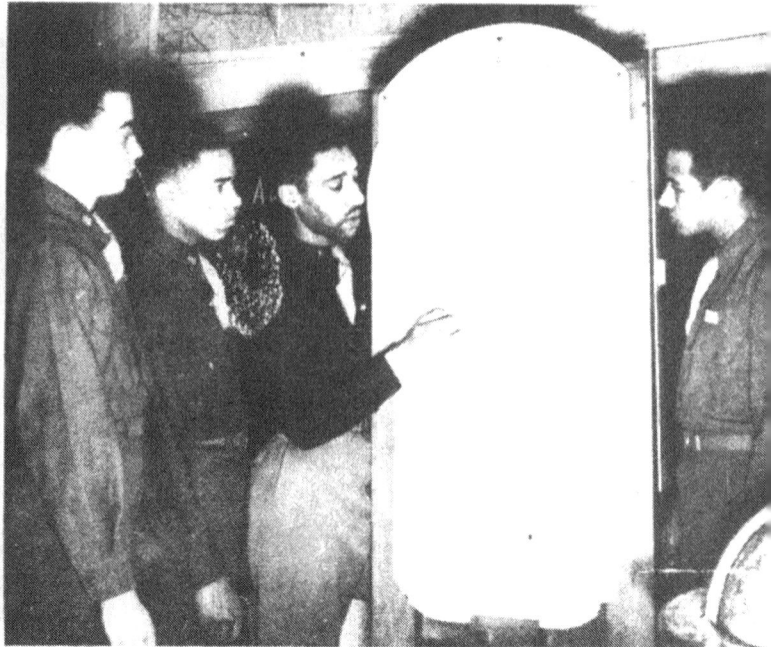

CADET OFFICERS
"44-F"

HUGH WHITE
Cadet Captain

LEWIS J. LYNCH
Cadet Adjutant

EUGENE EDMONDS
Cadet Lieutenant

JAMES EWING
Cadet Lieutenant

LT. A. A. BELLAMY

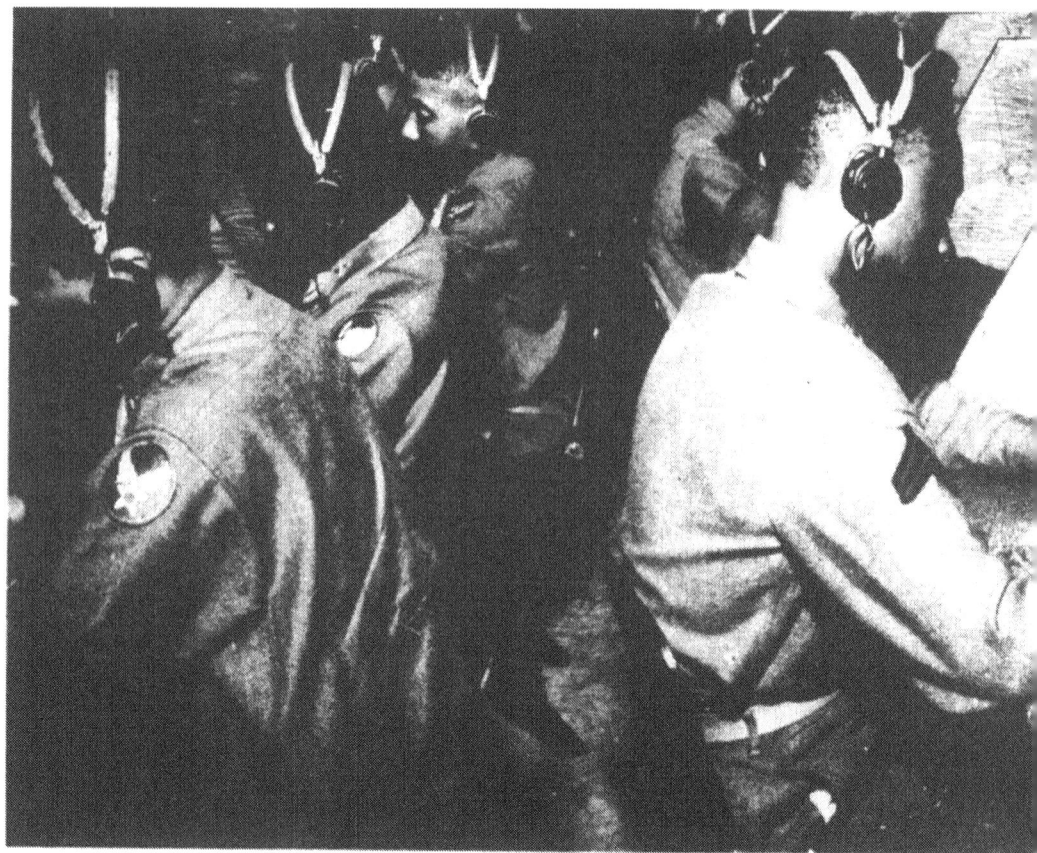

CLASS

LT. R. W. LAWRENCE

RICHARD S. ARMSTEAD

LeROY CAIN

GEORGE R. CATLIN

CLARENCE C. CONWAY

CARL F. ELLIS

WILLIAM C. FISHER

WILBUR I. GEORGE

CHARLES A. HILL

4 4 - F

LINCOLN T. HUDSON

WILLIAM A. JENKINS

RUPERT C. JOHNSON

SAMUEL E. KEITH

FRANK L. LEE

GEORGE A. LYNCH

HIRAM E. MANN

ULYSSES G. MATHIS

WALTER H. MILLER

JAMES T. MITCHELL

ROBERT J. MURDIC

DELANEY OLIVER

ANDREW PERIZ

JOHN R. PERKINS

WALTER H. REVELL

THOMAS P. ROCK

MAJOR M. ROSS

LEON W. SPEARS

HARRY T. STEWART

BONITA H. SMITH

WYRSON T. SHELL

JOHN B. TURNER

EDGAR K. WADSWORTH,

ARTHUR W. WARD

SAMUEL L. WASHINGTON

RHODIE J. WEBB

YENWITH K. WHITNEY

CLEVELAND J. WILLIAMS

EDWARD W. WOODWARD

FRANK N. WRIGHT

JAMES W. WRIGHT

W.O. Robert R. Snead

BOOK STAFF—Left to Right: Celestus King, Editor; Lewis J. Lynch, LT. S. S. Parker,
Advisor; Leonelle Bonam, Layout; William T. Jackson, Assistant Editor

Our grateful acknowledgmnt is made to the Base Photograph Section of Tuskegee
Army Air Field for their supervision in preparing the contents of this book.

The Editor.

TUSKEGEE ARMY AIR FORCE (TAAF)

TUSKEGEE, ALABAMA   CLASS   44-H   8 SEPTEMBER 1944

L to R

REAR ROW: Robert M Johnson   Charles W Cooper   Felix M McCrory   John W Squires   George E Franklin   Charles A Lane, Jr.   Albert L Lieteau   Herbert C Barland

CENTER: Edward E Manley   Carl E Carey   James Coleman   Morris E Gant   Samuel G Leftenant   Samuel Matthews, Jr   William H Holloman III   Stephen S Jenkins

KNEELING: George E Hardy   Edward Bishop   William M Cousins   Lawrence I Miller   Milton S Washington   Emet R Anders   John L Whitehead   William P Armstrong

151

LAST INSTRUCTIONS ★

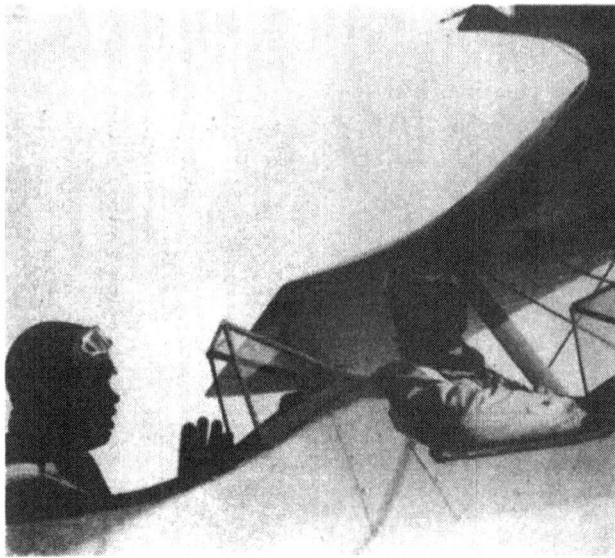

332nd
FIGHTER
GROUP

Lineage: Constituted as 332nd Fighter Group on 4 July 1942. Activated on 13 October 1942. Trained with P-39 and P-40 aircraft. Moved to Italy, arriving early in February 1944. Began operations with Twelfth Air Force on 5 February. Used P-39's to escort convoys, protect harbors, and fly armed reconnaissance missions. Converted to P-47's during April-May and changed to P-51's in June. Operated wtih Fifteenth Air Force from May 1944 to April 1945, being engaged primarily in protecting bombers that struck such objectives as oil refineries, factories, airfields, and marshalling yards in Italy, France, Germany, Poland, Czechoslovakia, Austria, Hungary, Yugoslavia, Rumania, Bulgaria, and Greece. Also made strafing attacks on airdromes, railroads, highways, bridges, river traffic, troop concentrations, radar facilities, power stations, and other targets. Received a Distinguished Unit Citation (DUC) for a mission on 24 March 1945 when the group escorted B-17's during a raid on a tank factory at Berlin, fought the interceptors that attacked the formation, and strafed transportation facilities while flying back to the base in Italy. Returned to the United States in October 1945. Inactivated on 19 October 1945.

Activated: 1 July 1947, Equipped with P-47's. Inactivated on 1 July 1949.

Squadrons: 99th, 1944-1945; 1947-1949. 100th, 1942-1945; 1947-1949. 301st, 1942-1945; 1947-1949. 302nd, 1942-1945.

Stations: Tuskegee, Alabama, 13 October 1942; Selfridge Field, Michigan, 29 March 1943; Oscoda, Michigan, 12 April 1943; Selfridge Field, Michigan, 9 July - 22 December 1943; Montecorvino, Italy, 3 February 1944; Capodichino, Italy, 15 April 1944; Ramitelli Airfield, Italy, 28 May 1944; Cattolica, Italy, c. 4 May 1945; Lucera, Italy, c. 18 July - September 1945; Camp Kilmer, New Jersey, 17-19 October 1945; Lockbourne Army Air Base, Ohio, 1 July 1947 - 1 July 1949.

Commanders: Lieutenant Colonel Sam W. Westbrook, Jr., 19 October 1942; Colonel Robert R. Selway, Jr., 16 May 1943; Colonel Benjamin O. Davis, Jr., 8 October 1943; Major George S. Roberts, 3 November 1944; Colonel Benjamin O. Davis, Jr., 24 December 1944, Major George S. Roberts, 9 June 1945 - unknown; Unknown, 1 July - 28 August 1947; Major William A. Campbell, 28 August 1947 - 1 July 1949.

Campaigns: American Theater; Air Combat, EAME Theater; Rome-Arno; Normandy; Northern France; Southern France; North Apennines; Rhineland; Central Europe; Po Valley.

Decorations: Distinguished Unit Citation, Germany, 24 March 1945.

Insigne - Shield: Azure on a fess nebule or, a panther passant sable armed and incensed gules.

Motto: SPIT FIRE (Approved 15 January 1943)

99th
FIGHTER
SQUADRON

Lineage: Constituted as 99th Pursuit Squadron pm 10 March 1941. Activated on 22 March 1941. Redesignated 99th Fighter Squadron on 15 May 1942. Inactivated on 1 July 1949.

Assignments: Army Air Corps, 22 March 1941; Technical Training Command, 26 March 1941; Southeast Air Corps (later Southeast Army Air Forces) Trainig Center, 5 November 1941 (attached to III Fighter Command, 19 August 1942); Twelfth Air Force, 24 April 1943; XII Air Support (later Tactical Air) Command, 28 May 1943 (attached to 33rd Fighter Group, 29 May 1943; 324th Fighter Group, c. 29 June 1943; 33rd Fighter Group, 19 July 1943; 79th Fighter Group, 16 October 1943; 324th Fighter Group 1 April - 6 June 1944); 332nd Fighter Group, 1 July 1947 - 1 July 1949

Stations: Chanute Field, Illinois, 22 March 1941; Maxwell Field, Alabama, 5 November 1941; Tuskegee, Alabama, 10 November 1941 - April 1943; Casablanca, French Morocco, 24 April 1943; Oued N'ja, French Morocco, 29 April 1943; Fardjouna, Tunisia, 7 June 1943; Licata, Sicily, 28 July 1943; Termini, Sicily, 4 September 1943; Barcellona, Sicily, 17 October 1943; Madna, Italy, 22 November 1943; Capodichino, Italy, 16 January 1944; Cerola, Italy, 2 April 1944; Pignataro, Italy, 10 May 1944; Ciampino, Italy, 11 June 1944; Orbetello, Italy, 17

June 1944; Ramitelli, Italy, 6 July 1944; Cattolica, Italy, c. 5 May 1945; Godman Field, Kentucky, 22 June 1945; Lockbourne Army Air Base, Ohio, 13 March 1946 - 1 July 1949.

Aircraft: P-40, 1943 - 1944; P-39, 1944; P-51, 1944-1945; P-47, 1944, 1945 - 1949.

Operations: Combat in Mediteranean Theater of Operations and European Theater of Operations, 2 June 1943 - 30 April 1945.

Service Streamers: American Theater.

Campaigns: Sicily; Naples-Foggia; Anzio; Rome-Arno; Normandy; Northern France; Southern France; North Apennines; Rhineland; Central Europe; Po Valley; Air Combat, EAME Theater.

Decorations: Distinguished Unit Citations: (Sicily, June - July) 1943; Cassino, 12-14 May 1944; Germany; 24 March 1945.

Emblem: Over and through a medium blue disc, border of nine golden orange segments fimbriated of the field, issuing out a sinister chief toward dexter base a golden orange winged panther in striking position, proper, between four yellow stars in dexter chief, and five like stars in sinister base (Approved 24 June 1944)

100th
FIGHTER
SQUADRON

Lineage: Constituted 100th Pursuit Squadron on 27 December 1941. Activated on 19 February 1942. Redesignated 100th Fighter Squadron on 15 May 1942. Inactivated on 19 October 1945. Activated on 1 July 1947. Inactivated on 1 July 1949.

Assignments: Southeast Air Corps (later Army Air Forces) Trainig Center, 19 February 1942; Third Air Force, 4 July 1942; 332nd Fighter Group, 13 October 1942 - 19 October 1945. 332nd Fighter Group, 1 July 1947 - 1 July 1949.

Stations: Tuskegee, Alabama, 19 February 1942; Selfridge Field, Michigan, 29 March 1943; Oscoda, Michigan, 29 October 1943; Selfridge Field, Michigan, 8 November - 22 December 1944; Montecorvino, Italy, 3 February 1944, Capodichino, Italy, 21 February 1944; Ramitelli Airfield, Italy, 6 June 1944; Cattolica, Italy, c. 4 May 1945; Lucera, Italy, c. 18 July - September 1945; Camp Kilmer, New Jersey, 17 - 19 October 1945; Lockbourne Army Air Base, Ohio, 1 July 1947 - 1 July 1949.

Aircraft: P-39, 1943 - 1944; P-40, 1943 - 1944; P-47, 1944; P-51, 1944 - 1945; P-47, 1947 -1949.

Operations: Combat in Mediterranean Theater of Operations and European Theater of Operations, 19 February 1944 - 26 April 1945.

Service Streamers: American Theater.

Campaigns: Rome-Arno; Normandy; Northern France; Southern France; North Apennines; Rhineland; Central Europe; Po Valley; Air Combat, EAME Theater.

Decorations: Distinguished Unit Citation: Germany, 24 March 1945.

Emblem: An ultramarine bllue disc, border red, piped white, circularly pierced with ragged edges, exposing a white glove in base market with light gray land areas and dark gray lines of latitude and longitude, supporting a crouching tan and brown panther, affronte, proper, winged white, in front of a yellow orange background segment (Approved 25 November 1944)

301st
FIGHTER
SQUADRON

Lineage: Constituted 301st Fighter Squadron on 4 July 1942. Activated on 13 October 1942. Inactivated on 19 October 1945. Activated on 1 July 1947. Inactivated on 1 July 1949.

Assignments: 332nd Fighter Group, 13 October 1942 - 19 October 1945. 332nd Fighter Group, 1 July 1947 - 1 July 1949.

Stations: Tuskegee, Alabama, 13 October 1942; Selfridge Field, Michigan, 29 March 1943; Oscoda, Michigan, 21 May 1943; Selfridge Field, Michigan, 10 July - 23 December 1943; Montecorvino, Italy, 8 February 1944, Capodichino, Italy, 15 April 1944; Ramitelli Airfield, Italy, 18 May 1944; Cattolica, Italy, c. 4 May 1945; Lucera, Italy, c. 18 July - September 1945; Camp Kilmer, New Jersey, 17 - 19 October 1945; Lockbourne Army Air Base, Ohio, 1 July 1947 - 1 July 1949.

Aircraft: P-39, 1943 - 1944; P-40, 1943 - 1944; P-47, 1944; P-51, 1944 - 1945; P-47, 1947 -1949.

Operations: Combat in Mediterranean Theater of Operations and European Theater of Operations, 15 February - 26 April 1945.

Service Streamers: American Theater.

Campaigns: Rome-Arno; Normandy; Northern France; Southern France; North Apennines; Rhineland; Central Europe; Po Valley; Air Combat, EAME Theater.

Decorations: Distinguished Unit Citation: Germany, 24 March 1945.

Emblem: On a light turquoise blue disc, edged black, a carucatyred cat wearing a red cape, brown aviator's hellmet and white goggles, piloting a gray, .50 caliber aerial machine gun with red and white tail, winged yellow orange, with an auxiliary gray wing tank under each wing, all in flight toward dexter, in front of a large, white cloud formation (Approved 29 June 1945)

302nd
FIGHTER
SQUADRON

Lineage: Constituted 302nd Fighter Squadron on 4 July 1942. Activated on 13 October 1942. Inactivated on 6 March 1945. Activated 302nd Tactical Fighter Squadron on 1 July 1987.

Assignments: 332nd Fighter Group, 13 October 1942 - 6 March 1945. 944th Tactical Fighter Group, 1 July 1987.

Stations: Tuskegee, Alabama, 13 October 1942; Selfridge Field, Michigan, 29 March 1943; Oscoda, Michigan, 19 November 1943; Selfridge Field, Michigan, December 1943; Montecorvino, Italy, 7 February 1944, Capodichino, Italy, 6 March 1944; Ramitelli Airfield, Italy, c. 28 May 1944 - 6 March 1945; Luke Air Force Base, 1 July 1987.

Aircraft: P-39, 1943 - 1944; P-40, 1943 - 1944; P-47, 1944; P-51, 1944 - 1945.

Operations: Combat in Mediterranean Theater of Operations and European Theater of Operations, 17 February 1944 - 20 February 1945.

Service Streamers: American Theater.

Campaigns: Rome-Arno; Normandy; Northern France; Southern France; North Apennines; Rhineland; Air Combat, EAME Theater.

Decorations: None.

Emblem: On a light blue disc, border red, a red devil, proper, winged white, trimmed yellow, running toward dexter over white cloud formation, edged yellow, in base, holding in left hand a white and yellow pitchfork with skull on tip of handle, and holding a white and yellow aerial machine gun under the right arm (Approved 2 November 1944)

PRISONERS OF WAR

GENE BROWN	HAROLD BROWN	ALFRED CARROL	ROBERT DANIELS
RED DRIVER	THURSTON GAINES	**ROGER GAITOR**	NEWMAN GOLDEN
ALFRED GORHAM	CORNELIUS GOULD	WILLIAM GRIFFIN	LLOYD HATCHCOCK
LINCOLN HUDSON	ALEXANDER JEFFERSON	LANGDON JOHNSON	GEORGE ILES
JOE LEWIS	WILBUR LONG	RICHARD MACON	WALTER McCREARY
ARMOUR McDAMOE:	WOODROW MORGAN	STERLING PENN	LEWIS SMITH
LUTHER SMITH	FLOYD THOMPSON	HUGH WHITE	HENRY WISE
C. WILLIAMS	KENNY WILLIAMS	CAROL WOODS	

M.I.A.s RETURNED TO STATES

CHUCK LACKSON	RUEL BELL	CHUBBY GREEN	ROBERT ONEIL
ROBERT MARTIN	LEON SPEARS	JAMES WALKER	SAMUEL WASHINGTON

M.I.A.s RETURNED TO COMBAT

ROBERT CHANDLER	FREDDIE HUTCHINS	ANDREW MARSHALL	SHELBY WESTBROOK

HERBERT V. CLARK HAD RETURNED TO ITALY FOR A SECOND COMBAT TOUR. RETURNING FROM A MISSION OVER MUNICH, GERMANY, HIS AIRCRAFT WAS DAMAGED BY FLACK OVER BALZANO IN NORTHERN ITALY. HE BAILED OUT, AND LANDED IN A SECTOR CONTROLLED BY THE ITALIAN UNDERGROUND KNOWN AS THE PARTISANS. UNABLE TO TRAVEL 300 MILES THRU THE GERMAN LINES, CLARK EVADED CAPTURE AND FOUGHT FOR EIGHT MONTHS WITH THE PARTISAN FORCES.

KILLED IN ACTION

WILLIAM ARMSTRONG Providence, RI	FRED BREWER Charlotte, NC	SIDNEY BROOKS Cleveland, OH
JAMES BROWN Los Angeles, CA	ROGER BROWN Glenco, IL	SAMUEL BRUCE Seattle, WA
JAMES CALHOUNE Bridgeport, CT	JOHN CHAVIS Raleigh, NC	JAMES COLEMAN Detroit, MI
HARRY DANIELS Indianapolis, IN	ALFONSO DAVIS Omaha, NB	ALWAYNE DUNLAP Washington, DC
MAURICE ESTERS Webster City, IO	WILLIAM FAULKNER Nashville, TN	SAMUEL FOREMAN Tulsa, OK

KILLED IN ACTION (Continued)

FREDERICK FUNDERBURG
Monticello, GA

JOE GORDON
Brooklyn, NY

EARL HIGHBAUGH
Indianapolis, IN

WELLING IRVING
Belzuni, MS

EDGAR JONES
New York, NY

ERWIN LAWRENCE
Cleveland, OH

WALTER MANNINGS
St. Louis, MO

ANDREW MAPLES
Orange, VA

ELTON NIGHTENGALE
Tuskegee, AL

HENRY POLLARD
Buffalo, NY

EMORY ROBBINS
Chicago, IL

CORNELIUS ROGERS
Chicago, IL

ALFONSO SIMMONS
Jacksonville, FL

NORVELL STOUDMIRE
St. Louis, MO

WALTER WESTMORELAND
Atlanta, GA

MORRIS GANT
Chicago, IL

MACEO HARRIS
Boston, MA

WENDELL HOCKADAY
Norfolk, VA

SAMUEL JEFFERSON
Galveston, TX

EDWARD LAIRD
Brighton, AL

SAMUEL LEFTENANT
Amityville, NY

ANDREW MARSHALL
Cambridge, MA

MAC ROSS
Dayton, OH

LELAND PENNINGTON
Rochester, NY

JOHN PROWELL, JR.
Lewisburg, AL

RONALD REEVES
Washington, DC

ROGER ROMINE
Oakland, CA

ARNETT STARK
Los Angeles, CA

ELMER TAYLOR
Pittsburgh, PA

LEONARD WILLETTE
Belleville, NJ

CLEMENCEAU GIVINGS
Richmond, VA

THOMAS HAWKINS
Glen Ridge, NJ

OSCAR HUTTON
Chicago, IL

CHARLES JOHNSON
Philadelphia, PA

CARROLL LANGSTON
Chicago, IL

WAYNE LEGGINS
Springfield, OH

GEORGE McCRUMBY
Cartersville, GA

NESL NELSON
Amarillo, TX

JAMES POLKINGHORNE
Pensacola, FL

JAMES RAMSEY
Augusta, GA

ROBERT ROBINSON
Ashville, NC

LEON ROBERTS
Pritchard, AL

ROOSEVELT STIGER
Jackson, MI

ROBERT TRESVILLE
Germantown, PA

SHERMAN WHITE
Montgomery, AL

KILLED IN ACTION (Continued)

WILLIAM F. WILLIAM
Cleveland, OH
BERYL WYATT
Independence, KS
ALBERT YOUNG
Memphis, TN

ROBERT WIGGINS
Elmsford, NY
CARL WOODS
Mars, PA

FRANK WRIGHT

QUITMAN WALKER
Indianola, MS

PURPLE HEART RECIPIENTS

ROGER GAITOR
WILBUR LONG
LEE RAYFORD

JOHN HAMILTON
RICHARD MACON
JOHN SLOAN

CHARLES HILL
ANDREW MARSHALL

DAY	FROM	TO	MAKE AND MODEL OF AIRCRAFT	MAKE OF ENGINE	H.P.	CERTIFICATE NUMBER	DURATION HRS	MIN	INST HRS	CLASS TRANS	CLASS Combat	CLASS	REMARKS	PILOT SIGNAT.
Aug. 3	Foggia, Italy		P-51-C	V-1763-7	1570		1	05					Checkout P-51	
" 4	"	"	"	V-1763-7	1760		1	55					X-Country Alt.	
" 5	"	ELBA - ROME	"	"	"		3	20						
" 7	"	Yugoslavia-Grosselija	"	"	"		5	25						
" 9	"	Gyor Hungary	"	"	"		5	00						
" 10	"	Ploesti Roumania	"	"	"		5	35						
" 12	"	Lyon France	"	"	"		5	10						
" 13	"	Avignon France	"	"	"		4	40						
" 16	"	Sou Germany	"	"	"		5	15						
" 17	"	Ploesti Rumania	"	"	"		5	45						
" 19	"	Ploesti Romania	"	"	"		5	05						
" 20	"	Blechhammer Ger.	"	"	"		5	15						
" 22	"	Avignon France	"	"	"		5	10						
" 23	"	Vienna Austria	"	"	"		4	35						
" 29	"	Toulon France	"	"	"		3	45						
Aug 31	"	Bucharest Roumania	"	"	"		6	10				6:10		Bombers pick up of US Air men from capital of Romania	
						TOTALS	73	10					Certified by Shelly F. Westbrook O-821921	

YEAR 1944

DAY	FROM	TO	MAKE AND MODEL OF AIRCRAFT	MAKE OF ENGINE	H.P.	CERTIFICATE NUMBER	DURATION HRS	MIN	INST HRS	CLASS TRANS	CLASS Combat	CLASS	REMARKS	PILOT SIGNAT.
1	Foggia	Bucharest	P-51-C	V-1763-7	1760		6	10			6:10		Same mission as yesterday	
2	"	Nis Yugoslavia	"	"	"		4	05			4:05		Straffing	
3	"	Zagreb	"	"	"		4	45			4:45		Bombing Bridges	
5	"	Budapest, Hung.	"	"	"		4	50			4:50		Oil Storage & Bridges	
6	"	Ovenia, Hung.	"	"	"		5	40			5:40		R.R. yards & Bridges	
11	"	Local	"	"	"		2	00			2:00		Pictures of the Group	
12	"	Munich, Germany	"	"	"		5	35			5:35		Jet aircraft Plant	
13	"	Blechhammer Ger.	"	"	"		5	50			5:50		Synthetic oil plants	
15	"	Local but Z.Z. Job	"	"	"		2	00			2:00		Exhibit & Pictures	
16	"	Budapest Hungary	"	"	"		4	50			4:50		Oil Refineries	
18	"	Budapest Hungary	"	"	"		5	25			5:25		Railroad bridge	
21	"	Debrezia Hung.	"	"	"		5	15			5:15		Railroad Bridge	
22	"	Munich, Germany	"	"	"		5	35			5:35		Jet aircraft Factory	
24	"	Athens Greece	"	"	"		6	00			6:00		Fighter Sweep X-Drink at ...	
4	"	Athens Greece	"	"	"		5	05			5:05		Strafted hanger + field ...	
6	"	"	"	"	"		6	25			6:25		Strafted two J-88 ... landed at B-17 Field	
						TOTALS	79	30					Certified by Shelly F. Westbrook O-821974 2nd Lt. A.C.	

YEAR 1944

DAY	FROM	TO	MAKE AND MODEL OF AIRCRAFT	MAKE OF ENGINE	H.P.	CERTIFICATE NUMBER	DURATION HRS	MIN	INST HRS	CLASS Combat	CLASS	CLASS	REMARKS	PILOT SIGNAT.
16	Foggia	Benevta	P-51-C	V-1760-7	1760		2	40		2:40			Early Return	
17	"	Blechhammer	"	"	"		5	00		5:00			Escort Bomb ...	
20	"	Vincenza Italy	"	"	"		3	30		3:30				
21	"	Gyor	"	"	"		3	20		3:20				
23	"	Regensburg Ger.	"	"	"		4	50		4:50				
						TOTALS				19:20			Certified by Shelly F. Westbrook O-821974 1st Lt. A.C.	

YEAR 1944

Table 1 (Year 1945)

NO	DAY	FROM	TO	MAKE AND MODEL OF AIRCRAFT	MAKE OF ENGINE	H.P.	CERTIFICATE NUMBER	DURATION HRS.	MIN.	CLASS	CLASS	CLASS	REMARKS	PILOT SIGNA.
1	3	Foggia	Local	P-51-D	Merlin	1570		1	30				Lufberry with B-17s to B-38	
1	4	"	"	"	"	"		0	00				Cracked up taking off - not injured	
1	7	"	Lenzt	P-51-Q	"	"		3	50				Escort - B-24	
1	12	"	Local	"	"	"		2	00				Local	
1	15	"	Vienna, Aust.	P-51-C	"	"		5	25				Vienna - B-24	
1	16	"	Local	P-51-D	"	"		1	00				Flew my new job today	
1	20	"	Regenceburg, Ger.	"	"	"		5	30				My old Waterloo	
1	21	"	Vienna - Austria	"	"	"		5	30				Bad visibility. Haze as hell	
2	1	"	Mooshberdinem & Vienna	"	"	"		5	00				Went to gras instead of assigned tgt Aust.	
2	2	"	Local	"	"	"		1	00				Real hot - very lazy	
2	5	"	Salzburg, Aust.	"	"	"		2	05				Early return - engine trouble	
2	8	"	Vienna, Aust.	"	"	"		6	00				Escorted B-17 from target	
2	8	"	Mooshberdithan	"	"	"		5	05				Escort & cover	
2	9	"	Local	"	"	"		3	25				Transition	
2	13	"	Vienna Aust.	"	"	"		5	05				Escort + cover	
2	14	"	Vienna, Aust.	"	"	"		5	00				Escort & cover	
		YEAR 1945					TOTALS	57	25				CERTIFIED BY Shelby Weathrok O-821421 1st AC	

Table 2

NO	DAY	FROM	TO	MAKE AND MODEL OF AIRCRAFT	MAKE OF ENGINE	H.P.	CERTIFICATE NUMBER	DURATION HRS.	MIN.	INST HRS.	CLASS	CLASS	CLASS	REMARKS	PILOT SIGNA.
2	15	Foggia	Vienna, Aust.	P-51-D	Merlin	1750		5	00					Escort & cover Bad weather	
2	16	"	Munchen, Ger.	"	"	"		5	10					Strafing escorted pillow	
2	17	"	Lintz, Aust.	"	"	"		3	35					Bad weather - did not com k.	
3	18	"	Lintz-Wels	"	"	"		3	15					Pretty good mission saw B-17	
2	19	"	Vienna, Aust.	"	"	"		5	35					Routine escort	
2	20	"	Bologna, Italy	"	"	"		4	55						
2	21	"	Vienna, Trieste	"	"	"		3	25					Special mission - Sup.	
2	22	"	M. Ger.	"	"	"		5	20					Early - oxygen leak	
2	23	"	Vienna area	"	"	"		1	15					Rec - mosquito - engine	
2	26	"	Munich, Ger.	"	"	"		1	15					Gunnery	
2	27	"	Local	"	"	"		1	15					Escort - 300' H. Ts	
2	28	"	Verona, Italy	"	"	"		5	30					Rec - saw 85 in action	
3	1	"	Stuttgart, Ger.	"	"	"		5	00					Escorted B-24 to Russian lines	
3	12	"	Vienna, Aust.	"	"	"		5	00					Section leader - not bad	
3	13	"	Regenceburg, Ger.	"	"	"		5	10					Strafed airfield target 2000	
3	14	"	Styre & Braer, Aust.	"	"	"		4	30					Hunting	
		YEAR					TOTALS	65	20					CERTIFIED BY Shelby Weathrok O-821421 1st AC	

Table 3

NO	DAY	FROM	TO	MAKE AND MODEL OF AIRCRAFT	MAKE OF ENGINE	H.P.	CERTIFICATE NUMBER	DURATION HRS.	MIN.	INST HRS.	CLASS	CLASS	CLASS	REMARKS	PILOT SIGNA.
3	15	Foggia	Khurlan, Ger.	P-51-D	Merlin	1760		5	50					Lonely raid to middle 300 - near Berlin	
3	16	"	Prague, Czech.	P-51-C	"	"		5	30					Rec - mosquito - nice ship	
3	20	"	Prague, Czech.	P-51-D	"	"		5	05					Escort & strafed loco bad weather. Ruhland, Ger.	
3	21	"	Nürnberg, Ger.	"	"	"		5	10					Led Sqd. - 5000 mission	
3	22	"	Ruhland, Ger.	"	"	"		5	30					Rec. between Berlin & Dresden - bad track	
3	23	"	Ruhland, Ger.	"	"	"		5	50	30				Ruhland - Braunes Dam weather killed Rec.	
3	24	"	Berlin, Ger.	"	"	"		2	20					Early return - bad ship	
3	25	"	Prague, Aust.	"	"	"		6	00					Led Sqd. again today 5000 mission	
3	27	"	Local	"	"	"		3	10					Local show time	
3	28	"	Local	"	"	"		3	25					Chased A-26 & B-17	
4	1	"	Prague & Lintz Rec.	"	"	"	Finis	4	05	30				Bad weather - incomplete	
														Total Ftr. 464 Total Time 689	
		YEAR					TOTALS							CERTIFIED BY L.F. Westbrook O-821421 1st AC	

S. Westbrook

(A) FLYING STATUS		(B) DATE OF ACTIVE SERVICE
X ☐		8 Feb 44
F NF		

(C) FLYING RESTRICTIONS		
Date	Length	Reasons

(D) PILOT ENGINE QUALIFICATIONS	
Engine	Basis of Qualifications
Over 4-Engine	
4-Engine	
2-Engine	
1-Engine	Grad of Adv.SE Fly.Sch.

(E) TYPE EXPERIENCE AND TYPE EQUIPMENT

	PURSUIT	BOMBER	DIVE	OTHER	TRANSPORT	APPROXIMATE INCL. DATES	AREA
TACTICAL-COMBAT	P-51					Mar 45	MTOUSAAF
	P-39					Mar 44	USA
TACTICAL-NONCOMBAT	P-47					Jul 44	USA
	P-40					Aug 43	USA
TRAINING				PT17,BT13A AT6		Feb 44	
OTHER							

(F) FLYING HOURS

HOURS	APPROXIMATE DATES	HOURS
— 250	Feb 44	1,000 – 1,500
250 – 500	Dec 44	1,500 – 2,000
500 – 750		2,000 – 3,000
750 – 1,000		+ 3,000

36. CIVILIAN FLYING EXPERIENCE

TYPE EQUIPMENT	H. P.	HOURS	NATURE OF ACTIVITY

37. AIR FORCE SPECIALTIES

(A) AIR CORPS RATINGS														(B) RATED, NONPILOT SPECIALTIES							
P	SP	CP	GP	LP	SVP	SSVP	BP	SBP	AO	SAO	TO			NAV.	BOR.	GNR.	ABMR.	WEA.	ENGR.	CUM.	PHOTO.
X																					

38. CHRONOLOGICAL RECORD OF MILITARY EXPERIENCE (incl. Brief Summary of any Enlisted Experience)

APPROXIMATE INCL. DATES	TYPE AND NUMBER OF ORGANIZATION AND LOCATION	POSITION AND DESCRIPTION OF DUTIES (incl. Type Equipment and Approx. Flying Hours Where Applicable)	PERFORMANCE RATING		OCCUPATIONAL CODE AND TITLE (AR 605-95)
14 Oct 42 8 Feb 44	AAFTS (See 30)	EM: Active duty 6 Mar 43. Basic Trng & CTD Aptd A/C 15 May 43. Pilot Trng,PT17,65 hrs. BT13,70 hrs. AT6, 80 hrs.			
9 Feb 44 28 Feb 44	Trans.Sch.TAAF Alabama	Student Officer: P-40,8 hrs. Trans. Trng.			2700 Student Officer
29 Feb 44 7 May 44	553 Ftr Sq Selfridge Fld Mich.	Pilot P-39; 66 hrs. RTU (Lt Col. C.A.Gale,Sq CO)	VS	CAG	1055 Ftr Pilot SE
8 May 44 14 Jul 44	Ftr Trng Unit Walterboro S.C.	Pilot P-39; 44 hrs P-47, 5 hrs. RTU. (Lt Col. S. Triffey,Sq CO)	VS	ST	1055 Ftr Pilot SE
15 Jul 44 31 Jul 44	Casual	Casual; Stag & Processing.Dep US 15 Jul 44. Arr. in MTO. 29 Jul 44.			1055 Ftr Pilot SE
1 Aug 44 31 Aug 44	99 Ftr Sq 332 Ftr Gp MTOUSAAF	Pilot P-51; 73 hrs. 13 c/missions 68 c/hrs. Wing-ship.(Capt.E.B.Lawrence,Sq CO)	VS	EBL	1055 Ftr Pilot SE
1 Sep 44 20 Oct 44	99 Ftr Sq 332 Ftr Gp MTOUSAAF	Pilot P-51; 89 hrs. 16 c/missions 84 c/hrs. Wing-ship.(Major G.S. Roberts,Sq CO)	Ex	GSR	1055 Ftr Pilot SE
21 Oct 44 22 Oct	99 Ftr Sq 332 Ftr Gp MTOUSAAF	Pilot P-51; 6 hrs. 2 c/missions 3 c/hrs. Wing-ship.(Capt. A. W. Davis,Sq CO)	Ex	AWD	1055 Ftr Pilot SE

39. CIVILIAN EXPERIENCE (Begin With Last And List Most Recent 4 Employers or Last 10 Years, Whichever Is Least)

INCL. DATES & MONTHLY SALARY ON LEAVING	NAME, PLACE AND NATURE OF INDUSTRY, PROFESSION OR BUSINESS	POSITION HELD AND DESCRIPTION OF DUTIES		OCCUPATIONAL CODE AND TITLE (AR 605-99)
23 Oct 44 24 Nov 44	Enemy Occupied Terr.	Missing in Action: Shot down 23 Oct 44. Returned to Allied Control 24 Nov 44.	Evadee:	Not to be used outside Cont US(Exclu-sive of Alaska) unless so auth by War Dept.
25 Nov 44 31 Dec 44	99 Ftr Sq 332 Ftr Gp MTOUSAAF	Pilot P-51; No duties. (Capt. W. A. Campbell,Sq CO)	S WAC	
1 Jan 45 4 Mar 45	99 Ftr Sq 332 Ftr Gp MTOUSAAF	Pilot P-51; 106 hrs. 18 c/missions 103 c/hrs. Wingship.(Capt. W.A.Campbell,Sq CO)	Ex WAC	1055 Ftr Pilot SE
5 Mar 45 22 Mar 45	99 Ftr Sq 332 Ftr Gp MTOUSAAF	Flt Comdr P-51 43 hrs. 8 c/missions 40 c/hrs. 8 Sq leads.(Capt.W.A.Campbell,Sq CO)	Ex WAC	1055 Ftr Pilot SE
23 Mar 45 12 Apr 45	99 Ftr Sq 332 Ftr Gp MTOUSAAF	Flt Comdr P-51; 24 hrs. 3 c/missions 18 c/hrs. 2 Sq leads. 1 Dep Gp lead. (Major W.A.Campbell, Sq CO)	Ex WAC	1055 Ftr Pilot SE
13 Apr 45 12 JUN 1945	AAFRS#1, Atl City NJ	Returnee: Ret to US 5 May 45. Leave,processing & assignment. (Robert L. Young,1st Lt,AC)	Unk RLY 40.	
Apr 1941 Feb 1943 $200.00	Erie Ordnance Depot LaCarne,Ohio	Welder: Electric & Acetylene.Repair & maintenance of test mounts for light & heavy artillery. Also general main-tenance on machine shop equipment.		Welder 04.651

PRINCIPAL OCCUPATIONS PREVIOUS TO LAST 4 EMPLOYERS or LAST 10 YEARS

Dec 1940 Apr 41 $75.00	Secor,Hotel,Toledo,Ohio	Waiter & Bus Boy: Catering services & dining room work.		Waiter 02.270

40. SPORTS (P—Participate; XL—Excel; C—Coach)	41. ACTIVE HOBBIES	42. ORGANIZATIONS AND SOCIETIES; SPEC. ACCOMP.; AWARDS AND DECORATIONS
(P) Football (P) Basketball (P) Softball (P) Volley Ball (XL) Equitation	Model Airplanes	45 Cal Pist 1 Qualified Score 74% Mkms EAME Theatre Ribbon WD Cir 62 1944 1 Star Rome Arno SDG080 1944 1 Star Southern France WDG080 1944 1 Star Germany WDG080 1944 Air Medal 15AG3102 7 Sep 1944 4 OLC to AM 15AF001040 1 Mar 45 0 Auth to wear (1) service bar for (9) mos overseas service from 15 Jul 44 to 3 May 45 WD Cir 268 1944 1 Star: Central Europe;1 Star:North Appenines per GO 40 21 May 45

HE CAN'T FORGET—Wearer of the Air Medal and Purple Heart, First Lieut. Henry A. Wise Jr., Chariton, Va., has been awarded the Certificate of Valor. Shot down over the Ploesti oil fields, captured and made prisoner by the Nazis in Bulgaria, the officer was freed in three weeks by Russian troops. A former fighter pilot with the 332nd Fighter Group in Italy, Lieutenant Wise is now a student at the Command and General Staff school, Fort Leavenworth, Kan.—U. S. Signal Corps Photo.

Members of the 332nd Fighter Group are shown at their base in Italy as they received their final instructions before starting on their 100th combat mission against the enemy.

H. Wise

Nelson, Ellington
Roberts, Grey, Driver

FIRST TRIP TO NAZI CENTER IS SUCCESSFUL

Ohio Pilot Bags Rocket Plane On History-making Mission

MAX JOHNSON
AFBO War Correspondent
WITH 15TH AIR FORCE IN ITALY—For the first time in the European war, Col. Benjamin O. Davis, Jr., and his fighter pilot squadron were over Berlin Saturday, scoring decisive victories over three of Hitler's jet-propelled aircraft and accounting for four more probables.

Col. Davis led his group on this record-breaking mission over 1,600 miles and providing protection for the 15th Army Airforce flying fortresses which bombed the Daimler Benz Tank Works in Berlin.

Th group's three victories were accredited to 1st Lt. Roscoe C. Brown, Jr., of New York, Lt. Earl Lane, of 1165 E. 294 St., Wickliffe, Ohio, and F-O. Charles Brantley, of 4263 Fairfax avenue, St. Louis. This marked the group's second encounter with the German jet-propelled planes. The first encounter came during the second week of last December when the group escorted bombers to targets in the vicinity of Munich, Germany. On this occasion, one small formation of jet-propelled planes made a pass at the bombers and darted away without scoring hits or being hit by chasing fighters.

The run to Berlin came as a surprise to participating bomber and fighter crew personnel. This was not deemed feasible due to adverse weather conditions.

When news reached Col. Davis' group that the target for the day was Berlin, every pilot wanted to fly the mission.

Jet-propelled planes encountered were in numerous groups ranging from two to twenty on this run 50 miles South of Berlin on into the target. These aircraft, mostly ME-262 and a few tailless rockets, attacked the bombers mostly from the rear in sections of two to eight aircraft.

(Continued on Page THREE-A).

FIGHTER SQUADRON

(Continued From Page ONE—A)
Lt. Brown, who was among the group's personnel participating in this mission, gave the newsmen first hand account in a press conference. He said that he fought for forty minutes over Berlin and that the jet-propelled planes seemed to be everywhere. Brown said that the Nazi pilots seemed reluctant to fight the escorting fighter planes and tried to capitalize on their plant excessive speed to make passes at the bombers and then dart away.

Lt. Brown said that the first jet he spotted the pilot was bailing out when he realized the tight position, while his companion died in the plane.

"I still haven't seen Berlin," he said in answer to an inquiry as to how the German capital looked. "I kept so busy that I just didn't have time."

During the entire run, thirteen planes were shot down but the others were credited to another accompanying fighter group and the various bomber personnel. The mission to Berlin is believed to be one of the most successful yet taken by the 15th AAA and sets the record for aerial victories over jet planes.

(Call-Post reporters contacted the parents of Lt. Lane. The pilot attended Wilberforce University a year and was studying at Western Reserve University here when he joined the air corps. He has a sister, Miss Barbara Lane. According to Mr. Lane, his son completed 35 missions over a month ago. The family attend Antioch

332nd Escorts Bombers to Hungary on 100th Mission

Pilots of the group have been awarded eight Distinguished Flying Crosses, one Legion of Merit and over 100 Air Medals and clusters.

The group has destroyed 75 enemy aircraft in aerial combat, 17 of which were destroyed while the outfit was with the 12th Air Force. It has destroyed 214 enemy aircraft on the ground, as well as a large amount of rolling stock.

Its pilots also hold the distinction of having sunk an enemy destroyer which was sighted and bombed in the harbor of Trieste

15th AAF IN ITALY — The 332nd Fighter Group, commanded by Col. B. O. Davis, Jr., "chalked up" its 100th mission against the enemy with the 15th Air Force recently when it provided escort for heavy bombers to their target in Gyor, Hungary.

The group began operations with the 15th Air Force on June 7, 1944, while still flying P-47 Thunderbolts. Soon after its initiation, however, the group changed to its present type of fighter, the P-51 Mustang.

Mission assignments have been varied slightly, but bomber escort has been the principal task. The group has participated in strafing attacks, provided air-sea rescue and escorted C-47's evacuating Allied airmen from enemy occupied countries.

8 DFC's, Other Awards
on June 25.
Commanded by Officers
The group has often been paid

visits by bomber personnel of the 15th Air Force Bomb Groups who wished to express their appreciation for the fine escort work done by the pilots.

Under the skillful guidance of Col. Davis, the flyers have moulded themselves into a combat team with one express purpose, "to keep the bombers flying and the Allies winning."

OHIO FLIER SHARES IN AIR VICTORIES—First Lt. Harold (left) of Columbus, Ohio, brought down two German Focke 190's last week while escorting bombers over Southern France. Officer Cornelius Gould, Jr. (right), former Pittsburgh Court player, wingman, was largely responsible for the air victories gave protection to Lieutenant Sawyer and other fighter pilots under the command of Lt. Col. B. O. Davis, Jr. The flyers shot 12 enemy planes during four missions.

H. Sawyer, C. Gould

LLIES HAIL FLIERS . . . CHEER DARING AIRMEN WHO OUTSMARTED GERMAN FIGHTERS WITH INFERIOR PLANES

Piloting inferior and outmoded planes—P-40 Warhawks—the 99th Fighter Squadron, all-Negro segment of the 12th Air Force umpells covering the expanding beachhead south of Rome, was being acclaimed by the Allies this week.

When the daring bronze pilots shot down twelve enemy planes in two days, they established one of the best records ever turned in by any fighter squadron. White officers were quick to admit the excellence of these pilots in their P-40 fighter-bomb-

ers, by no means the most modern aerial weapon or the easiest fighting craft to pile up victories.

The entire world was watching the 99th. Nearly nine months overseas and the squadron had only one enemy craft to its credit. Doubting Thomases began to spread rumors. They said the 99th hadn't shown anything, and wouldn't . . . But, those boys of the 99th didn't give up hope. They knew they had the training. They had ambition, intestinal stamina and teamwork.

They were not worried about

the slower and inferior planes. They only wanted a chance to meet the Germans in battle. It hadn't been their fault that Nazi planes refused to engage them in combat.

But, then came January 27-28. The Germans came in droves and 99th pilots went out to meet them. Their score: enemy planes destroyed, 12; probably destroyed 2; damaged 4.

In photo at left, Capt. Clarence Clifford Jamison, Little Rock, Ark., gives details of a day's mission to members of the

99th Fighter Squadron at an airfield somewhere in Italy. Pilots of the 99th have done every type of fighter plane work.

Scene at top, right, shows 99th pilots, eager for the command that will send them off to meet the enemy in the skies above Italy, in a "briefing" session. Among the pilots in this group are First Lieuts. Hammond A. Lawson, Maryville, Calif.; William A. Walker, Carbondale, Ill., and George T. McCrumby, Fort Worth, Texas.

Bottom photo, right, shows the

ground crew of a P-40 Warhawk of the 99th Fighter Squadron in Italy bringing up the bombs that soon will go diving through space toward some Nazi target.—U.S. Army Signal Corps Photos.

THEY'RE WRITING HISTORY WITH BULLETS AND BOMBS . . . THESE ADVENTUROUS 99TH FLIERS SET PACE FOR OTHER AMERICAN WINGMEN

The 99th Fighter Squadron, all-Negro unit of the Twelfth Air Force, is making history as well as headlines. The Squadron's biggest accomplishment was reported on January 27-28 when the bronze airmen shot down twelve Nazi planes over an Italian beachhead.

Pictured here are nine of the daring young airmen who had a hand in bagging the 12 German fighters:

First Lt. Edward L. Topping, San Francisco, Calif., left; 2nd Lt. Wilson V. Eagleston, Bloomington, Ind., second from left; 1st Lt. Leon C. Roberts, Pritchard, Ala., third from left; 1st Lt. Robert W. Deitz, Portland, Ore., fourth from left; 2nd Lt. Louis C. Smith, Los Angeles, Calif., fifth from left, at top; Capt. Rodney Custis, Hartford, Conn., shown in plane; 2nd Lt. Charles P. Bailey, Punta Gorda, Fla., sixth from

left; 1st Lt. Willie Ashley, Sumter, S. C., seventh from left, and 1st Lt. Howard Baugh, Petersburg, Va.

Lieutenant Deitz was credited with shooting down two planes during the two-day air battle with the Nazis; Lieutenant Baugh and 2nd Lt. Clarence Allen (not shown here) were credited with equal share in the destruction of one plane in the January 27 engagement, and other officers

shown here were each credited with one enemy plane.

Captain Charles (Buster) Hall, Brazil, Ind., pictured on the front page of The Courier last week, shot down two enemy planes January 28, running up his total to three.

COMBAT RECORD OF NEGRO AIRMEN

June 9, 1945

	DESTROYED	DAMAGED	TOTAL
Aircraft (aerial)	150	25	136
Aircraft (ground)	150	123	273
Barges and Boats	16	24	40
Box cars, Other Rolling Stock	58	561	619
Buildings & Factories	0	23	23
Gun Emplacements	3	0	3
Destroyers	1	0	1
Horsedrawn Vehicles	15	100	115
Motor Transports	6	81	87
Power Transformers	3	2	5
Locomotives	57	69	126
Radar Installations	1	8	9
Tanks on Flat Cars	0	7	7
Oil and Ammunition Dumps	2	0	2
Total Missions	12th Air Force		1267
Total Missions	15th Air Force		311
Total Sorties	12th Air Force		6381
Total Sorties	15th Air Force		9152
Grand Total Missions			1578
Grand Total Sorties			15533
Total number of pilots sent overseas			450
Total number of pilots graduated at Tuskegee			992

Awards:

Legion of Merit	1
Silver Star	1
Soldier Medal	2
Purple Heart	8
Distinguished Flying Cross	95
Bronze Star	14
Air Medal and Clusters	744

*Final total of Distinguished Flying Crosses awarded to Negro pilots estimated at: 150

FIFTEENTH AIR FORCE BOMBING MISSIONS

June 1944

2nd B-24s: Szolnok, Hun M/Y; Miskolc, Hun M/Y; Szeged, Hun M/Y; Simeria, Rum M/Y; Cluj, Rum M/Y

      B-17s: Debreczen, Hun M/Y (FRANTIC); Oradea, Rum M/Y

3rd B-24s: Omis, Yugo

4th B-24s: Genoa M/Y; Turin M/Y; Savona M/Y; Novi Ligure M/Y; Recco Viaduct; Orelle and Gad RRBr's

      B-17s: Antheor..... Var R., Fr RRBr

5th B-24s: Br..... giore M/Y; Forli
          M/..... M/Y; and four
          It.....

      B-17s: Pi.....

6th B-24s: Plo..... Rum M/Y

      B-17s: Bel..... Installations, Yugo.....

7th B-24s: Volt.....

8th B-17s: Pola.....

9th B-24s: Munic..... ..., etc.; Porto Margh.....

      B-17s: Munich Ger I/Area and A/D

10th B-24s: Trieste I/O; Ferrara A/D; Ancona

      B-17s: Mestre M/Y; Porto Marghera M/Y and I/O

11th B-24s: Giurgiu, Rum Oil Loading Quay and I/O (1,024 tons); Constanta, Rum

      B-17s: Smederevo, Yugo M/Y and I/O; Foscani, Rum A/D (FRANTIC)

13th B-24s: Munich, Ger M/Y and Industry; Porto Marghera I/O

      B-17s: Munich, Ger A/D

14th B-24s: Five Oil Targets (1,005 tons)--one at Pardubice, Czech and four in the Balkans

      B-17s: Budapest, Hun I/O (210 tons)

16th B-24s: Bratislava, Czech I/O (369 tons); Vienna area Oil Refineries--Lobau (256 tons) and Schwechat (101 tons)--and Oil Depot--Winterhafen (94 tons)

      B-17s: Vienna area Oil Refineries--Kragan (192 tons) and Florisdorf (195 tons)

22nd B-24s: Six M/Y's and two Br's in Italy; Turin M/T works; Chivasso M/T Depot

      B-17s: Fornova di Taro M/Y; Modena M/Y; Parma M/Y

23rd B-24s: Ploesti, Rum I/O; Giurgiu, Rum I/O (487)

      B-17s: Ploesti, Rum I/O

24th B-24s: Ploesti, Rum I/O; Craiova, Rum RR Depot

      B-17s: Piatra, Rum RRBr

25th B-24s: Sete, Fr I/Os; Avignon, Fr M/Y; Toulon, Fr

      B-17s: Sete, Fr M/Y and I/Os

26th 17&24: Five of the seven Oil Refineries in the Vienna area--Moosbierbaum (276 tons), Florisdorf (245), Lobau (222), Korneuberg (236), Schwechat (156)--and Oil Depot-- Winterhafen (60)

27th B-24s: Brod, Yugo M/Y; Drohobycz, Po I/O (140)

      B-17s: Budapest, Hun M/Y

28th B-24s: Karlova, Bul A/D; Bucharest, Rum I/O (265)

30th 17&24: Major targets abandoned; hit rail and airdrome targets in Hun and Yugo

July 1944

2nd B-24s: Budapest, Hun I/O, A/D and M/Y

      B-17s: Almasfuzito, Hun I/O; Bleckhammer, Ger I/O; Brod and Vinkovci, Yugo M/Y's

3rd B-24s: Giurgiu, Rum I/O (280); Bucharest, Rum I/O (84); Belgrade, Yugo I/O (70)

      B-17s: Arad, Rum Repair Shops; Piatra, Rum RRBr

4th B-24s: Pitesti, Rum M/Y and RRBr

      B-17s: Brasov, Rum I/O (426 tons)

5th B-24s: Toulon, Fr Docks and Sub Pens; Bezier, Fr M/Y

      B-17s: Montpellier, Fr M/Y

6th 17&24: Italian M/Y's, RRBr's, I/O's and Bergamo Steel Works targets for 711 heavies

7th B-24s: Bleckhammer N, Ger I/O; Odertal, Ger I/O; Dubnica, Czech Armament Works; Zagreb, Yugo M/Y and A/D

      B-17s: Bleckhammer S, Ger I/O

8th B-24s: Vienna, Aus A/D's; Vienna, Korneuberg (166 tons) and Florisdorf (219) I/O's

      B-17s: Vienna, Aus, Vosendorf I/O (162 tons)

9th 17&24: Ploesti, Rum I/O

10th B-24s: Minor rail targets in Italy

11th B-24s: Toulon, Fr Harbor Area (200 tons)

12th B-24s: Miramas and Nimes, Fr M/Y's (760 tons); Theoule and Var River, Fr Br's (300 tons)

13th B-24s: Brescia M/Y; Mantova M/Y; Verona M/Y; Trieste I/Os; Fiume

---

      B-17s: Mestre M/Y; Latisana, Pinzano and Venzone RRBr's

14th 17&24: Four I/O and a M/Y at Budapest, Hun

15th 17&24: Ploesti, Rum I/O

16th 17&24: Vienna, Aus Oil Storage, Aircraft Engine Works, A/D and M/Y

17th B-24s: Avignon, Fr M/Y; Arles, Fr RRBr; Tarascon Fr RRBr

18th 17&24: Friedrichshafen, Ger Jet Aircraft Plants; Memmingen, Ger A/D; Casarsa RRBr

19th B-24s: Neuaubling (Munich Area), Ger I/A

      B-17s: Munich, Ger Ordnance Depot

20th B-24s: Friedrichshafen, Ger I/A and Aircraft Engine Works

      B-17s: Memmingen, Ger A/D

21st B-24s: Brux, Czech I/O; Mestre M/Y

      B-17s: Brux, Czech I/O

22nd 17&24: Ploesti, Rum I/O

23rd B-24s: Berat, Alb I/O

24th B-24s: Les Chanoines, Fr A/D; Valence, Fr A/D; Genoa Harbor Area

      B-17s: Turin I/BB and Tank Works

25th 17&24: Linz, Aus Tank Works

26th B-24s: Vienna Area: Markersdorf, Aus A/D; Graz, Aus A/D; Zwolfaxing, Aus A/D

      B-17s: Vienna, Aus I/Ac

27th 17&24: Budapest, Hun Armament Works

28th 17&24: Ploesti, Rum I/O

30th B-24s: Lispe, Hun I/O

      B-17s: Budapest, Hun A/D; Brod, Yugo M/Y

31st B-24s: Targoviste, Rum I/O; Bucharest, Rum I/Os

      B-17s: Ploesti, Rum I/O

August 1944

2nd B-24s: Genoa M/Y and Harbor Area

      B-17s: Portes les Valences, Fr M/Y and Torpedo Factory; Le Pouzin, Fr I/Os

3rd B-24s: Friedrichshafen, Ger I/A's; Brenner Br's

      B-17s: Friedrichshafen, Ger I/A and Chemical Works; Immenstadt, Ger M/Y

6th B-24s: Toulon, Fr Sub Pens; Rail Bridges and Oil Storage in France

      B-17s: Portes les Valences, Fr M/Y; Le Pouzin, Fr I/Os and RRBr

7th B-24s: Blackhammer N, Ger I/O; Novi Sad, Yugo I/Os; Alibunar, Yugo A/D

      B-17s: Blackhammer S, Ger I/O

9th B-24s: Refineries, Oil Storage, A/D's in Hungary

      B-17s: Gyor, Hun I/A and Wagon Works; Brod, Yugo M/Y

10th 17&24: Ploesti, Rum I/O

12th B-24s: Gun Positions around Sete, Toulon and Marseille, Fr and around Genoa

      B-17s: Gun Positions in Savona area

13th 17&24: Gun Positions and Bridges in southern France and (B-17s) Pec, Yugo

14th 17&24: Gun Positions near Toulon, Fr, Genoa and Savona

15th 17&24: Southern France invasion beaches

16th 17&24: Rail Bridges in southern France

17th B-24s: Ploesti, Rum I/O

      B-17s: Nis, Yugo A/D

18th 17&24: Ploesti, Rum I/O

19th B-17s: Ploesti, Rum I/O (last attack)

20th B-24s: Oil Refineries in Czech; Szolnok, Hun M/Y

      B-17s: Oswiciem, Po I/O

21st B-24s: Hadju Boszormeny, Hun A/D

22nd B-24s: Vienna, Lobau I/O; Bleckhammer S, Ger I/O

      B-17s: Odertal, Ger I/O

23rd B-24s: Vienna, Aus I/O's and A/D; Ferrara RRBr

      B-17s: Vienna, Aus I/Ac and I/Area

24th 17&24: Oil Refineries in Germany and Czechoslovakia, Pardubice, Czech A/D (B-17s) and Bridges in Hungary, Yugoslavia and Italy attacked by 600 heavies

25th B-24s: Brno, Czech I/A

      B-17s: Brno, Czech I/A and A/D

26th B-24s: Bucharest, Rum A/D and Army Barracks; Giurgiu, Rum Ferry

      B-17s: Avisio, Latisana, Venzone RR Viaducts

27th B-24s: Bleckhammer S, Ger I/O; Avisio Viaduct; Ferrara Br

      B-17s: Bleckhammer, Ger I/O

28th B-24s: Rail Bridges and M/Y's in Hungary & Italy

      B-17s: Vienna, Moosbierbaum I/O

29th 17&24: Oil Storage and Rail Targets in Czechoslovakia, Hungary and Italy

30th B-24s: Cuprija, Yugo Br

      B-17s: Brod, Yugo M/Y; Novi Sad, Yugo M/Y

31st B-17s: Novi Sad, Yugo RRBr; Ploesti Evacuation Mission

FIFTEENTH AIR FORCE BOMBING MISSIONS

September 1944

1st	B-24s:	Kraljevo & Mitrovica, Yugo Br's; Debreczen, Hun M/Y; Ferrara RRBr
	B-17s:	Nis, Yugo A/D; Moravia, Yugo RRBr; Evacuation Mission
2nd	B-24s:	Bridges and M/Y's in Yugoslavia
3rd	B-24s:	Bridges in Yugoslavia and Italy
	B-17s:	Belgrade, Yugo RRBr's; Evac Mission
4th	B-24s:	Bridges, Viaducts and M/Y's in Italy
	B-17s:	Genoa Docks and Submarines (490 tons)
5th	B-24s:	Bridges in Italy, Hungary, Yugoslavia
	B-17s:	Budapest, Hun RRBr's
6th	B-24s:	Novi Sad, Yugo M/Y; Leskovac, Yugo M/Y and Troop Concentration
8th	17&24:	Bridges and M/Y's in Yugoslavia
10th	B-24s:	Vienna, Aus Ord Depot and I/Area; Horsching, Hun A/D; Trieste Harbor
	B-17s:	Vienna, Lobau and Schwechat I/O's
12th	B-24s:	Munich, Ger Aircraft Engine Works; Lechfeld, Ger A/D
	B-17s:	Lechfeld, Ger A/D
13th	B-24s:	Odertal, Ger (Oswiecim, Po I/O; Avisio Br; Mezza Corona Br
	B-17s:	Bleckhammer N, Ger I/O (287 tons)
15th	B-24s:	Athens, Gr M/Y; Athens, Eleusis and Tatoi A/D's
	B-17s:	Athens, Kalamaki A/D; Salamis, Gr Sub Base
17th	17&24:	Budapest, Hun M/Y
18th	17&24:	Bridges and M/Y's in Hungary & Yugo
19th	B-24s:	Kraljevo and Mitrovica, Yugo Br's
20th	B-24s:	Bratislava, Czech I/O; Malacky, Czech A/D; Gyor, Hun I/Ac and M/Y
	B-17s:	Budapest and Szob, Hun RRBr's
21st	17&24:	Bridges and M/Y's in Hungary & Yugo
22nd	B-24s:	Munich, Ger A/D; Larissa, Gr M/Y
	B-17s:	Munich, Ger Aircraft Engine Works
23rd	B-24s:	Rail Bridges and Viaducts in Italy
	B-17s:	Brux, Czech I/O and M/Y
24th	B-24s:	Athens, Gr Kalamaki and Tatoi A/D's
25th	B-24s:	Athens, Gr Harbor Facilities

October 1944

4th	17&24:	Munich, Ger M/Y; Bridges in Italy and on the Brenner Pass route
7th	B-24s:	Vienna, Aus Schwechat, Winterhafen and Komara I/Os; Gyor, Hun A/D
	B-17s:	Vienna, Lobau I/O; Ersekuvar, Hun M/Y
10th	17&24:	Bridges and M/Y's in Italy
11th	B-24s:	Vienna, Aus Motor Works
	B-17s:	Vienna, Aus Ord Depot; Graz, Aus Motor Works
12th	17&24:	Bologna Troop Con, Bivouac Area and Stores (698 heavies, 1271 tons)
13th	B-24s:	Vienna, Aus Motor Works and I/Area; M/Y's in Aus, Czech and Hungary
	B-17s:	Vienna, Aus I/O's; Bleckhammer S, Ger I/O
14th	B-24s:	Odertal, Ger I/O; Maribor, Yugo Br
	B-17s:	Bleckhammer N, Ger I/O; Ersekuvar, Hun M/Y
16th	B-24s:	St. Valentin, Aus Tank Works; Linz, Aus Benzol Plant; Steyr and Graz, Aus Aero Engine Works
	B-17s:	Brux, Czech I/O; Pilsen, Czech Skoda Works; M/Y's in Austria
17th	B-24s:	Vienna, Aus M/Y
	B-17s:	Bleckhammer S, Ger I/O
20th	B-24s:	Innsbruck, Aus M/Y; Bad Aibling, Ger A/D
	B-17s:	Brux, Czech I/O; Regensburg, Ger I/Os
21st	B-24s:	Gyor and Szombathely, Hun M/Y and A/D
23rd	B-24s:	Plauen, Ger Arms Works (100 tons); Regensburg, Ger I/Os; M/Y's and Rail Targets in Italy and Brenner Pass
	B-17s:	Pilsen, Czech Skoda Works; Rosenheim, Ger M/Y
25th	B-17s:	Klagenfurt, Aus I/Ac
26th	B-17s:	Innsbruck, Aus M/Y
28th	B-17s:	Klagenfurt, Aus I/Ac; Munich, Ger M/Y
29th	B-24s:	Munich, Ger M/Y

November 1944

1st	B-24s:	Graz, Aus Ord Depot
	B-17s:	Graz, Aus M/Y & A/D; Vienna Ord Depot
2nd	B-17s:	Vienna, Moosbierbaum I/O; Klagenfurt
3rd	B-24s:	Vienna, Moosbierbaum I/O; Klagenfurt, Aus I/Ac
	B-17s:	Vienna, Aus Ord Depot

4th	B-24s:	Munich & Augsburg, Ger M/Y's; Linz M/Y
	B-17s:	Regensburg, Ger I/Os
5th	17&24:	Vienna, Florisdorf I/O (1100 tons); Podgorica, Yugo M/Y; Mitrovica, Yugo Troop Concentrations
6th	17&24:	Vienna, Aus Moosbierbaum I/O (403 tons) and Ord Depot; Bruck, Aus Steel Works; Maribor, Yugo M/Y
7th	B-24s:	Brenner Pass; Yugoslav Troop Con's
	B-17s:	Vienna, Florisdorf I/O; Maribor M/Y
8th	B-24s:	Mitrovica and Prijepolje, Yugo Troop Concentrations
11th	17&24:	Brux, Czech I/O; Rail Targets in Austria and Italy
12th	B-24s:	Bridges in northern Italy
13th	17&24:	Bleckhammer, Ger I/O
14th	B-24s:	Linz, Aus Benzol Plant
15th	B-24s:	Novi Pazar, Yugo Troop Con; Linz, Aus Benzol Plant
	B-17s:	Linz, Aus Benzol Plant
16th	B-24s:	Munich, Ger M/Y; Visegrad, Yugo Troops
	B-17s:	Munich, Ger M/Y; Innsbruck, Aus M/Y
17th	B-24s:	Vienna, Florisdorf I/O (402 tons); Bleckhammer S, Ger (199 tons); Graz, Aus & Gyor, Hun & Maribor, Yugo M/Y's
	B-17s:	Brux, Czech I/O; Salzburg, Aus M/Y
18th	17&24:	Vienna, Aus Florisdorf and Korneuberg I/O's (510 tons); Aviano A/D; Vicenza A/D; Yugoslav Troop Concentrations
19th	17&24:	Vienna, Aus I/O's; Linz, Aus Benzol Plant; Rail Targets in Italy and Yugo
20th	B-24s:	Rail Targets in Yugo and Czech
	B-17s:	Bleckhammer S, Ger (314 tons) I/O; Brno, Czech M/Y
22nd	17&24:	Rail Targets in Germany, Austria, Italy
23rd	B-24s:	Zenica and Brod, Yugo RRBr's
24th	B-17s:	Linz, Aus Benzol Plant; Klagenfurt M/Y
25th	B-24s:	M/Y's in Germany and Austria
	B-17s:	Linz Benzol Plant; Klagenfurt, Aus M/Y
30th	B-24s:	Munich, Ger M/Y; Innsbruck, Aus M/Y
	B-17s:	Linz, Aus Benzol Plant

December 1944

2nd	17&24:	Bleckhammer N & S, Odertal, Ger and Vienna, Florisdorf I/O's (450 heavies)
3rd	17&24:	Linz, Aus I/Area; Villach, Aus M/Y and Goods Station
6th	B-24s:	Szombathely & Sopron, Hun M/Y's; Graz
	B-17s:	Zagreb, Yugo M/Y; Brod, Yugo HWYBr
7th	B-24s:	Innsbruck and Salzburg, Aus M/Y's; Klagenfurt, Aus I/Area
	B-17s:	Salzburg and Klagenfurt, Aus M/Y's; Linz, Aus and Spittal, Ger Benzol Plants; Athens, Gr Supply Mission
8th	17&24:	Rail Targets Klagenfurt, Villach, Graz and Volkermarkt, Aus; Moosbierbaum I/O
9th	3-24:	Linz, Aus I/Area; Vienna, Moosbierbaum I/O; Brux, Czech I/O
	B-17s:	Regensburg, Ger M/Y and I/O
10th	B-17s:	Brux, Czech I/O
11th	17&24:	Vienna, Moosbierbaum I/O & Goods Yard
12th	17&24:	Bleckhammer S, Ger I/O
15th	17&24:	M/Y's in Austria and Germany
16th	17&24:	Brux, Czech I/O; Linz, Aus Benzol Plant; Innsbruck, Aus M/Y
17th	B-24s:	Odertal, Ger I/O; Bleckhammer S, Ger I/O; M/Y's in Austria and Germany
	B-17s:	Bleckhammer N, Ger I/O
18th	B-24s:	Vienna, Florisdorf, Oswiecim, Po and Bleckhammer, Ger I/O's; Graz, Aus
	B-17s:	Odertal, Ger I/O
19th	B-24s:	M/Y's in Germany and Austria
	B-17s:	Bleckhammer N, Ger I/O; Vienna, Aus M/Y; Sopron, Hun M/Y
20th	B-24s:	Salzburg, Aus M/Y; Villach, Aus M/Y; Pilsen, Czech Skoda Works
	B-17s:	Brux, Czech I/O; Regensburg, Ger I/Os; Linz, Aus M/Y; Salzburg, Aus M/Y
21st	B-24s:	Rosenheim, Ger M/Y
25th	B-24s:	Innsbruck, Hall & Wells, Aus M/Y's
	B-17s:	Brux, Czech I/O
26th	B-24s:	Oswiecim, Po I/O; Brenner Pass
	B-17s:	Bleckhammer S & Odertal, Ger I/O's
27th	B-24s:	Bruck and Klagenfurt, Aus M/Y's; Maribor, Yugo M/Y; Brenner Pass
	B-17s:	Vienna, Aus Vosendorf I/O; Linz and Wiener Neustadt, Aus M/Y's
28th	B-24s:	Brenner Pass; Pardubice, Czech I/O
	B-17s:	Regensburg, Ger I/Os; Salzburg, Aus M/Y
29th	B-24s:	Brenner Pass; M/Y's Austria & Germany
	B-17s:	Innsbruck, Aus M/Y; Castel Franco and Udine Locomotive Repair Depots

Lt. Col. Benjamin O. Davis, Commanding Officer, 99th Fighter Squadron, posed with the first pilots to be assigned to the unit at Tuskegee Air Base, 1942. L to r, front row: Lt. Herbert E. Carter, Lt. Les Rayford, Lt. George S. Roberts, Col. B. O. Davis, Lt. Lemuel R. Custis, Lt. Clarence Jamison, and Lt. Charles B. Hall. Second row: Lt. Walter I. Lawson, Lt. Spann Watson, Lt. Alan Lane, Lt. Paul G. Mitchell, Lt. Leon Roberts, Lt. John W. Rogers, Lt. Louis R. Purnell, Lt. James Wiley, and Lt. Graham Smith. Third row: Lt. Willie Ashley, Lt. Charles Dryden, Lt. Erwin Lawrence, Lt. William A. Campbell, Lt. Willie H. Fuller, Lt. Richard Davis, Lt. Sidney Brooks, Lt. Sherman White, and Lt. George R. Bolling.

Col. B. O. Davis, Jr.

Mac Ross

Brigadier General Benjamin O. Davis Sr., presents Silver Star to his son, Col. B. O. Davis Jr., and DFCs to Captain Joseph Elsberry, Lts. Jack Holsclaw, and "Lucky" Lester.

Top: Allen Lane, Graham Smith, Bill Campbell, Faith McGinnis Paul Mitchell, Spann Watson, Willie Ashley, Louis Purnell Erwin Lawrence, Charles Hall, George Bolling, Herbert Clark

GROUND CREW OF THE 99TH FIGHTER SQUADRON

Alva Temple

Flight Surgeons of the 332nd Fighter Group. L to R, Major Vance Marchbanks, Chief Surgeon, and Capts. William K. Allen, Arnold Moloney, and Bascomb Waugh.

Edward Gleed, Nelson Brooks, B.O. Davis, Jr., George Roberts Denzal Harvey, Cyrus Perry, Ray Ware

Conway Waddy

Pfc. John T. Fields, Armorer of the 100th FS

Crew Chiefs - 302 Sqd.

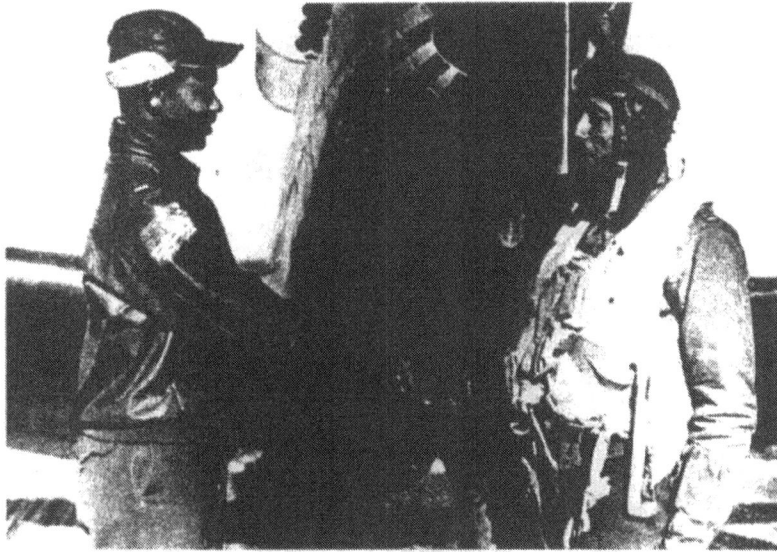

John Briggs, Wendell Pruitt

Joseph Elsberry

Alexander Jefferson

Robert Martin

Back row - Lieutenant Colonel N. S. Brooks and Captain D. W. Stevenson

Front row - Major E. D. Jones and Captain W. R. Thompson

Maj. Gen. John K. Cannon, commander 12th USAAF, congratulates Capt. C.B. Hall, Brazil, IND., who shot down two German planes over bridge head south of Rome. Hall flies with 99th Negro Fighter Squadron which knocked down 12 German fighters in 2 days. Capt. L.R. Curtis, Hartford, Conn., and Lt. W. V. Eagleson, Bloomington, Inc., (background) each got one.

Col. Roberts, Col. Brooks, Capt. Lucas, Maj. Letcher

Lt. Charles Tate, and P-51C Mustang. The 99th began flying Mustangs after being attached to the 332nd FG in July, 1944 at Ramitelli, Italy.

Edith and Co-worker

D.F.C. Awards: Robert Martin, Edmund Thomas, Charles Tate, Richard Harder, Spurgeon Ellington, Clarence Dart

Wilson, Perry, Lacy

Bernard Ponder

Major George "Spanky" Roberts, Commander, center standing, and members of the 99th Fighter Squadron. Top row, L to R: Heber Houston, William Alsbrook, Wilson Eagleson, Charles Bailey, Albert Manning, Alva Temple, George Greay, Clarance Dart, Herman "Ace" Lawson, Bill Campbell, Edward Thomas. Kneeling: L to R: Charles Jamerson, Charles Tate, "Herky" Perry, and Leonard "Black" Jackson.

Charles Hall

Herman Lawson

Lee Archer

Capt. Armour McDaniel inspects flack damage to his Mustang incurred during a straffing mission along the Danube. L to R, S/Sgt. Richard Adams, McDaniel, Lt. James McFatridge, and Lt. Ulysses Taylor

Captain Andrew D. Turner, OK for take off.

Men of the 100th FS, L to R, Lt. Dempsey Morgan, Lt. Carroll Woods, Lt. Bob Nelson, Captain Andrew Turner, CO, and Lt. "Lucky" Lester. Mustang "Skippers Darlin' " belongs to Turner.

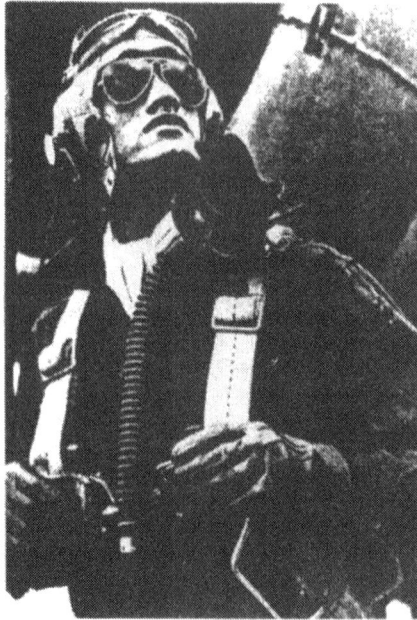
1st Lt. John "Mr. Death" Whitehead, of the post war 332nd FW, 100th F.S.

Capt. Elwood T. Driver, CO of the 100th at Lockbourne.

Hannibal Cox

Lt. Alphonso Davis of the 99th FS.

Joe Chinworth, Sanford Perkins, Bob Williams, Howard Gamble, Henry Bowman

Captains Jack Holsclaw, Lowell Steward, and Clarence Lester, all of the 100th FS.

HARRIS

HENRY
PEOPLES

ARMOUR
M'DANIEL

JOE
MERTON

JOHNSON

ALTON
BALLARD

BOB
FRIEND

Edward Toppings

Capt. Ed Toppins, and his TOPPER III. Toppins confirmed 4 victories during his tour with the 99th.

Robert Diez

Col. Elmer Jones
Graham Smith

Lt. Curry, Melvin Jackson, Howard Baugh, John Gibson Charles De Bow, Richard Caesar

Captain Wendell O. Pruitt of the 302nd,

Charles McGee, Nathaniel Wilson

Walter Downs

Captain "Luke" Weathers of the 302nd FS, (on Wing 2nd from left) and the crew chiefs of the 302nd. Sgts., Eli, Riddley, Johnson, Blevins, Lightfoot, Farr, Teamer, Strothers, Jacobs, Johnson, Suttle, and Thomas. All are members of "A" Flight.

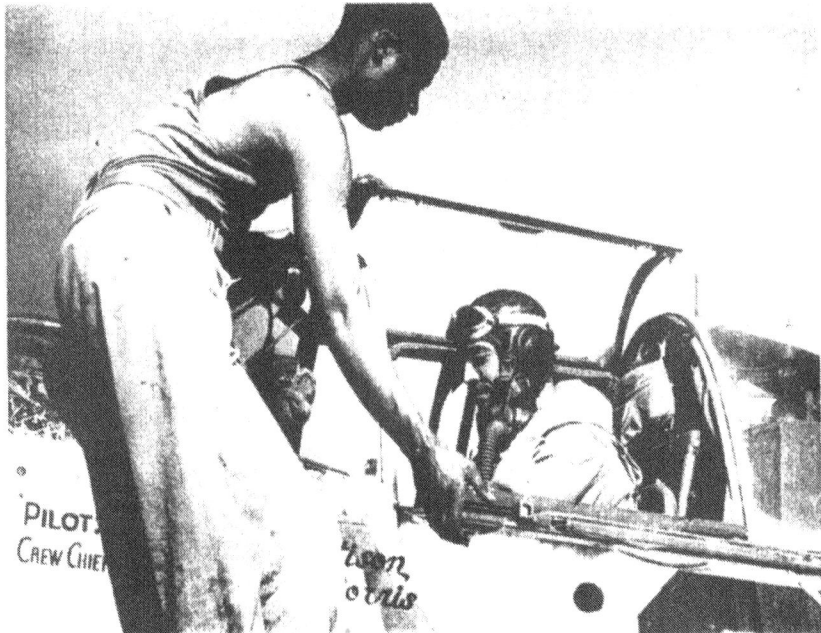

Captain William T. Mattison, Operations Officers 100th FS, and his crew chief, S/Sgt. Alfred D. Morris.

Kneeling: Emil Clifton, Edward Thomas, Henry Wise, Richard Harder
Standing: Howard Baugh, Clarence Dart, Shelby Westbrook, Marion Rogers, Roger Galther, Leonard Willette, Charles Jamison, Thomas Patton, Noel Alsbrook, Quitman Walker, Ace Lawson, Albert Manning

Andrew Marshall

William Holloman

Maj. Lee Rayford, Henry Scott, Red Driver Robert Oneil
Maj. Erwin Lawrence, Fred Hutchings, Spurgeon Ellington, Howard Gamble

Flex Kirkpatrick

Clarence Jamison

Wendell Pruitt

Crew Chiefs
301 Ftr. Sqd.

Tanker Crew
301st Sqd.

Crew Chiefs
301st Sqd.

Lewis Craig
99th Sqd.

Bill Campbell
"Ace" Lawson

Capt. Alvin Temple
99th Sqd.

'Hooks'' Jones

Spurgeon Ellington

William Mattison

WILLIAM (BILL) THOMPSON
Lt. Colonel U.S.A.F. (Retired)

Chaplain Perry & Aid

Freddie Hutchins
302nd Sqd.

Col. Taylor
Sgt. Lucas
Lt. Lucas

Capt. Daniels
Capt. Thomas
Lt. Merton

191

Edward Thomas
99th Sqd.

Major Gleed

Major William Campbell
99th Sqd.

Pilot Joe Lewis
Crew Chief Allie Peek
301st Sqd.

Pilot S. Westbrook
Crew Chief Chas. Hensley

Lt. Allen, Sgt. Jackson - Sqd. Op's.
Robert Chandler
99th Sqd.

Clarence Dart
Charles Tate
99th Sqd.

FISH HOUSE

M/Sgt. "Shag" Crawford
& Crew Chiefs

99th Ftr. Sqd.
Col. William Campbell C. O.

R & R

M/Sgt. Dansby

De Marcus Ray, Col. B.O. Davis, Jr., Maj. William Campbell, Lt. Felix Kirkpatrick, and Lt. Spann Watson

LT. LEAHR
Cincinnati, O.

LT. BUSSEY
Los Angeles, Calif.

Major James T. Wiley

George L. Knox

George E. Hardy

Lemuel R. Custis

Vernon V. Haywood

CAPT. DANIELS
Chicago, Ill.

CAPT. JACKSON
Warrenton, Va.

CAPT. McCREARY
San Antonio, Tex.

LT. BAILEY
Tampa, Fla.

P. T. Braswell   Frank Wright
99th Sqd.

Col. "Spanky" Roberts

Roy E. LaGrone

"Tommy" and Archer
99th Sqd.

Pilots of the 332 Fighter Group, 15th Air Force in Italy, August 1944
Capt. Clarence Dart, Capt. Alvin Temple, Capt. John Daniels, Lt. Wilbur Long, Lt. Marion Rodgers,
Lt. Robert Chandler, Lt. Leonard Willette, Sgt. Thomas Jackson

99th FS P-40L "NONA II" bellied in with loss of port wing after completing mission though damaged on take-off.

Richard Harder

Major Erwin Lawrence

K. I. Williams, Emile Clifton, Frank Moody

NOTES

GODMAN FIELD

HEADQUARTERS BUILDING

FORT KNOX, KENTUCKY

HEADQUARTERS, ARMY AIR BASE
Godman Field, Ft. Knox, Kentucky
Office of the Base Commander

★

27 September 1945

Greetings to all Members of this Command:

I wish to take this opportunity to express my sincere appreciation for the high calibre of service rendered by you since I have had the honor to command Godman Field.

The short time I have been here has been a difficult period for all of us. We have prepared intensively for war and have seen the end of the war. We are now experiencing the difficult transition from war to peace.

I am proud to be able to say, that in spite of these difficult times, there has been a steady and sharp rise in the efficiency of all activities of this field. In spite of the many uncertainties in almost everyone's mind, morale is at high pitch. In less than three short months a tradition has been born that will serve all of us in good stead; whether we choose to remain in the service or whether we return to civilian ranks.

To those of you who are leaving the Army, I wish you every success in whatever undertaking you may pursue. For those who elect to remain, may you carry on in the best traditions of our Armed Forces.

B. O. Davis, Jr.

B. O. DAVIS, JR.,
Colonel, Air Corps,
Commanding.

B. O. DAVIS, JR.

COLONEL, AIR CORPS

Commanding

Born 18 December 1912, Washington, D. C. Appointed to U. S. Military Academy 1 July 1932 from Illinois, graduating in June 1936. Assigned to 24th Infantry Regiment at Ft. Benning, Ga., 1936-37. Attended Infantry School at Ft. Benning 1937-38. Professor of Military Science and Tactics at Tuskegee Institute, Ala., from 1938 to 1940. Spent several months with Fourth Cavalry Brigade in 1941 at Ft. Riley, Kan. As a Captain, he transferred to the Air Corps and to Tuskegee Army Air Field, Ala., for flight training. Graduated with first class of P-40 pilots in 1942. Assumed command of the overseas-bound 99th Pursuit Squadron, arriving in Casablanca, April 1943. Returned to U. S., in Novem-

ber 1943, to take command of 332nd Fighter Group at Selfridge Field, Mich. Second tour of overseas duty in World War II: CO of 332nd Fighter Group in Sicily and Italy. Returned June 1945, to command 477th Bombardment Group (M), later re-designated 477th Composite Group at Godman Field, Ky. Assumed command of the entire base 1 July 1945.

Awards and decorations: Legion of Merit, Silver Star, Distinguished Flying Cross, Air Medal with 4 Oak Leaf clusters, Distinguished Unit Citation, European Theater ribbon, and the American Defense and American Theater ribbons.

HISTORY OF GODMAN FIELD

★

Godman Field, Army Air Base, is located 30 miles south of Louisville, Kentucky and is under the jurisdiction of First Air Force Headquarters, Mitchel Field, L. I.

Since May 6, 1944 the primary mission of Godman has been the training of the 477th Bombardment Group (changed to 477th Composite Group—26 June 1945). In addition, the runways serve adjacent Fort Knox as a landing field.

Godman attracted worldwide attention on 1 July 1945 when the present Commanding Officer, Colonel B. O. Davis, Jr., assumed command, taking over from Colonel Robert R. Selway, Jr.

The field is unique in that it is the first and only Army installation, within continental USA to be commanded and staffed by all Negro personnel.

Many of those stationed at Godman Field have served overseas in actual combat and are proud wearers of decorations representing many theatres of operation and major campaigns.

Through training and actual on-the-job experience at various Air Forces Technical Training Schools, the men and women of Godman hold a wide variety of Military Occupational Specialties. They are qualified to perform all of the many different and complex tasks required to operate an Air Forces installation. Measured by the same high standard of U. S. Army Air Forces that have applied the world over, they compare favorably with the best.

Among the technicians to be found at Godman are:

Bombardier-Navigator, Armament Specialist, Airplane Mechanic, Bombsight Mechanic, Sheet Metal Worker, Machinist, Radar Specialist, Meteorologist, Control Tower Operator, Ordnance Specialist.

The value of this training, both to the soldiers themselves and to a brighter peacetime America is obvious. Many of the members of this command have already been discharged to civilian life to carry on in their specialties. Others are looking forward to the time when they will follow.

Of Godman Field it can be truthfully said:

"We Did Our Share For Victory."

STAFF OFFICERS

477TH COMPOSITE GROUP STAFF OFFICERS
Col. B. O. Davis, Jr. (in front).

First row, left to right: Major Vance H. Marchbanks, Major Thomas J. Money, Major Andrew D. Turner, Major Douglas L. T. Robinson.
Second row: Captain Charles I. Williams, Major William A. Campbell, Captain Elmore Kennedy.
Third row: Lt. Henry V. Moore, Captain William B. Thompson, Captain John R. Beverly, Captain Robert L. Smith, Lt. Carl B. Taylor, Lt. John D. Silvera, not present, Major Edward C. Gleed.

View of barracks on 10th street looking from Second avenue.

P O S T   B U I L D I N G S

Below: A view down 10th street.
Bottom: Theatre.

Below: Base chapel.
Bottom: Headquarters building.

WAR DEPARTMENT THEATER Nº 9

BASE HEADQUARTERS
GODMAN FIELD

BASE FLAG SHIP

ON THE LINE

Godman Field hangar line.

Twin-engine Mitchell bombers ready for inspection.

ON THE WAY TO REVIEW

R E V I E W

At the top of opposite page, Band passing in review; below, other review scenes.

Colonel B. O. Davis and staff on the reviewing line.

Colonel Davis decorates Major Vance H. Marchbanks with Bronze Star.

Top row: Major Elmer D. Jones, Air Service Group director; Major V. H. Marchbanks, Base surgeon; Captain Elizabeth C. Hampton, commanding officer of WAC squadron. Bottom row: Major W. B. Edelin, executive officer of Base Unit; Captain J. W. Redden, director of service and administration; Lt. John H. Jones, traffic officer; Lt. George Lima, Base photographic officer.

Top row: Captain C. J. Williams and office force in Base surgical office; headquarters office. Bottom row: Major D. L. T. Robinson, Chaplain, and staff; Captain George E. Pannell, director of operations and training, and secretary; Lt. M. E. G. Allen, WAC adjutant.

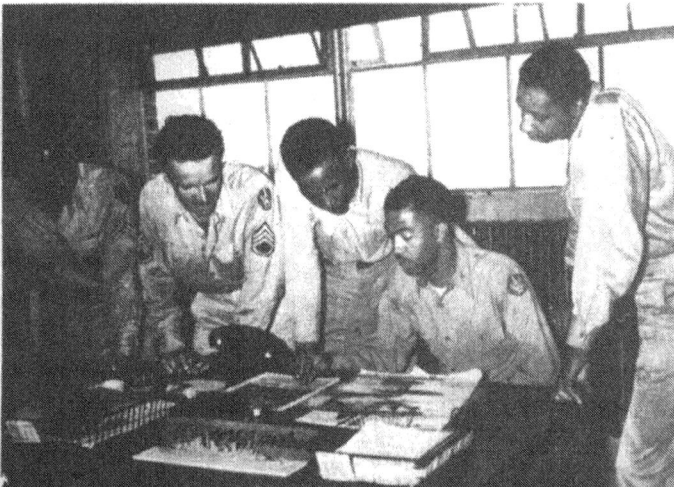

Top row: Base medical supply personnel; Lieutenant Harllee and Lieutenant Williams, Intelligence officers, and staff. Bottom row: Classification clerk; Clerk in the office of transportation and maintenance; Special orders clerk.

IN THE OFFICES

Top row: Motor pool dispatchers office; Adjutant's section; Motor pool main office. Bottom row: Personnel section.

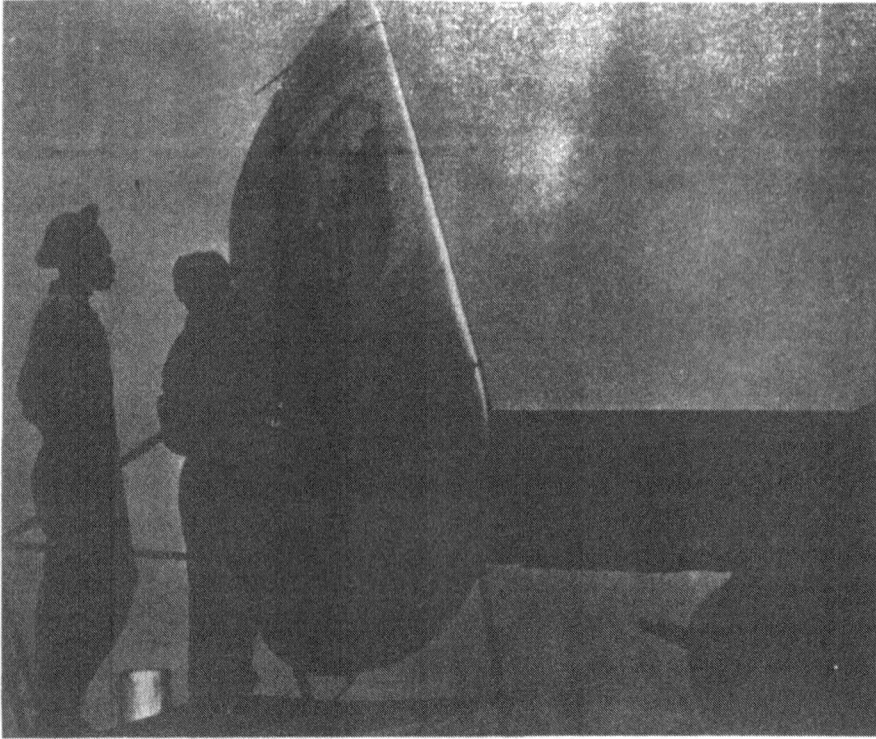

MAINTENANCE MEN

Painting field identification on plane.

Below: Working on engine.
Bottom: Checking manifold pressure gauge.

Below: Mechanics of motor pool.
Bottom: An engine overhaul.

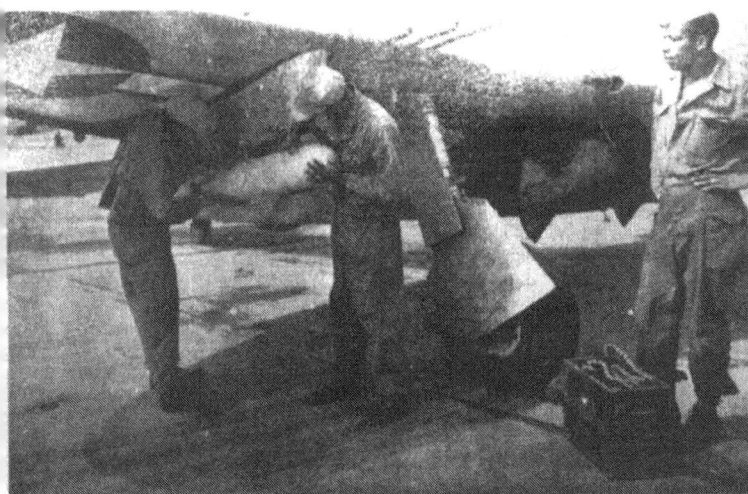

Top, left: Loading bombs in wing racks of P-47.
Top, right: Maintenance crew of B-25 working on wheel.
Right: Refueling bomber.

Below: Adjusting bomb rack.
Bottom: Mechanics at work on plane parts.

Below: Truck repair.
Bottom: Cleaning airplane parts.

Camera technicians issues repaired speed graphic camera to photographer.

WAC First Sergeant M. B. Gay and chief clerk.

Below: Sgt. John Wilson and Cpl. Joseph Jefferson, mail clerks in Headquarters, 477th Composite Group.

Bottom: Base classification office.

Below: Teletype operator in signal office at Western Union machine.

Bottom: . . . plotting a synoptic map in Base weather station.

Below: Sergeant Scipio and WAC Pvt. Elise Alexander working out an office problem.

Bottom: Looking over the flight schedule for the day.

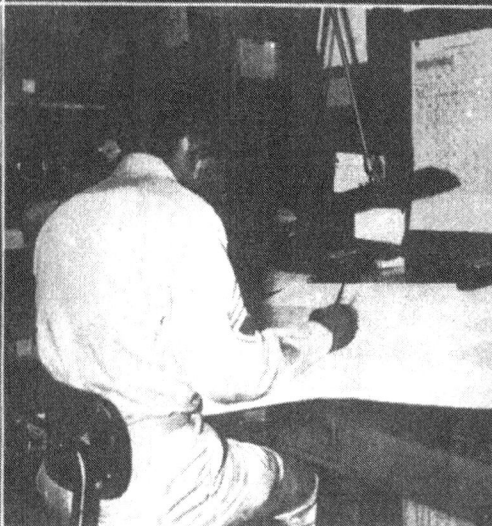

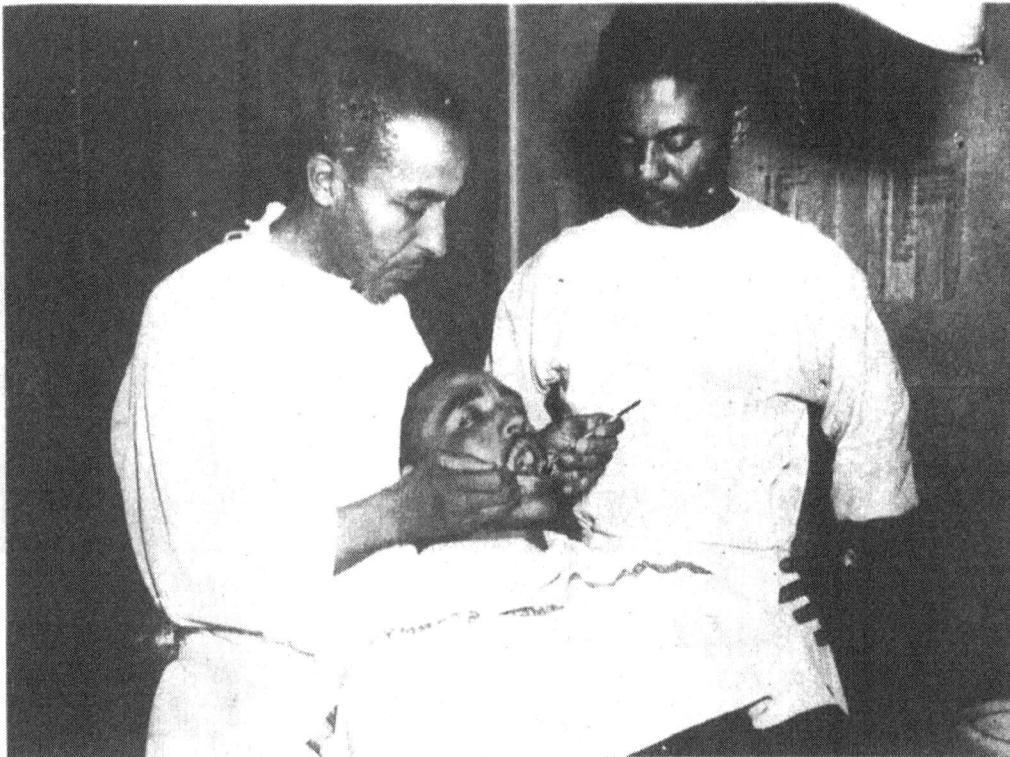

Lieutenant Charles A. Newsome, chief of dental clinic, working on patient's teeth.

Below: A massage in the physiotherapy department.
Bottom: Captain Brooks gives a special physical examination for flyers.

Below: Molar trouble in the dental clinic.
Bottom: An eye examination in the flight surgeon's office.

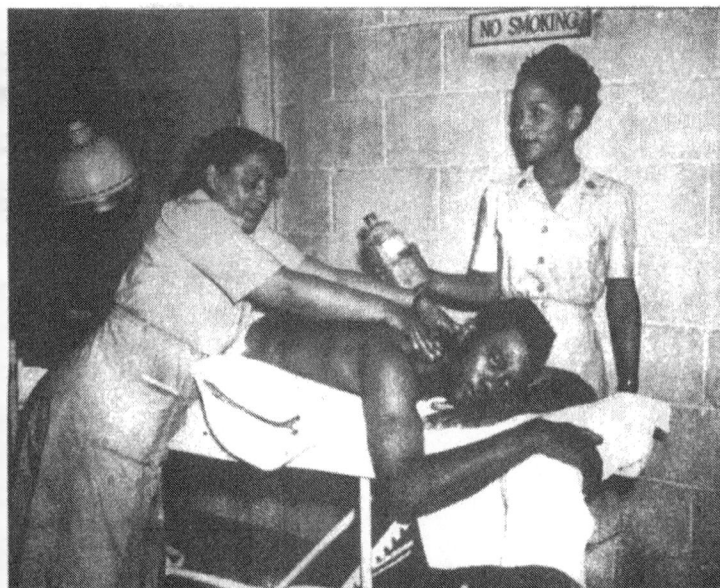

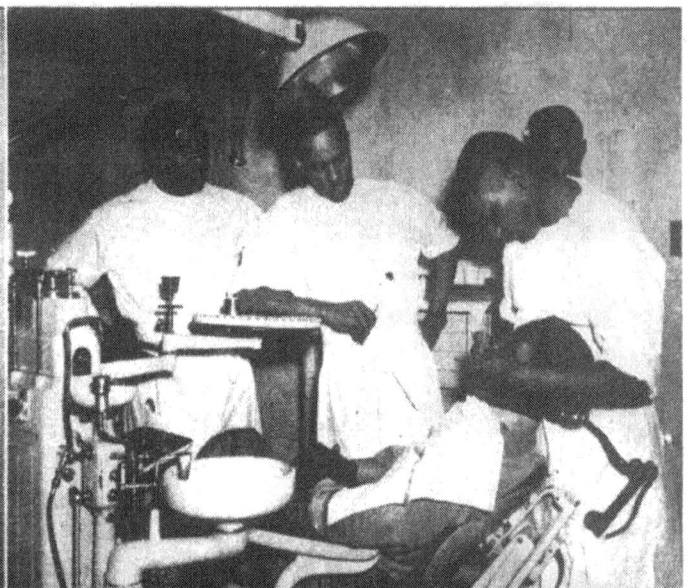

A group of 477th men.

Colonel Davis beside his plane.

SEEN AROUND THE FIELD

Squadron G on the march.

602nd Air Engineering squadron en route to parade grounds.

387TH AIR SERVICE GROUP STAFF OFFICERS

First row, left to right: Captain L. S. Carter, Major Elmer D. Jones, Major George W. Webb.

Second row: Captain Omar D. Blair, Captain John H. Williams.

Third row: First Lt. James A. Grant, First Lt. Emmett J. Rice, First Lt. Clarence S. Lewis, First Lt. Robert S. Lawery.

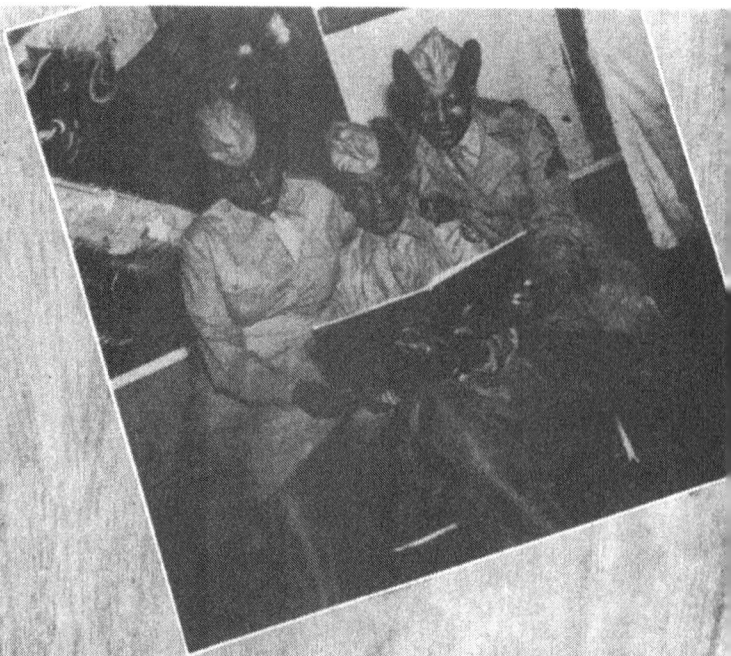

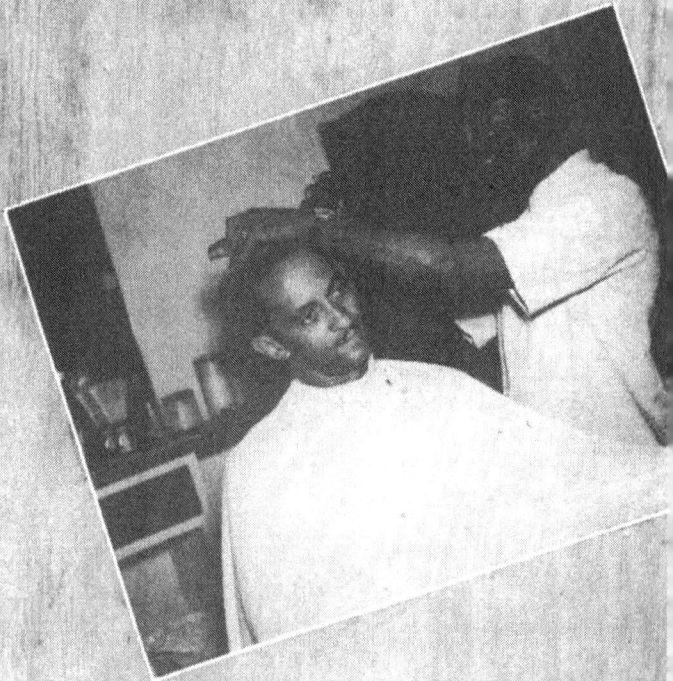

THE ETERNAL CHOW LINE

C H O W

Below: Mess sergeant Bell gives directions to cooks.
Bottom: Almost ready to serve.

Below: Dishing out to hungry 617th EM.
Bottom: Its cake for dessert.

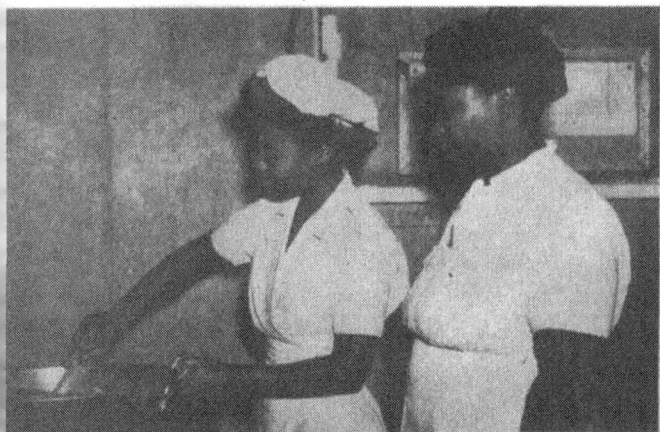

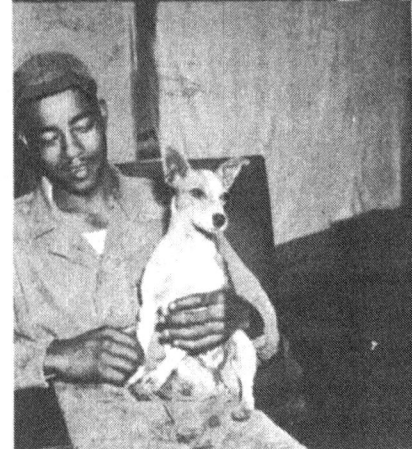

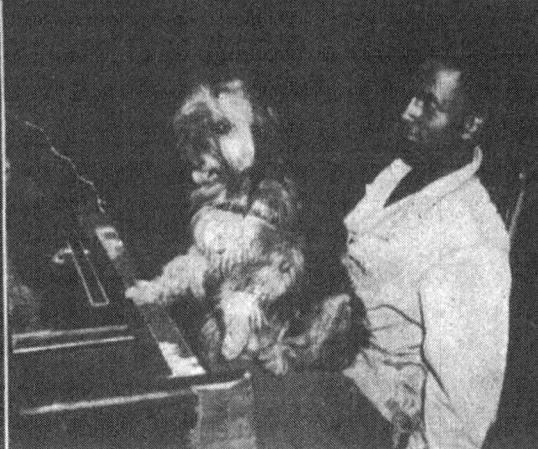

477TH COMPOSITE GROUP

EDWARD C. GLEED
Major
Group Operations Officer

VANCE H. MARCHBANKS, JR.
Major
Base Surgeon

DOUGLAS L. T. ROBINSON
Major
Chaplain

ANDREW D. TURNER
Major
Deputy Group Commanding
Officer

JOHN R. BEVERLY, JR.
Captain
Group Intelligence Officer

GEORGE E. PANNELL
Captain
Group Gunnery Officer

JAMES B. RAY
Captain
Base Signal Officer

ROBERT L. SMITH
Captain
Group Engineering Officer

CHARLES R. STANTON
Captain
Director for Operations and
Training

WILLIAM R. THOMPSON
Captain
Group Armament Officer

ELLIOTTE J. WILLIAMS
Captain
Medical Administrative Officer

WILLIAM N. BROWN
First Lieutenant
Special Service Officer

ALBERT E. COLLIER
First Lieutenant
Cryptographic Officer

GEORGE B. GREENLEE, JR.
First Lieutenant
Assistant Group Intelligence
Officer

WILLIS J. HUBERT
First Lieutenant
Statistical Control Officer

HORACE M. KING
First Lieutenant
Group Weather Officer

WILLIAM H. LEWIS
First Lieutenant
Assistant Statistical Officer

GEORGE S. LIMA
First Lieutenant
Photographic Officer

THOMAS N. MALONE
First Lieutenant
Group Personal Equipment
Officer

HENRY D. MOORE
First Lieutenant
Group Ordnance Officer

JAMES T. WILEY
Captain
Assistant Group Operations
Officer

THEODORE E. MORAN	JOHN D. SILVERA	JOSEPH W. CONNOLLY	REGINALD A. FREEMAN	LUNA I. MISHOE
First Lieutenant	First Lieutenant	Second Lieutenant	Second Lieutenant	First Lieutenant
Group RADAR Officer	Public Relations Officer	Group Bomb Officer	Group Navigation Officer	Group Photographic Intelligence Officer

477TH COMPOSITE GROUP

FIRST ROW:

AGARD, George B., M/Sgt., 470 W. 150th St., New York, N. Y.

JOHNSON, Sidney L., M/Sgt., 129 W. Southern Ave., Springfield, Ohio.

PAIGE, Doward W., M/Sgt., Jasper, Tex.

PETERSON, Joseph, T/Sgt., 1051 Boston Rd., New York, N. Y.

ROSS, Coxie E., T/Sgt., 2821 Highland Ave., Kansas City, Mo.

BIVINS, George A., S/Sgt., Rt. 1, Box 45, McKeesport, Pa.

SECOND ROW:

DIRICKSON, John T., S/Sgt., 163 Catherine St., Red Bank, N. J.

ROBINSON, Melvin C., S/Sgt., 2518 Caldwell St., Omaha, Neb.

THOMPSON, Leon, S/Sgt., 3621 Second Ave., Los Angeles, Calif.

WHITE, Roy F., S/Sgt., 1672 Post St., San Francisco, Calif.

ANDERSON, John E., Sgt., 20470 Kentucky, Detroit, Mich.

BAKER, Gilbert L., Sgt., 12006 E. Marginal Way, Seattle, Wash.

477TH COMPOSITE GROUP

★

FIRST ROW:

BRADLEY, Louis C., Sgt., 1629 Monsvier Pl., Lynchburg, Va.
BUCHANAN, James W., Sgt., 706 Tayco St., Menasha, Wis.
CARTER, William H., Sgt., 1957 19th St., Santa Monica, Calif.
COLES, Russell L., Sgt., 33 Convent Ave., Apt. 18, New York, N. Y.
MARSHALL, Roscoe, Sgt., 3304 E. Alabama St., Houston, Tex.

SECOND ROW:

MILLER, James, Jr., Sgt., 40 Rutgers St., Newark, N. J.
OLIVER, Ellsworth R., Sgt., 390 W. Elm St., New Bedford, Mass.
PARKER, Edwin, Sgt., 159 Fisher Ave., Neptune, N. J.
SMITH, George F., Jr., Sgt., 18 Leroy St., Dayton, Ohio.
SMITH, Otis M., Sgt., 822 E. Carton St., Flint, Mich.

THIRD ROW:

WILKS, Samuel D., Sgt., Rt. 4, Box 52, Chester, S. C.
WILSON, John H., Sgt., 1304 Pierre Ave., Shreveport, La.
BERRY, Solomon S., Cpl., 434 Grand Ave., Bronx, N. Y.
CARY, John E., Cpl., 3040 Champa St., Denver, Colo.
DANIEL, Wiley B., Jr., Cpl., 3421 Hale Ave., Louisville, Ky.

FOURTH ROW:

FREEMAN, James E., Cpl., 437 Manhattan Ave., New York, N. Y.
GIBBS, James R., Cpl., 2711 Georgia Ave., Washington, D. C.
GIBSON, John T., Cpl., 261 Evergreen Ave., Morristown, N. J.
GRIMES, Clyde H., Cpl., 1148 E. 43rd Pl., Los Angeles, Calif.
HOWARD, Wendell H., Cpl., 919 W. State St., Springfield, Ohio.

FIFTH ROW:

HUBBARD, Maurice, Cpl., 1120 Waco St., Corpus Christi, Tex.
JEFFERSON, Joseph E., Cpl., 1815 Second St., N.W., Washington, D. C.
JOHNSON, John, Cpl., 5602 S. Calumet Ave., Chicago, Ill.
JOHNSON, Louis. Cpl., 4205 Langley Ave., Chicago, Ill.
LEWIS, Earl M., Cpl., 2347 W. Lake St., Chicago, Ill.

SIXTH ROW:

LIPSCOMB, Lawrence T., Cpl., 7714 Susquehanna St., Pittsburgh, Pa.
MILLER, Houston M., Cpl., 820 State St., Springfield, Ohio.
MOSELEY, Alexander D., Cpl., 508 West 147th St., New York, N. Y.
PERRY, Richard H., Cpl., 1 West Hamilton Ave., Englewood, N. J.
PILGRIM, Earle M., Cpl., 206 Macon St., Brooklyn, N. Y.

SEVENTH ROW:

RICHARDSON, Ellis, Cpl., 3011 Alms Pl., Cincinnati, Ohio.
SMITH, Harold D., Cpl., 376 Hamilton Ave., Columbus, Ohio.
CARRELL, Richard, Pfc., 1519 . . . . . , Kansas City, Mo.
COOK, Walter H., Pfc., 1342 Grove St., Chattanooga, Tenn.
CORNELIUS, Leroy A., Pfc., 837 Freeman St., Bronx, N. Y.

EIGHTH ROW:

DAVIS, Tyrone C., Pfc., 251 Eloit St., Detroit, Mich.
FORD, Richard L., Pfc., 26 North Main, Woodstown, N. J.
GILLESPIE, Otis W., Pfc., 536 N. Upper St., Lexington, Ky.
GREER, Cornelius B., Pfc., 5619 Michigan Ave., Chicago, Ill.
JACKSON, Milton, Pfc., 21 Trent, Pittsburgh, Pa.

NINTH ROW:

LYONS, Irving, Pfc., 490 St. Nicolas Ave., New York, N. Y.
MAYWEATHER, Ben, Pfc., 605 Carpenter St., Memphis, Tenn.
MILLER, Edward C., Pfc., Rt. 2, Cumberland St., Morristown, Tenn.
ROSE, Wallace B., Pfc., 27 Hollander St., Boston, Mass.
SPURLOCK, Jethro, Pfc., 2433 Franklin St., Omaha, Neb.

TENTH ROW:

THOMPSON, John B., Pfc., 1945 Seventh Ave., New York, N. Y.
WALKER, Anthony, Pfc., 811 Howard Ave., Mamaroneck, N. Y.
WHITE, Frank P., Pfc., 534 E. Forest Ave., Detroit, Mich.
WISE, Robert L., Pfc., 541 W. 13th St., Chicago, Ill.
MOORE, Clarence M., Pvt., 774 Union St., Montgomery, Ala.

617TH BOMBARDMENT SQUADRON

★

CHARLES I. WILLIAMS
Captain
Commanding

JAMES Y. CARTER
Captain
Flight Leader

Fil- State RR

Col.

RICHARD B. HIGHBAUGH
Captain
Flight Leader

HUBERT L. JONES
Captain
Pilot

Col MATS

FITZROY NEWSUM
Captain
Operations Officer

WINSTON A. ADKINS
First Lieutenant
Pilot

HARVEY R. ALEXANDER
First Lieutenant
Pilot

CLARENCE W. BANTON
First Lieutenant
Ordnance Officer

ELLIOTT H. BLUE
First Lieutenant
Pilot

KIA Korea "52"

VIRGIL BRASHEARS, JR.
First Lieutenant
Pilot

HERMAN R. CAMPBELL
First Lieutenant
Pilot

FRANCIS B. COLLIER
First Lieutenant
Navigation Officer

RAYMOND K. DEWBERRY
First Lieutenant
Armament Officer

WILLIAM B. ELLIS
First Lieutenant
Pilot

HENRI F. FLETCHER
First Lieutenant
Pilot

Col

JOHN L. HARRISON, JR.
First Lieutenant
Pilot

LOUIS G. HILL, JR.
First Lieutenant
Flight Leader

General 1970

DANIEL JAMES, JR.
First Lieutenant
Pilot

OBIE E. JEFFERSON
First Lieutenant
Supply Officer

SAMUEL LYNN
First Lieutenant
Pilot

HENRY P. MILES
First Lieutenant
Communications Officer

HARVEY N. PINKNEY
First Lieutenant
Pilot

ARTHUR SAUNDERS
First Lieutenant
Armament and Chemical Officer

DAVID A. SMITH
First Lieutenant
Intelligence Officer

HAROLD E. SMITH
First Lieutenant
Co-Pilot

JEROME D. SPURLIN
First Lieutenant
Pilot

CHARLES E. WALKER
First Lieutenant
Pilot

HAROLD E. WARD
First Lieutenant
Assistant Navigation Officer

HERBERT J. WILLIAMS
First Lieutenant
Pilot

LOUIS H. ANDERSON
Second Lieutenant
Bombardier-Navigator

AUGUSTUS G. BROWN
Second Lieutenant
Pilot

ROBERT S. BROWN
Second Lieutenant
Pilot

RICHARD B. CARTER
Second Lieutenant
Bombardier-Navigator

EUGENE C. CHEATHAM
First Lieutenant
Pilot

JAMES R. CHICHESTER
Second Lieutenant
Pilot

LEON V. CREED
Second Lieutenant
Bombardier-Navigator

VIRGIL A. DANIELS
Second Lieutenant
Pilot

CHARLES E. DARNELL
Second Lieutenant
Pilot

EDWARD T. DIXON
Second Lieutenant
Pilot

HARRISON R. DUKE
Second Lieutenant
Bombardier

MARCUS L. GITTENS
Second Lieutenant
Bombardier

DUDLEY M. GLASSE
Second Lieutenant
Bombardier-Navigator

LLOYD R. GOLDSON
Second Lieutenant
Bombardier

ARGONNE F. HARDEN
Second Lieutenant
Pilot

ORGRETTE B. GRAHAM
Second Lieutenant
Bombardier

ARCHIE H. HARRIS
Second Lieutenant
Pilot

THOMAS W. HAYWOOD, JR.
Second Lieutenant
Bombardier-Navigator

WARREN E. HENRY
Second Lieutenant
Pilot

CHARLES D. HILL
Second Lieutenant
Pilot

VORIS S. JAMES
Second Lieutenant
Pilot

NATHANIEL A. JONES, JR.
Second Lieutenant
Bombardier

FRANK LEE
Second Lieutenant
Pilot

EDDIE A. McLAURIN
Second Lieutenant
Electronics Officer

IVAN J. McRAE
Second Lieutenant
Pilot

GEORGE H. O. MARTIN
Second Lieutenant
Navigator-Bombardier

JOHN W. MOSLEY
Second Lieutenant
Pilot

ISAAC S. NIXON
Second Lieutenant
Bombardier

ROGER C. TERRY
Second Lieutenant
Pilot

JAMES F. TROTTER
Second Lieutenant
Bombardier-Navigator

JOSEPH H. WILLIAMS
Second Lieutenant
Pilot

OSCAR H. YORK
Second Lieutenant
Pilot

REGINALD A. BRUCE
Flight Officer
Pilot

JAMES E. BROTHERS
Flight Officer
Pilot

MARCEL CLYNE
Flight Officer
Pilot

GAMALIEL M. COLLINS
Flight Officer
Pilot

MARTIN L. COOK
Flight Officer
Pilot

LLOYD J. EUGENE
Flight Officer
Bombardier

HENRY T. FEARS
Flight Officer
Pilot

ALFONSO C. FULLER
Flight Officer
Bombardier-Navigator

GEORGE P. HARBERT, JR.
Flight Officer
Bombardier-Navigator

EDWARD HARRIS
Flight Officer
Pilot

CHARLIE A. JOHNSON
Flight Officer
Pilot

ALVIN B. LaRUE
Flight Officer
Bombardier-Navigator

DOUGLAS H. McQUILLAN
Flight Officer
Pilot

GEORGE B. MATTHEWS
First Lieutenant
Pilot

CHARLES C. MAXWELL
Flight Officer
Pilot

KENNETH G. MAY
Flight Officer
Bombardier-Navigator

OSCAR T. MILLER
Flight Officer
Bombardier

WILLARD B. MILLER
Flight Officer
Pilot

FLARZELL MOORE
Flight Officer
Pilot

ALLEN MORTON, JR.
Flight Officer
Bombardier-Navigator

JOHN I. MULZAC
Flight Officer
Pilot

ROBERT M. PARKEY
Flight Officer
Pilot

EDWARD S. PRESSLY
Flight Officer
Navigator-Bombardier

AMOS A. ROGERS
Flight Officer
Pilot

DAVID A. SHOWELL
Flight Officer
Bombardier

WENDELL R. SMITH
Flight Officer
Navigator-Bombardier

ALFONSO C. TOLER
Flight Officer
Bombardier

WESLEY C. WALKER
Flight Officer
Bombardier-Navigator

RAYMOND M. WHITE
Flight Officer
Pilot

ROBERT E. WILLIAMS
Flight Officer
Pilot

NASHBY WYNN, JR.
Flight Officer
Pilot

617TH
BOMBARDMENT
SQUADRON

FIRST ROW:
GAINES, Thomas H., T/Sgt., 1711 Arctic Ave., Atlantic City, N. J.
HORNE, Edward A., T/Sgt., 1037 S. Orleans St., Memphis, Tenn.
LATIMER, Merle O., T/Sgt., 501 Decatur St., Brooklyn, N. Y.
SMITH, James A., T/Sgt., 330 Second Ave., Columbus, Ga.
AUSTIN, William H., S/Sgt., 2036 W. Ogden, Chicago, Ill.
BORDERS, Luther C., S/Sgt., 2410 10th St., Riverside, Calif.

SECOND ROW:
BROWN, James N., S/Sgt., 572 Breckinridge, Lexington, Ky.
COOPER, Leonard C., S/Sgt., 211 Sycamore St., Oxford, N. C.
DAVIS, Benjamin F., S/Sgt., Box 113, Holt, Ala.
GILLIAM, Leonard A., S/Sgt., 216 Forest St., Suffolk, Va.
HOLMES, Lester N., S/Sgt., 103-20 32nd Ave., Corona, L. I., N. Y.
JONES, Elmore, S.Sgt., Box 169, Blythe, Calif.

THIRD ROW:
LAWSON, Joseph R., S/Sgt., 1330 Cornell Ave., Indianapolis, Ind.
LIGGETT, John W., S/Sgt., First and Lovely St., Kingston, Tenn.
McCRAE, James E., S/Sgt., 67 Trowbridge, Detroit, Mich.
MOSBY, Quinten L., S/Sgt., Morgantown, W. Va.
OLIVER, Raymond A., S/Sgt., 425 N. First St., Vinita, Okla.
PERRY, Lee E., S/Sgt., 5810 Hawthorne Ave., Cleveland, Ohio.

FOURTH ROW:
PHILLIPS, Arthur W., S/Sgt., 11724 Imperial Ave., Cleveland, Ohio.
PINKARD, Finley B., S/Sgt., 102-06 32nd Ave., Corona, L. I., N. Y.
REAVES, Emmitt N., S/Sgt., 9 Gregory Ave., Akron, Ohio.
REESE, Harry S., S/Sgt., Munford, Ala.
RICE, Marcus C., S/Sgt., 101 Watson Row, Clarksburg, W. Va.
ROBERTZ, Paul L., S/Sgt., 1709 Ninth Ave., Huntington, W. Va.

FIFTH ROW:
ROCHON, Clet T., S/Sgt., 702 French St., New Iberia, La.
WILLIAMS, Roy, S/Sgt., 53 Howell St., S.E., Atlanta, Ga.
ALBRITTEN, Cleveland, Sgt., 308 Pine St., N.E., Atlanta, Ga.
ALEXANDER, Elzie, Sgt., 119 Bank St., Dayton, Ohio.
ANDERSON, Willie J., Sgt., 508 Scott St., Cameron, Tex.
BAILEY, Samuel A., Sgt., 580 Mountain Ave., N. Plainfield, N. J.

SIXTH ROW:
BARNES, William J., Sgt.
BARTON, Roland A., Sgt.
BERRIEN, Clifford, Sgt., 373 Hensel Ave., Springfield, Ohio.
BOOKER, William L., Sgt., 2117 Lafayette St., Denver, Colo.
BROWN, Frank E., Sgt., 111-23 145th St., Jamaica, L. I., N. Y.
BRUNER, John B., Sgt., 1215 Eighth St., Oklahoma City, Okla.

SEVENTH ROW:
BRYANT, Clarence A., Sgt., 716 N. Bond St., Baltimore, Md.
BUCK, Melvin, Sgt., 266 W. 131st St., New York, N. Y.
BURGESS, David, Sgt., 941 Smith St., Gainesville, Fla.
BUSH, Isaac T., Sgt., 1683 W. 37th St., Los Angeles, Calif.
CALLOWAY, Thomas W., Sgt., 521 Washington Ave., Wellsville, Ohio.
CAMPBELL, Hubbard S., Sgt., Rt. 1, Box 95, Ponce De Leon, Fla.

EIGHTH ROW:
CAMPBELL, Ralph A., Sgt., 149 Monroe St., Buffalo, N. Y.
CAREY, Lester, Sgt., 3225 Bell Ave., St. Louis, Mo.
CHASE, Albert W., Sgt., 1614 E. Monument St., Baltimore, Md.
CHIEVES, William H., Sgt., 104 N. 50th St., Philadelphia, Pa.
CLACK, Wilbur, Sgt., Box 3, Yukon, W. Va.
CLARKE, Edgar A., Sgt., 41 Cunard St., Boston, Mass.

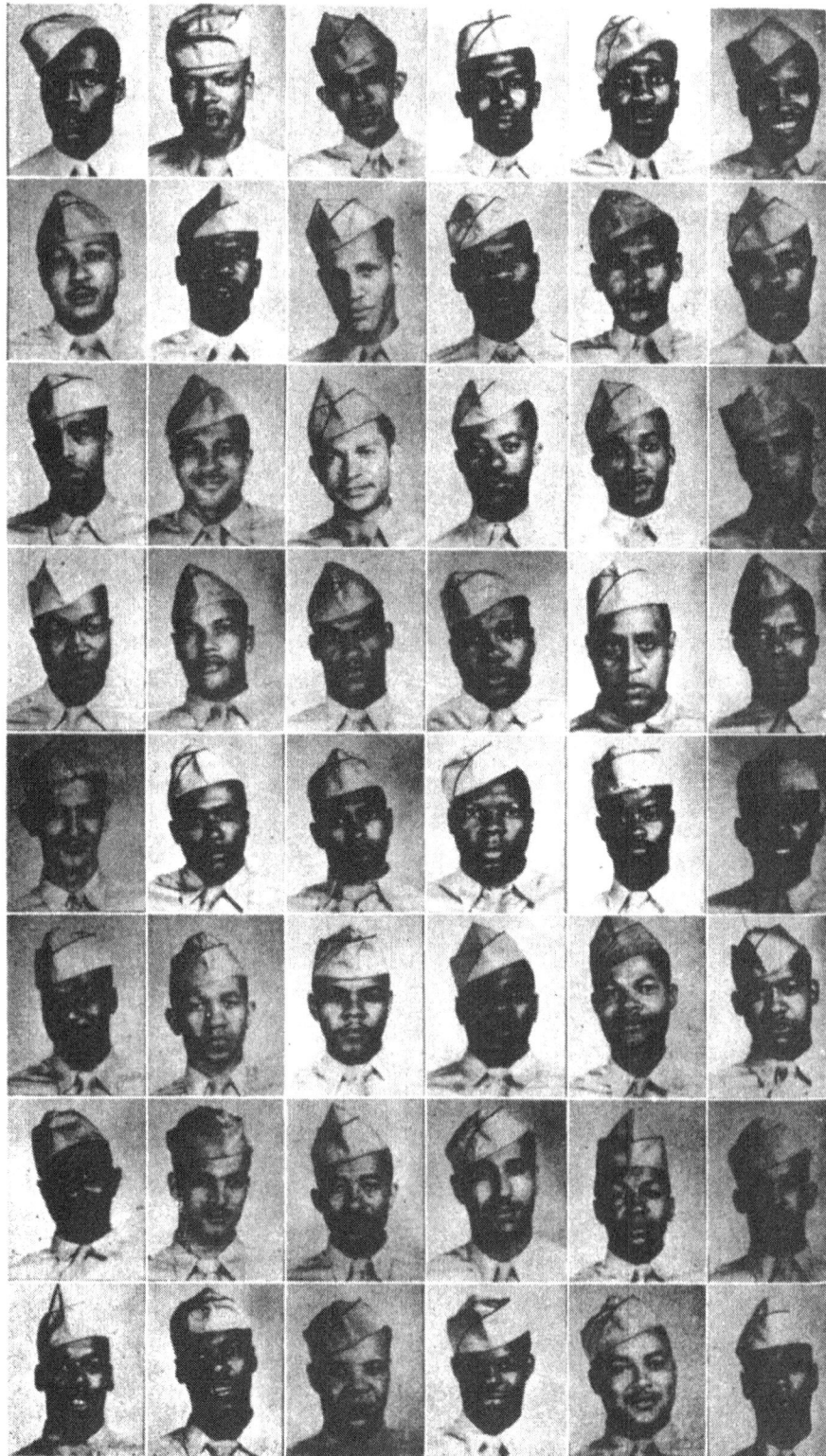

617TH BOMBARDMENT SQUADRON

WILLIAM D. PHEAN
Lieutenant

FIRST ROW:
COLBERT, George M., Sgt., 2712 Sherman Ave., N.W., Washington, D. C.
COLES, Calvin J., Sgt., 268 High St., Hackensack, N. J.
COULTHURST, Audley E., Sgt., 43 West 112th St., New York, N. Y.
CRAWFORD, Rudolph H., Sgt., 210 West 127th St., New York, N. Y.
CROWE, Hugh W., Sgt., 115 W. Penn St., Evansville, Ind.
CRUTCHER, Charles A., Sgt., 319 Prospect St., Wheaton, Ill.

SECOND ROW:
CURTIS, Frank N., Sgt., Parkersburg, W. Va.
DELFYETTE, Richard, Sgt., 62 West 115th St., New York, N. Y.
DICKEY, Earle L., Sgt., 115 N. Ninth St., Darby, Pa.
DILLARD, Harold, Sgt.
EDEY, Simeon A., Sgt., 279 River St., Cambridge, Mass.
EDWARDS, Leslie, Sgt.

THIRD ROW:
FLEMING, Jimmie L., Sgt., 1001 Alfred Dr., Ashtabula, Ohio.
FLOWERS, Jean, Sgt., 4311 N. Market St., St. Louis, Mo.
GILSTRAP, Waymon, Sgt., 295 Trenholm St., Atlanta, Ga.
GOODMAN, Charles S., Sgt., 473 Franklin Ave., Brooklyn, N. Y.
GRAGG, Robert J., Sgt., 4903 N.E. 29th Ave., Portland, Ore.
GREENE, Mitchell, Sgt., 507 Medbury, Detroit, Mich.

FOURTH ROW:
GREELEA, George H., Sgt., 114 Staley St., Opelika, Ala.
HACKETT, Holmes, Jr., Sgt., 354 Pacific Ave., Jersey City, N. J.
HAIRSTON, James T., Sgt., 414 Ross St., Danville, Va.
HAMPTON, Jerry T., Sgt., 3440 107th St., Corona, N. Y.
HARRIS, Daniel, Sgt., Rt. 2, Stuttgart, Ark.
HARVEY, Sylvester C., Sgt., Toledo, Ohio.

FIFTH ROW:
HOLMAN, Hubert L., Sgt., 617 Hudson St., Indianapolis, Ind.
HOYLES, Joseph M., Sgt., 239 Madison St., Brooklyn, N. Y.
HUDSON, George G., Sgt., 6633 S. Rhodes Ave., Chicago, Ill.
HYNES, Amos, Jr., Sgt., 318 E. 11th St., Newton, Kan.
JACKSON, Julius J., Sgt., 1635 Wharton St., Philadelphia, Pa.
JAMESON, Luther J., Sgt., 5209 Ward St., Cincinnati, Ohio.

SIXTH ROW:
JOHNSON, Gordon, Sgt., 30½ River St., Danbury, Conn.
JOHNSON, William T., Sgt., 49 Elmer St., Hartford, Conn.
JONES, John W., Sgt., 113 Oberlin Rd., Elyria, Ohio.
KELLER, Clarence R., Sgt., 790 E. 158th St., Bronx, N. Y.
KEYES, George, Sgt.
LEAVELLE, Raymond, Sgt., 666 St. Nicholas Ave., New York, N. Y.

SEVENTH ROW:
LEDBETTER, Charles W., Sgt., 86 Mather St., Hartford, Conn.
LONG, Clem, Sgt., 112 Douglas Way, San Antonio, Tex.
LOPES, Manuel A., Sgt., 62 Sherman St., S. Dartmouth, Mass.
LOWERY, Thomas L., Jr., Sgt., 914 W. French Pl., San Antonio, Tex.
McCADDEN, Charles F., Sgt., 3935 Fourth Ave., S., Minneapolis, Minn.
MITCHELL, Isaac T., Sgt., 2634 Wylie Ave., Pittsburgh, Pa.

EIGHTH ROW:
MOSLEY, James, Sgt., Box 1025, Brownfield, Tex.
OWENS, Clarence J., Sgt., 945 Grant St., Beaumont, Tex.
PALMER, Coleridge, Sgt., 1009 Whitted St., Durham, N. C.
PARKER, Reginald W., Sgt., 3802 S. Parkway, Chicago, Ill.
PARKEY, Kenneth L., Sgt., 937 15th St., Des Moines, Iowa.
PENN, David H., Sgt., 420 East Charles St., Sistersville, W. Va.

NINTH ROW:
PRADIA, Lawrence B., Sgt., 3107 Sampler St., Houston, Tex.
PURIFOY, Grant U., Sgt., Snow Hill, Ala.
REDDING, James W., Sgt., 817 N. Peters St., South Bend, Ind.
REED, George B., Sgt.
REEVES, Frank, Sgt.
ROBINSON, Roy A., Sgt., 1020 N. 21st St., St. Louis, Mo.

TENTH ROW:
ROSE, Alexander, Sgt., 1611 W. Lexington St., Baltimore, Md.
ROSS, George W., Sgt., 13 Edgerton Terr., East Orange, N. J.
ROWLETT, Charles G., Sgt., 307 N. Second St., Murray, Ky.
ROY, John S., Sgt. 1951 Logan St., Shreveport, La.
RUTLEDGE, Isaac V., Sgt., 340 56th St., Fairfield, Ala.
SANDERS, Christopher, Sgt., 2324 W. Comberland St., Philadelphia, Pa.

617TH BOMBARDMENT SQUADRON

FIRST ROW:
SEABROOK, Roy C., Sgt., 492 Convent Ave., New York, N. Y.
SCOTT, William A., Sr., Sgt., Patterson, La.
SHEPARD, Marion J., Sgt., 911 Adams St., Mobile, Ala.
SLAUGHTER, Thomas, Sgt., 914 S. Third Ave., Phoenix, Ariz.
SMITH, William A., Sgt., 169-17 110th Ave., Jamaica, N. Y.
SMITH, Woodie N., Sgt., 509 Larkin St., S.W., Atlanta, Ga.

SECOND ROW:
SPARKS, Joe W., Sgt., 815 E. Second St., Fort Worth, Tex.
THOMAS, Clarence E., Sgt., 65 West 135th St., New York, N. Y.
THOMAS, Winfred, Sgt., 3615 Meadow St., Dallas, Tex.
TOOMBS, Percy H., Sgt., 16 N. 36th St., Philadelphia, Pa.
WALKER, Delmar E., Sgt., 2101 N. Seventh St., Kansas City, Kan.
WALKER, Philip S., Sgt., 1703 Marshall Ave., Newport News, Va.

THIRD ROW:
WATKINS, Johnny B., Sgt., 1637 E. Adams Blvd., Los Angeles, Calif.
WILLIAMS, Thompson E., Sgt., 716 Dickinson St., Elmira, N. Y.
WILSON, George H., Sgt., 726 E. 37th Pl., Chicago, Ill.
WOODS, Robert W., Sgt.
WRIGHT, John K., Sgt., 3418 North 28th St., Kansas City, Kan.
YORK, Virtree L., Sgt., 1732 Conners Ave., East St. Louis, Ill.

FOURTH ROW:
ALEXANDER, John D., Cpl., 17826 Mitchell Ave., Detroit, Mich.
BARNES, Sidney D., Cpl., 1712 Bienville Ave., New Orleans, La.
BARZEY, George E., Cpl., 1650 Park Ave., New York, N. Y.
BATCHELOR, Jethro D., Cpl.
BAYSMORE, Clarence, Cpl., 510 Summit, Portsmouth, Va.
BELL, Albert Q., Jr., Cpl., 405 S. Third St., Seneca, S. C.

FIFTH ROW:
BELLOWS, James C., Cpl., 2728 W. Fletcher St., Philadelphia, Pa.
BOSTICK, William A., Cpl., 25 N. Delaware Ave., Atlantic City, N. J.
BOSTON, Oliver A., Cpl., 5631 Roosevelt St., Detroit, Mich.
BROWN, Arthur D., Cpl., 12 Plainfield Ave., Scotch Plains, N. J.
BROWN, John E., Jr., Cpl., Rt. 1, Newark, Del.
CAGNOLATTI, Calvin M., Cpl., 3831 St. Bernard Ave., New Orleans, La.

SIXTH ROW:
CALLAWAY, Harold J., Cpl., 290 Ogden St., Orange, N. J.
CARTER, Archie L., Cpl., 360 Nostrand Ave., Brooklyn, N. Y.
CARTER, James L., Cpl., 1112 N. Eden St., Baltimore, Md.
CHUBE, David D., Cpl., 1344 N. 28th St., Baton Rouge, La.
COLEMAN, Emerson, Cpl., 23 S. Enterprise St., Union, S. C.
COUSINS, Craig R., Cpl., 2448 Fafayeet St., Denver, Colo.

SEVENTH ROW:
CUMMINGS, Melvin T., Cpl., 542 W. Vine St., Milwaukee, Wis.
CUNNINGHAM, John, Cpl., 565 Willis St., Detroit, Mich.
DAVIS, Leroy, Cpl., 1042 42nd St., Newport News, Va.
DEMPSEY, David L., Cpl., 1228 French St., Wilmington, Del.
DILLARD, Calvin C., Cpl., Rt. 2, Box 111, Como, Miss.
DODSON, Granville M., Cpl., 805 N. Everest, Oklahoma City, Okla.

EIGHTH ROW:
DOTSON, Richard A., Cpl., 512 30th St., Denver, Colo.
DOUGLAS, Herbert M., Cpl., 15 Center St., Toms River, N. J.
DRIVER, David S., Cpl., 37 Riverside Dr., Baltimore, Md.
DUNCAN, John E., Cpl., 162 Pine St., Buffalo, N. Y.
DYER, Elijah M., Cpl., 2421 Poplar St., Oakland, Calif.
FINLEY, Charles R., Cpl., 324 T St., Washington, D. C.

NINTH ROW:
FOGG, Henry, Cpl., 3936 Evan Ave., St. Louis, Mo.
FRAZIER, James B., Cpl., 1417 Clerland St., Jacksonville, Fla.
GOLER, William F., Cpl., 813 S. Jefferson St., Dublin, Ga.
HAMILTON, Verdell D., Cpl., Lloyd, Fla.
HARRELL, Samuel R., Cpl., 4328 Michigan Ave., Chicago, Ill.
HARRIS, Sherman, Cpl., 1328 N.E. Seventh St., Oklahoma City, Okla.

TENTH ROW:
HARRISON, Edward, Cpl., 208 S. Grant Ave., Columbus, Ohio.
HAUSLEY, John R., Cpl., 1542 Lewis St., Indianapolis, Ind.
HILL, Wiley, Cpl., 1037 Princess Ann Rd., Norfolk, Va.
HOPPS, Porter, Cpl., 3575 Rhodes Ave., Chicago, Ill.
HOWARD, Walter O., Cpl., 30 W. 138th St., New York, N. Y.
HOY, Lee, Cpl., 1836 Payne St., Wichita, Kan.

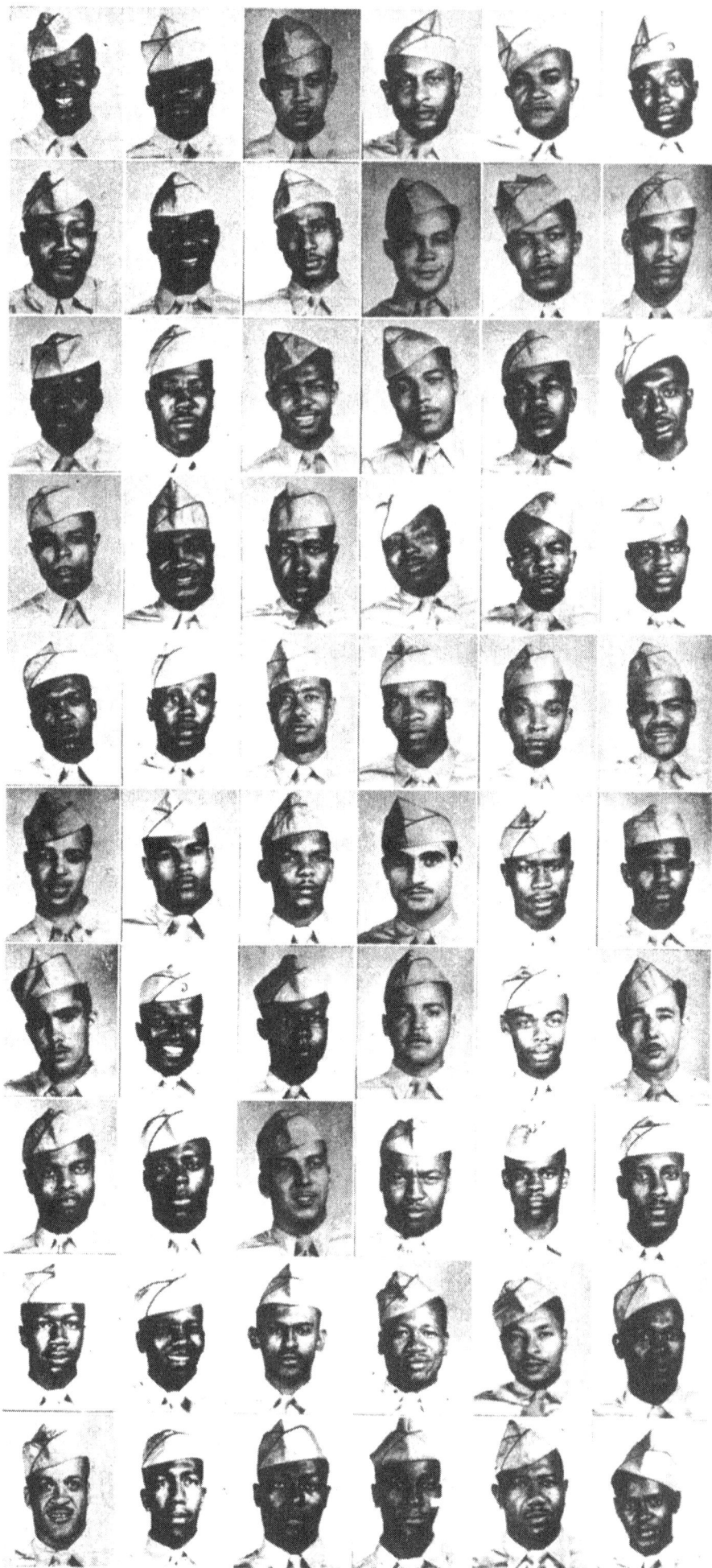

617TH BOMBARDMENT SQUADRON

FIRST ROW:

HUBBARD, Luther, Cpl., 1000 Bryant Ave., N., Minneapolis, Minn.
HUNT, Calvin, Cpl., 13938 Lumpkin Ave., Detroit, Mich.
HUTCHINS, Morris W., Cpl., 531 Franklin St., Danville, Va.
INMAN, Tracy C., Cpl., Rt. 2, Box 300, Fairmont, N. C.
JACKSON, Leroy, Cpl., Hodge, La.
JACKSON, Preston M., Cpl., 1100 Second Ave., Leavenworth, Kan.

SECOND ROW:

JOHNSON, Lawrence, Cpl., 6238 S. Parkway, Chicago, Ill.
JOHNSON, L. M. Cpl., Rt. 5, Lumberton, N. C.
JOHNSON, Nelson, Cpl., 6141 Enens Ave., Chicago, Ill.
JONES, Harold L., Cpl., Charleston, S. C.
JONES, Henry, Jr., Cpl., 1008½ Oak St., Monroe, La.
JONES, Roderic A., Cpl., 8 Retford Ave., Cranford, N. J.

THIRD ROW:

KENNEDY, Benny L., Cpl., 538 Lincoln Ave., Youngstown, Ohio.
KIMBERLIN, William A., Cpl., 25 North Lane St., Lebanon, Ohio.
KIRK, Solomon R., Cpl., St. Louis, Mo.
LANDRUM, Jefferson, Cpl., 414 N. Second St., Vinita, Okla.
LEE, Noble, Cpl., 939 Clay St., Detroit, Mich.
LOTHLON, Charles D., Cpl., 2008 E. 24th St. Terr., Kansas City, Mo.

FOURTH ROW:

LUCAS, John C., Cpl., 14 Buffington Ave., Pittsburgh, Pa.
MALONE, Isaac, Cpl., 507 Carpenter St., Mt. Pleasant, Tenn.
MARABLE, John L., Cpl., 11365 Cameron St., Detroit, Mich.
McCOY, William E., Cpl.
McDONALD, Walter T., Cpl., 613 18th St., Washington, D. C.
MENDES, Benjamin A., Cpl., 74 Bainbridge St., Roosevelt, N. Y.

FIFTH ROW:

MITCHELL, Howard, Cpl., 204 Morris Ave., Hamilton, Ohio.
MOORE, Ivory V., Cpl., 616 Burkett St., Taylor, Tex.
MORGAN, Jackie R., Cpl., 1174 E. 21st St., Los Angeles, Calif.
NEW, Albert J., Cpl.
NICHOLS, Clifton V., Cpl., 5446 Michigan, Chicago, Ill.
NORMAN, Henry, Cpl., 204 Troy Ave., Kansas City, Kan.

SIXTH ROW:

PASCHAL, Patron E., Cpl., 347 N.W. Eighth St., Miami, Fla.
PATTERSON, William B., Cpl., 3116 Miami St., Omaha, Neb.
PAYNE, William H., Cpl., Rt. 1, Ripley, Ohio.
PRICE, Nathaniel, Cpl., 5007 Sheriff Rd., N.E., Washington, D. C.
PROTHO, Leroy B., Cpl., 37 Peach Pl., Pasadena, Calif.
PRYOR, Ellsworth P., Cpl., 2025 Ohio St., Omaha, Neb.

SEVENTH ROW:

QUEEN, Melvin M., Cpl., 2307 M St., N.W., Washington, D. C.
REED, William E., Cpl.
REESE, William, Cpl.
RICHARDSON, Samuel L., Cpl.
RICHARDSON, Thomas L., Cpl., Box 276, Warrenton, N. C.
ROUSE, Willie, Cpl., 13601 Anderson Ave., Augusta, Ga.

EIGHTH ROW:

RUSSELL, Otis C., Cpl., 1416 McCulloch St., Fort Wayne, Ind.
SCOTT, Clarence E., Cpl., 622 Cawthorn Court, Louisville, Ky.
SCOTT, Walter H., Cpl., 26 East View Ave., White Plains, N. Y.
SHARPE, Leonard, Cpl., 524 E. Adams St., Detroit, Mich.
SHINGLES, Iders, Cpl., 17 E. North St., Akron, Ohio.
SIMMS, Waymon A., Cpl., 423 Clark St., Quincy, Fla.

NINTH ROW:

SIMON, Thomas J., Cpl., 440½ N.W. 15th St., Miami, Fla.
SIMMONS, Clarence, Cpl., 140 Mustill St., Akron, Ohio.
SMITH, Howard, Cpl., 21 Carpenter St., Woodbury, N. J.
SMITH, Joe, Cpl., 203 Mitchell St., Toledo, Ohio.
SMITH, John S., Cpl., 1734 N. Seventh St., Milwaukee, Wis.
SPENCER, Theodore, Cpl.

TENTH ROW:

STANIGAR, Keith I., Cpl., 2114 McDougall, Detroit, Mich.
STEELE, William J., Cpl., 1124 S. Second St., Camden, N. J.
STEWART, James, Jr., Cpl., 2511 Riverside Dr., Chattanooga, Tenn.
STONE, Richard, Cpl., 723 E. Pecan St., Sherman, Tex.
TAYLOR, Robert O., Cpl., 6598 Stanfor, Detroit, Mich.
THOMPSON, Cecil A., Cpl., 921 Bellevue, St. Joseph, Mo.

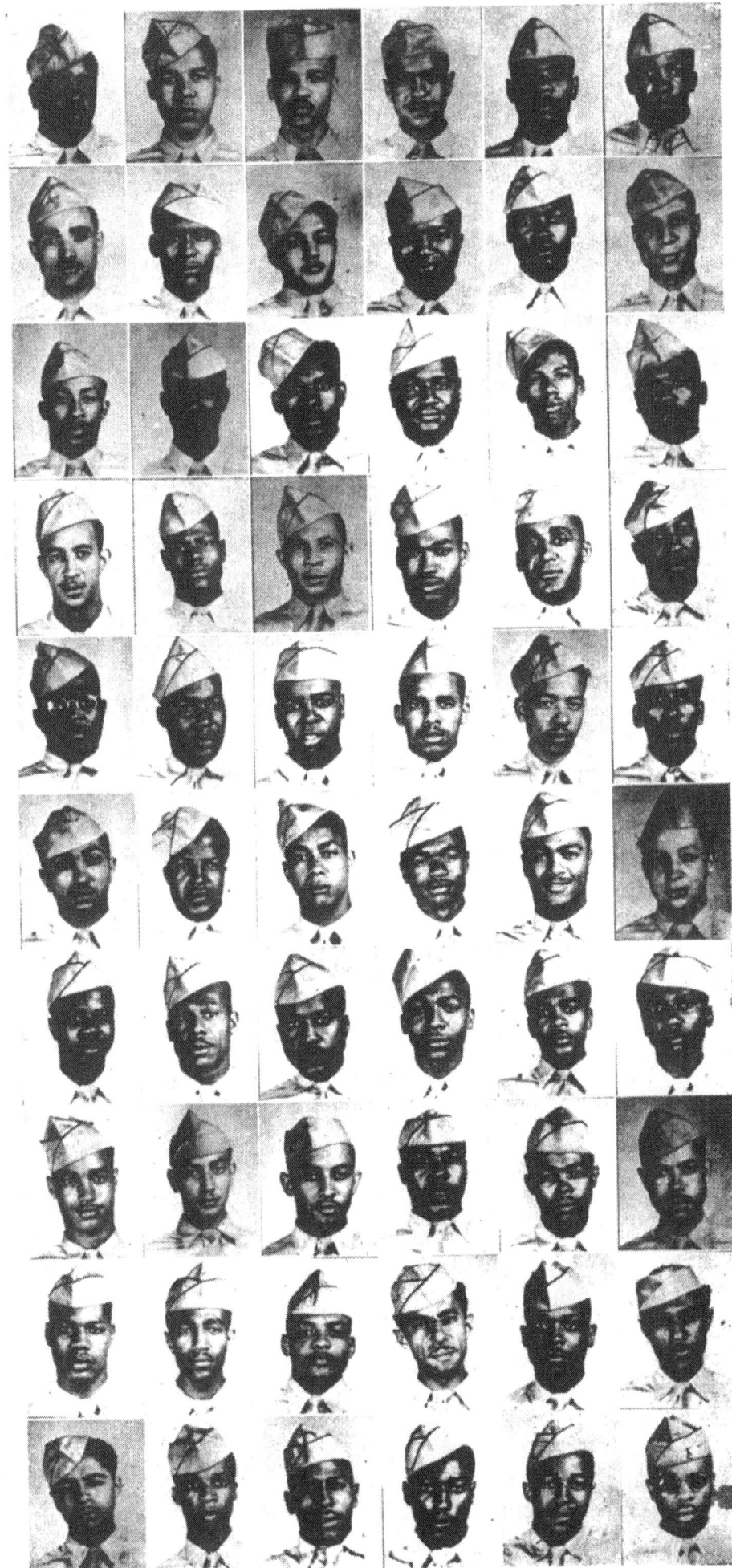

617TH BOMBARDMENT SQUADRON

FIRST ROW:
THOMPSON, David A., Cpl., 223 Galt St., New Albany, Ind.
TRAYLOR, Joseph H., Cpl., 812 East Ninth St., Chattanooga, Tenn.
TRICE, Frederick D., Cpl., 4506 Champlain Ave., Chicago, Ill.
VAUGHN, Abb R., Cpl., 4543 St. Ferdinand Ave., St. Louis, Mo.
WARE, Jesse, Cpl.
WASHINGTON, Clarence, Cpl., 1004-L Zion St., Mobile, Ala.

SECOND ROW:
WATSON, Eugene, Cpl.
WEBSTER, Sherman N., Cpl., Rt. 2, Box 138, Chesnee, S. C.
WELCH, Cornelius C., Cpl., 4160-A Albine Ave., St. Louis, Mo.
WELLS, James R., Cpl., 1120 Second St., Bradenton, Fla.
WHITE, Irvin W., Cpl., 1717 Butler St., Philadelphia, Pa.
WILLIAMS, Maurice, Cpl., 696 East St., Memphis, Tenn.

THIRD ROW:
WILLIAMS, Odie E., Cpl., 1630 Carver Lane, St. Louis, Mo.
WORMLEY, Lonnie, Cpl., 220 Connelly St., San Antonio, Tex.
AVERY, Wrochell E., Pfc., Rt. 42, Morganton, N. C.
BRINTLEY, Baxter L., Pfc., 302 Buffalo St., Shelby, N. C.
BROOKS, Alfred, Pfc., Georgetown, S. C.
BROWN, Eric D., Pfc., 1077 Fox St., The Bronx, N. Y.

FOURTH ROW:
BROWN, Lewis S., Pfc., R 1544 N.W. 10th Ave., Fort Lauderdale, Fla.
BROWN, Lionel B., Pfc., 5606 Perry Ave., Chicago, Ill.
COOPER, Onie, Pfc., Warden, La.
CRITTENDON, Sam L., Pfc., 1004 W. College St., Florence, Ala.
DIXON, Benjamin, Pfc., 1518 N. Mount St., Baltimore, Md.
FOY, Charlie, Pfc., Winston-Salem, N. C.

FIFTH ROW:
FRAZIER, Marion, Pfc., 500 West 157th St., New York, N. Y.
GREENE, Fletcher A., Pfc., 2020 Madison Ave., Baltimore, Md.
HART, Percy L., Pfc., 577 E. Warren Ave., Detroit, Mich.
GOUDY, John R., Pfc.
HOLMES, George S., Pfc., 2426-K N.W., Washington, D. C.
HURDLE, Esper L., Pfc., Box 111, Driver, Va.

SIXTH ROW:
JOHNSON, Archie, Pfc., 641 W. Ninth St., Cincinnati, Ohio.
KEARNEY, Junious, Pfc., Star Rt., Box 51, Warrenton, N. C.
LIDDELL, Lee F., Pfc., 758 Cherry St., Grenada, Miss.
MAYNARD, Frank, Jr., Pfc., Burlington, N. C.
McFADDEN, Robert, Pfc., 207½ Bladen St., Wilmington, N. C.
MOREHEAD, Norman, Pfc.

SEVENTH ROW:
NELSON, Roscoe, Pfc.
NEWMAN, J. B., Pfc., Rt. 1, Ozark, Ala.
NORTON, John E., Pfc., 835 S. Fayett St., Jacksonville, Ill.
ODEN, Thomas L., Pfc., 1125 S. 16th St., Philadelphia, Pa.
POLLARD, Arthur, Pfc., 271 Amhur St., E. Orange, N. J.
PORTER, Bennie, Pfc., 1010 N. Trade St., Winston-Salem, N. C.

EIGHTH ROW:
REQUER, Clinton C., Pfc., 354 Cuba St., Mobile, Ala.
REYNOLDS, Earl C., Pfc., 115 East Fifth Ave., Corsicana, Tex.
ROBERTS, Milton E., Pfc., 1408 Geary St., San Francisco, Calif.
SAMBRONE, John A., Pfc., 977 E. 48th St., Los Angeles, Calif.
WHITE, Eddie, Pfc., Rt. 7, Box 309 Marshall, Tex.
WILLIAMS, Earl L., Pfc., 801 Dakata St., Coffeyville, Kan.

NINTH ROW:
ALLEN, Henry J., Pvt., 219 Hopkinson Ave., Brooklyn, N. Y.
BASS, Merle, Pvt., 1814 Post St., San Francisco, Calif.
BIGGS, John, Pvt., 79 McDonough Blvd., Atlanta, Ga.
CARPENTER, Robert C., Pvt., 402 S. Olive St., San Antonio, Tex.
HAYGOOD, William K., Pvt., 15539 Twelfth St., Detroit, Mich.
KENYON, Lewis, Pvt., 107 Trowbridge St., Detroit, Mich.

TENTH ROW:
MOSS, Henry B., Pvt., 2427 East 59th St., Cleveland, Ohio.
SHEPHERD, Lewis, Pvt., 917 Ripley St., Davenport, Iowa.
THOMAS, Arnett J., Pvt., 3033 Indiana Ave., Chicago, Ill.
TUCKER, W. C., Pvt., 2233 Randolph St., St. Louis, Mo.
WHITTAKER, Henry, Jr., Pvt., Box 99 Centerville, La.

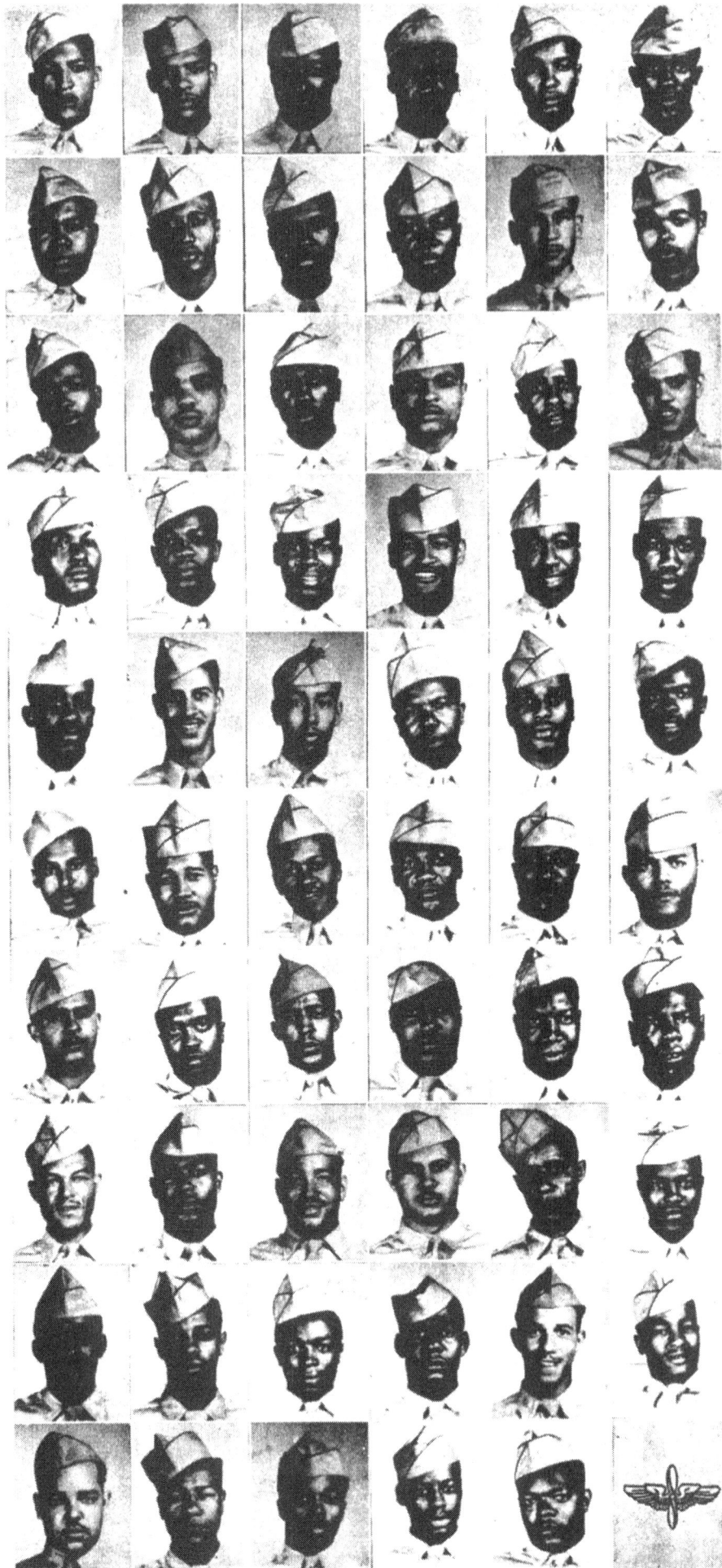

618TH BOMBARDMENT SQUADRON

Col SACK

ELMORE M. KENNEDY
Captain
Commanding

REYNOLD E. BURCH
Captain
Flight Surgeon

FREDERICK L. PARKER
Captain
Operations Officer

WILLIAM P. BROOKS, JR.
First Lieutenant
Adjutant

ROLIN B. BYNUM
First Lieutenant
Flight Commander

WILLIE L. BYRD
First Lieutenant
Pilot

TERRY J. CHARLTON
First Lieutenant
Engineering Officer

WILLIAM C. COLEMAN, JR.
First Lieutenant
Pilot

STEPHEN L. CUYJET
First Lieutenant
Ordnance Officer

WHITTIE ENGLISH
First Lieutenant
Communications Officer

WILLIAM H. FARLEY
First Lieutenant
Pilot

STEWART B. FULBRIGHT,
First Lieutenant
Pilot

GEORGE W. GIDDINGS
First Lieutenant
Navigator

LUTHER A. GOODWIN
First Lieutenant
Pilot

CHARLES R. HALL
First Lieutenant
Transportation Officer

MILTON T. HALL
First Lieutenant
Pilot

KENNETH R. HAWKINS
First Lieutenant
Pilot

WALTER B. HERRON
First Lieutenant
Pilot

Chica

HENRY P. HERVEY
First Lieutenant
Pilot

HAROLD A. HILLERY
First Lieutenant
Flight Commander

PERRY E. HUDSON, JR.
First Lieutenant
Pilot

CHARLES H. HUNTER
First Lieutenant
Flight Commander

JAMES A. HURD
First Lieutenant
Pilot

HALDANE KING
First Lieutenant
Flight Commander

GEORGE H. KYDD, II
First Lieutenant
Pilot

GEORGE McDONALD
First Lieutenant
Navigator-Bombardier

PAUL L. MOODY
First Lieutenant
Pilot

AHMED A. RAYNER, JR.
First Lieutenant
Pilot

MILTON B. RICHARDSON
First Lieutenant
Communications Officer

ARTHUR ROBINSON
First Lieutenant
Navigator-Bombardier

FENTON B. SANDS
First Lieutenant
Navigator-Bombardier

JUNIUS R. SAVAGE
First Lieutenant
Executive Officer

JAMES D. SOLOMON
First Lieutenant
Armament Officer

CLARENCE H. THOMAS
First Lieutenant
Intelligence Officer

WILLIAM D. TOMPKINS
First Lieutenant
Flight Leader

JOHN B. TURNER
First Lieutenant
Pilot

LEON L. TURNER
First Lieutenant
Flight Leader

JOSEPH D. WHITEN
First Lieutenant
Pilot

LESLIE A. WILLIAMS
First Lieutenant
Pilot

WILLIAM S. ANDERSON
Second Lieutenant
Bombardier-Navigator

KERMIT G. BAILER
Second Lieutenant
Navigator

PAUL J. BONSEIGNE
Second Lieutenant
Pilot

ROBERT W. BOYD
Second Lieutenant
Bombardier

HAROLD H. BROWN
Second Lieutenant
Pilot

IVAN G. BYNOE
Second Lieutenant
Bombardier-Navigator

STRATMAN COOKE
Second Lieutenant
Radar Officer

AUGUSTUS COUSINS, JR.
Second Lieutenant
Pilot

CHARLES W. DIGG
Second Lieutenant
Pilot

CHARLES J. DORKINS
Second Lieutenant
Pilot

CHARLES H. DRUMMOND, JR.
Second Lieutenant
Pilot

JAMES A. EVANS
Second Lieutenant
Bombardier-Navigator

CHARLES B. FANCHER
Second Lieutenant
Assistant Armament Officer

MELVIN S. HALL
Second Lieutenant
Navigator-Bombardier

BERNARD HARRIS
Second Lieutenant
Pilot

DONALD S. HARRIS
Second Lieutenant
Bombardier-Navigator

EUGENE R. HENDERSON
Second Lieutenant
Pilot

SAMUEL C. HUNTER, JR.
Second Lieutenant
Pilot

LOWELL H. JORDAN
Second Lieutenant
Pilot

CELESTINO S. MONCLOVA
Second Lieutenant
Navigator

ROGER V. PINES
Second Lieutenant
Navigator-Bombardier

WARDELL A. POLK
Second Lieutenant
Bombardier-Navigator

EVERETT E. RICHARDSON
Second Lieutenant
Navigator-Bombardier

WILLARD W. SAVOY
Second Lieutenant
Lead Navigator

LLOYD R. SHULTS
Second Lieutenant
Pilot

EDWARD W. WATKINS
Second Lieutenant
Pilot

JAMES W. WHYTE, JR.
Second Lieutenant
Pilot

WALTER H. ALLEN
Flight Officer
Pilot

WILLIAM L. CAIN
Flight Officer
Pilot

CLARENCE C. CONWAY
Flight Officer
Bombardier-Navigator

EDWIN T. COWAN
Flight Officer
Pilot

HARRY R. DICKENSON
Flight Officer
Bombardier

JAMES E. EDWARDS
Flight Officer
Pilot

JAMES EWING, JR.
Flight Officer
Pilot

HERVEN P. EXUM
Flight Officer
Pilot

THOMAS M. FLAKE
Flight Officer
Co-Pilot

RUTLEDGE H. FLEMING
Flight Officer
Co-Pilot

EDWARD M. GIBSON
Flight Officer
Bombardier-Navigator

JAMES L. GREEN
Flight Officer
Pilot

DONALD A. HAWKINS
Flight Officer
Pilot

THOMAS D. HILL, JR.
Flight Officer
Bombardier

McCRAY JENKINS
Flight Officer
Bombardier-Navigator

JAMES L. JONES
Flight Officer
Bombardier

CLAYTON F. LAWRENCE
Flight Officer
Bombardier

ROBERT S. LAWRENCE
Flight Officer
Bombardier

LEVERT V. MIDDLETON
Flight Officer
Bombardier

CHARLES J. QUANDER
Flight Officer
Pilot

HARRIS H. ROBNETT, JR.
Flight Officer
Pilot

JESSE H. SIMPSON
Flight Officer
Pilot

PAUL W. SCOTT
Flight Officer
Bombardier-Navigator

WAYMAN SURCEY
Flight Officer
Pilot

SAINT M. TWINE, JR.
Flight Officer
Pilot

FRED E. VELASQUEZ
Flight Officer
Pilot

MORRIS J. WASHINGTON
Flight Officer
Pilot

ALVIN X. WATERS
Flight Officer
Bombardier-Navigator

JOHN E. WILSON
Flight Officer
Bombardier

EUGENE L. WOODSO[...]
Flight Officer
Bombardier-Navigato[...]

618TH BOMBARDMENT SQUADRON

FIRST ROW:
DAVIS, Herbert, 1/Sgt., 701 Nebraska, San Antonio, Tex.
CRENCHAU, Charles M., M/Sgt., 1914 Denison St., Little Rock, Ark.
BEST, Eugene, T/Sgt., 622 E. Jackson St., Thomasville, Ga.
DUNLAP, James D., T.Sgt., 803 Washington St., Paducah, Ky.
MALLORY, Albert H., T/Sgt., 5817 St. Antoine St., Detroit, Mich.
McFERREN, Harold A., T/Sgt., 1335 W. Hastings St., Chicago, Ill.

SECOND ROW:
ATKINSON, Lionel, S/Sgt., 1352 Clinton Ave., Bronx, N. Y.
BAILEY, William S., S/Sgt., 1414 Sandusky St., Pittsburgh, Pa.
BATTEN, William T., S/Sgt., 210-K W. 153rd St., New York, N. Y.
CHRISTINE, John W., S/Sgt., 7322 Tioga, Pittsburgh, Pa.
GRIMES, Raymond N., S/Sgt., 1119 Lamont St., N.W., Washington, D. C.
HAILSTOCK, Frank M., Jr., S/Sgt., 409 Walnut St., Sewickley, Pa.

THIRD ROW:
HALL, James E., S/Sgt., 1614 Ninth Ave., Huntington, W. Va.
HARRIS, Lee, S/Sgt., 4412 South Parkway, Chicago, Ill.
HARRISON, Cornelius P., S/Sgt., 614 S. Adams St., Petersburg, Va.
HERBERT, Norman E., S/Sgt., 2313 N. Camac St., Philadelphia, Pa.
HICKS, Fred, S/Sgt., 401 S. Seminole St., Wewoka, Okla.
HUGHES, Clayton M., S/Sgt., 3820 Fifth Ave., S., Minneapolis, Minn.

FOURTH ROW:
JONES, James A., S/Sgt., 314 West 112th St., New York, N. Y.
KEENE, Frank K., S/Sgt., 526 N. Illinois Ave., Atlantic City, N. J.
LAKE, Willie, S/Sgt., 805 Caroline St., Jacksonville, Fla.
LEFROY, Albert, S/Sgt., 2309 Conti St., New Orleans, La.
LEROY, James B., S/Sgt., 327 E. Market St., Xenia, Ohio.
MACK, Alfred G., S/Sgt., 1618 Garfield St., Middletown, Ohio.

FIFTH ROW:
MARABLE, James P., S/Sgt., Rt. 1, Malone, Ala.
MATHIS, Robert L., S/Sgt., 306 Cherry St., Waco, Tex.
MILLS, Perry, S/Sgt., General Delivery, Lorado, W. Va.
MOORE, Edward C., S/Sgt., Uniontown, Ala.
NEWTON, Vernon J., S/Sgt., 1629 Westwood Ave., Baltimore, Md.
PORTER, George W., S/Sgt., Rt. 1, Box 45, Slidell, La.

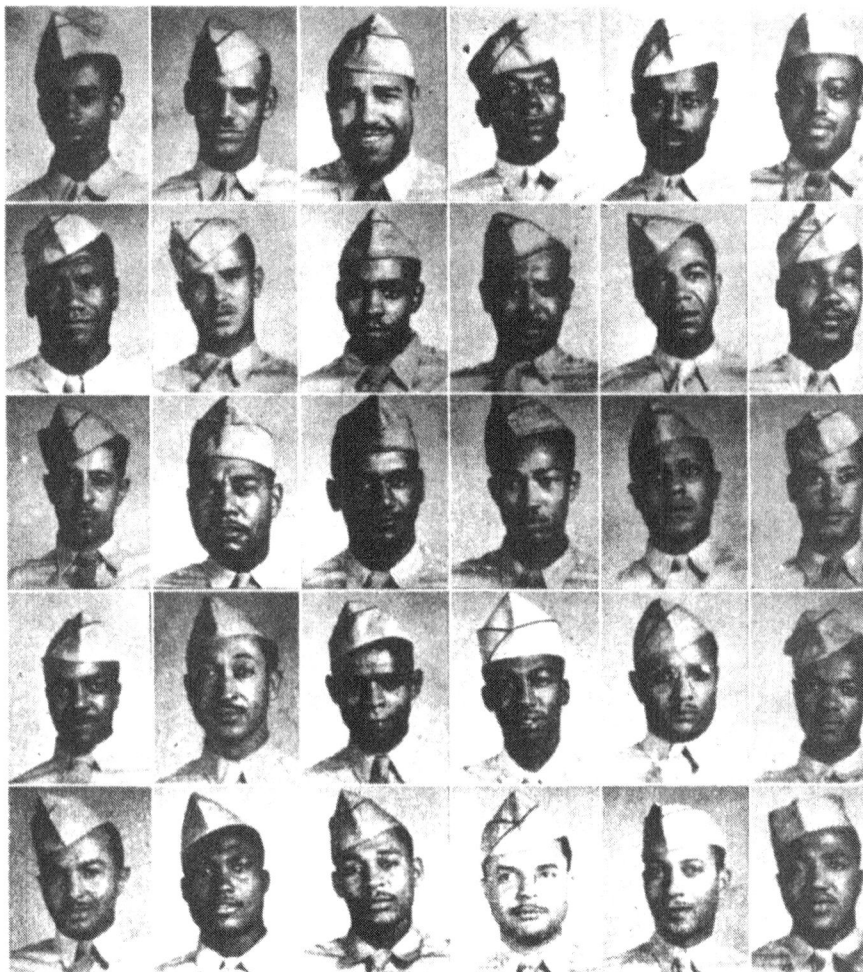

618TH BOMBARDMENT SQUADRON

HOWARD A. WOOTEN
Flight Officer
Pilot

ROY T. ROUTT
Second Lieutenant
Pilot

FIRST ROW:
RANDOLPH, Walter, S/Sgt., 789 Van Buren, Lockland, Ohio.
SLAUGHTER, McCoy, S/Sgt., 318 Lowell St., Pittsburgh, Pa.
STEWART, Meredith, S/Sgt., 344 W. 21st St., Indianapolis, Ind.
STRONG, Carl R., S/Sgt., 67 Winter St., Providence, R. I.
THIGPEN, Easie, S/Sgt., 2718 Calumet Ave., Chicago, Ill.
THORPE, Dorsey W., S/Sgt., 1065 W. North St., Piqua, Ohio.

SECOND ROW:
WHITEHEAD, J. H., S/Sgt., Wilson, N. C.
WOODLIFF, Hugh D., S/Sgt., 118 Seventh Ave., N.W., Roanoke, Va.
ABRAM, Johnie W., Sgt., 1031 East Eighth St., Oklahoma City, Okla.
ADAMS, Earl T., Sgt., 1755 W. Grand Blvd., Detroit, Mich.
ADAMS, Everlyn E., Sgt., Phillippi, W. Va.
ALLISON, Dewitt, Sgt., 11 Rutgers St., Newark, N. J.

THIRD ROW:
ALLEN, Floyd R., Sgt., 2527 W. Turner St., Philadelphia, Pa.
ANDERSON, Jack L., Sgt., Overock Rd., Poughkeepsie, N. Y.
ARRINGTON, Jason C., Sgt., Box 83, Hazard, Ky.
BAILEY, James R., Sgt.
BALLARD, John T., Sgt., 646 N. 56th St., Philadelphia, Pa.
BANKS, Elbert, Sgt., 51½ Spring St., White Plains, N. Y.

FOURTH ROW:
BARRETT, Allen L., Sgt., 631 Oxford St., Dalton, Ga.
BENNETT, William, Sgt., 2801 Cottonwood St., Portland, Ore.
BROWN, R. J., Sgt., 41 Princeton Ave., Bethlehem, Pa.
CATCHINGS, Dexter L., Sgt., 3012 Hadley Ave., Houston, Tex.
CHAMBERS, Frank H., Sgt., 37 S. Cecil St., Philadelphia, Pa.
CHANCELLOR, Jack C., Sgt., 6524 S. Langley Ave., Chicago, Ill.

FIFTH ROW:
COLEMAN, William, Sgt., 911 N. 19th St., St. Louis, Mo.
COPELAND, Lexie, Sgt., 32 Kearney Ave., Jersey City, N. J.
CRAIN, Charles A., Sgt., 200 Liberia St., Chillicothe, Mo.
DAILEY, Goodrich T., Sgt., 143 Fain St., Nashville, Tenn.
DANIELS, George W., Jr., Sgt., 5621 Calumet Ave., Chicago, Ill.
DANIELS, James, Sgt., 1328 S. Racine Ave., Chicago, Ill.

SIXTH ROW:
DAVIS, Samuel R., Sgt., Rt. 1, Box 1-A, Toone, Tenn.
DAYS, James, Sgt.
ELLIS, Lewis E., Sgt., 4837 Moore Pl., Detroit, Mich.
ESQUERRE, Jean R., Sgt., 919 Eagle Ave., Bronx, N. Y.
EWING, Edward, Sgt., 30 Downing St., Denver, Colo.
FIDDMONT, Robert L., Sgt., 7910 Bruno Ave., St. Louis, Mo.

SEVENTH ROW:
FIELDER, Willie, Sgt., 4407 Central Ave., Cleveland, Ohio.
FORREST, Leonard A., Sgt.
FOSTER, Percy, Sgt., 301 10th St., N., Birmingham, Ala.
FRANK, Robert A., Sgt., 923 N. 16th St., Philadelphia, Pa.
GIBBONS, Napoleon B., Sgt., 1335½ Ross St., Chattanooga, Tenn.
GIVNER, Napoleon U., Sgt., House No. 180, Indianola, Pa.

EIGHTH ROW:
GOLDEN, Charles L., Sgt., 256 Watson St., Buffalo, N. Y.
GREEN, Leroy, Sgt., 2924 Wyoming St., San Antonio, Tex.
GREENWOOD, Robert, Sgt., 1612 Geary St., San Francisco, Calif.
HARRIS, Thomas B., Sgt., 1607 E. Chase St., Baltimore, Md.
HARVEY, Alonzo, Sgt., Box 61, Brewton, Ala.
HIGHTOWER, Clarence T., Sgt., 5449 Indiana Ave., Chicago, Ill.

NINTH ROW:
HOBBS, Calvin, Sgt., 2418 Burdette St., Omaha, Neb.
HOBSON, Charles A., Sgt., 30 Hamilton Terr., New York, N. Y.
HODGES, Alonzo E., Sgt., 2110 W. Madison St., Louisville, Ky.
HOLMAN, Henry H., Sgt., 6751 37th Ave., S., Seattle, Wash.
JACKSON, George W., Sgt., 1901 East Ninth St., Kansas City, Mo.
JACKSON, Walter, Sgt., 530 21st N.E., Washington, D. C.

618TH BOMBARDMENT SQUADRON

FIRST ROW:
JEFFERSON, Luther, Sgt., Box 1483, Cotton Valley, La.
JOHNS, Alphonso, Sgt., 301 West 130th St., New York, N. Y.
JOHNSON, Harlan P., Sgt., 912 Douglass St., Huntington, W. Va.
JONES, Charley W., Sgt., 3923 Delmar Blvd., St. Louis, Mo.
JONES, Herbert, Sgt., 2636 S. Howard St., Philadelphia, Pa.
JONES, Leslie U., Sgt., 1107 Fourth St., N., Birmingham, Ala.

SECOND ROW:
KERN, Donald, Sgt., 900 W. 12th St., Newton, Kan.
KING, Roy B., Sgt., 13 S. Barton St., Martinsville, Va.
LEE, Wilbert E., Sgt., 909 Fulton St., Alexandria, La.
LIGON, Aldridge C., Sgt., 1056 S. Bellerine, Memphis, Tenn.
LINDSAY, John R., Sgt., 3202 Fredonia Ave., Cincinnati, Ohio.
LIPSY, Wardell, Sgt.

THIRD ROW:
LOMAX, James W., Sgt., Box 739, Gary, W. Va.
MASON, Charley, Sgt., 319 N. Grant, Marshall, Mo.
MAYES, Robert, Sgt., 1996-A Fulton St., Brooklyn, N. Y.
McCLAIN, James C., Sgt.
McGREGOR, Albert E., Sgt., 455 West Court, Louisville, Ky.
MEADOWS, Arthur V., Sgt., 710 East 218th St., Bronx, N. Y.

FOURTH ROW:
MICHAEL, Alfred L., Sgt., 272 Manhattan Ave., New York, N. Y.
MILES, James W., Sgt., 7233 Susquehanna St., Pittsburgh, Pa.
MITCHELL, Burrell P., Sgt., 1379½ Washburn Ave., Chicago, Ill..
MITCHELL, Leroy, Sgt., 810 Third Ave., Gallipolis, Ohio.
MOBLEY, Joseph, Sgt., 425 West Ave., Ocean City, N. J.
MOORE, Riley, Sgt., Birmingham, Ala.

FIFTH ROW:
MORGAN, Henry C., Sgt., 812 Fulton St., Brooklyn, N. Y.
MURRAY, John H., Sgt., 122 Etzel Pl., St. Louis, Mo.
OLLIE, Arlee, Sgt., 1400 East 13th St., Austin, Tex.
PATTON, Frederick H., Sgt., 2133 Pine, San Francisco, Calif.
PENN, Alfred, Sgt., 93 Union Ave., Hempstead, N. Y.
PERRY, Raymond H., Sgt., 854 Davis Ave., Mobile, Ala.

SIXTH ROW:
PICKETT, David F., Sgt., 1004 West 16th St., Des Moines, Iowa.
PORTER, Coleman, Sgt., 1015 21st St., N.W., Washington, D. C.
REED, Louis, Sgt., 59 Clayton St., Worcester, Mass.
ROBERTS, Eugene C., Sgt., 170-44 Douglas Ave., Jamaica, L. I., N. Y.
ROBERTS, Theophilus W., Sgt., 963 Texas St., Memphis, Tenn.
ROBINSON, Romeo R., Sgt., 140 42nd, N.E., Washington, D. C.

SEVENTH ROW:
ROBINSON, William D., Sgt., 532 State St. Lane, Jacksonville, Fla.
SCOTT, Nelson, Sgt., 214 W. Gray, Houston, Tex.
STROMAN, William H., Sgt., 2313 Webster Ave., Pittsburgh, Pa.
STRONG, Paul, Sgt., 1820 N. Norfolk, Tulsa, Okla.
TANNER, Ralph L., Sgt.
TAYLOR, Albert G., Sgt.

EIGHTH ROW:
TODD, Edward M., Sgt., 2334 Avenue O, Birmingham, Ala.
TONKINS, C. A., Sgt., 201 17th St., S.E., Washington, D. C.
TORAN, Charles B., Sgt., 268 McLean Ave., Woodlawn, Ohio.
TRAVIS, James F., Sgt., 1312½ E. 25th St., Kansas City, Mo.
TRICE, Roy G., Jr., Sgt., 465 W. 147th St., New York, N. Y.
VALENTINE, Henry W., Sgt., 632 E. 42nd St., Chicago, Ill.

NINTH ROW:
VAUGHN, Samuel, Sgt., 1244 S. Patton St., Philadelphia, Pa.
WALLACE, Robert E., Sgt., 517 West 160th St., New York, N. Y.
WASHINGTON, George, Sgt., 1117-H Seventh St., Harrisburg, Pa.
WATKINS, Levi A., Sgt., 122 Woodworth Ave., Yonkers, N. Y.
WESTRAY, Kenneth M., Sgt., 1625 East Capitol St., Washington, D. C.
WHITE, Waldo R., Sgt., 522 Marston St., Detroit, Mich.

TENTH ROW:
WINBORNE, Thomas J., Sgt., 328 First Ave., Portsmouth, Va.
YANCEY, Stanley A., Sgt., 212 W. Street, N.W., Washington, D. C.
ALLEN, David, Cpl., 1109 Spring St., Tampa, Fla.
ALSTON, Dabney J., Cpl., 359 Jerusalem Rd., Scotch Plains, N. J.
ANDERSON, Benjamin, Cpl., General Delivery, Smithville, Tex.
BAILEY, Rodger, Cpl., 75 Pelham St., Southampton, N. Y.

618TH BOMBARDMENT SQUADRON

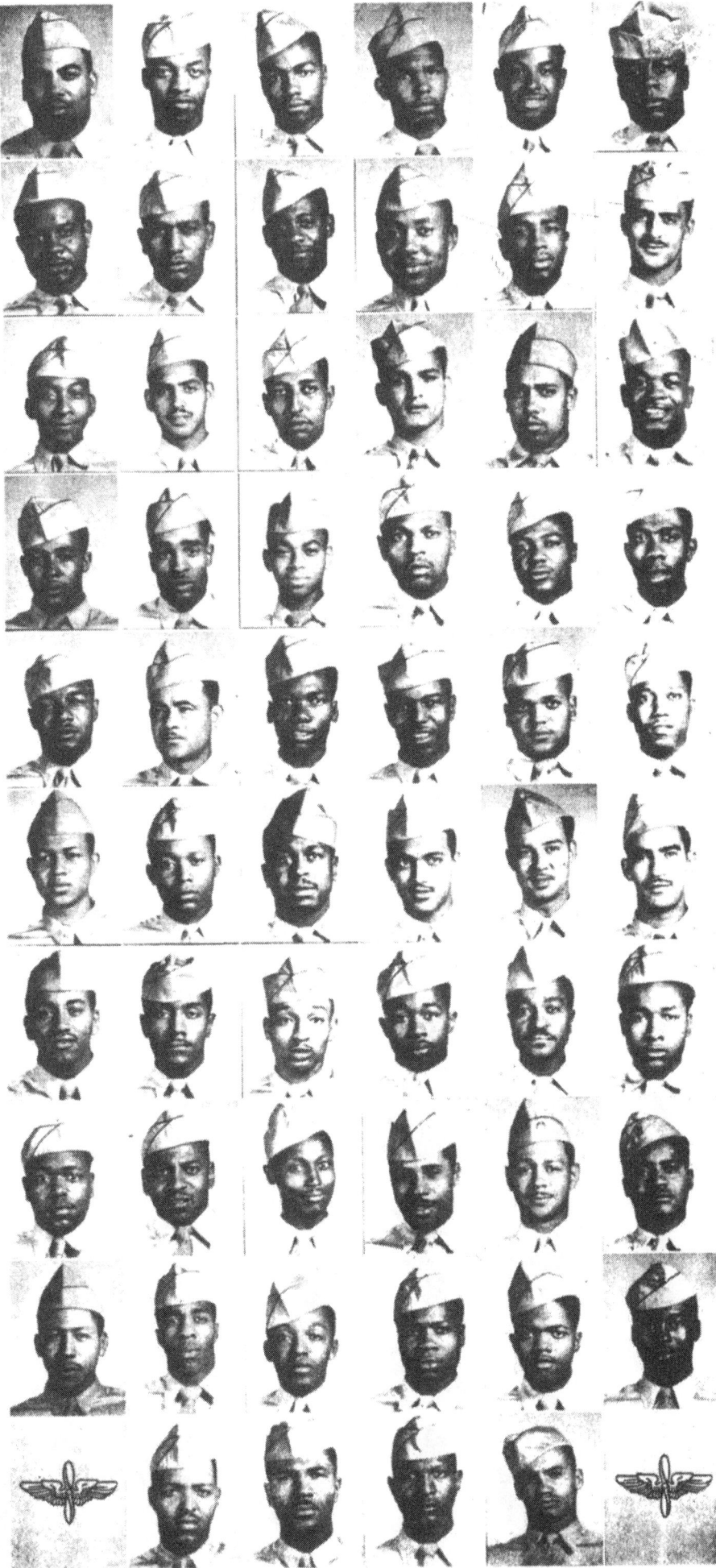

FIRST ROW:
BANKS, Haywood L., Cpl., 116 Ridge St., Reidsville, N. C.
BENNETT, Richard L., Cpl., 325 W. 11th St., Indianapolis, Ind.
BLACK, William, Cpl., 343 Deweest St., Lexington, Ky.
BLACKMON, Bernard, Cpl., 551 Weinacker Ave., Mobile, Ala.
BROWN, Charles L., Cpl., Thorpe, W. Va.
BROWN, Jimmie, Cpl.

SECOND ROW:
BROWN, Louis A., Cpl., 6414 Champlain, Chicago, Ill.
BURDINE, Warren B., Cpl., Ct. D-73 Austin Homes, Knoxville, Tenn.
CARTER, Frisby M., Cpl., 178 Mill St., New Bedford, Mass.
CAWTHON, Floyd J., Jr., Cpl., 780 Josephine St., Memphis, Tenn.
CHAMBERS, Stermidge, Cpl., 1017 17th St., Racine, Wis.
CLAYTON, Harold H., Cpl., 210 N. 60th St., Philadelphia, Pa.

THIRD ROW:
CHEW, Andrew, Cpl., 356-E S. Wellington St., Memphis, Tenn.
CLEMONS, Robert P., Cpl., 269 Belmont St., Detroit, Mich.
COBBS, Filbert H., Cpl., 619 W. Bowman, N.W., Roanoke, Va.
COUSIN, Warren J., Cpl., 1917 Lafitte St., New Orleans, La.
DAMERON, Victor L., Cpl., 1318 Indiana Ave., Wichita, Kan.
DAVIS, Walter L., Cpl., 1431 N.W. 69th St., Miami, Fla.

FOURTH ROW:
DE WEAVER, Fred, Cpl., 644 Greensferry, Apt. 381, Atlanta, Ga.
DIXON, Joseph H., Cpl., 1932 F. St., Fresno, Calif.
DOUGLAS, Arnold, Cpl., 1092 Franklin Ave., Bronx, N. Y.
EASLEY, Robert L., Cpl., Talladega, Ala.
EVANS, Luther E., Cpl., Rt. 2, Emmet, Ark.
GALES, G. M., Cpl., 425 W. Court Beecher Terr., Louisville, Ky.

FIFTH ROW:
GARDINER, James W., Cpl., 32-37 103rd St., Corona, L. I., N. Y.
GARDNER, Marcus P., Cpl., 211 Orrin St., Lake Charles, La.
GILBEAU, Alex, Cpl., 808 Meadow St., Houston, Tex.
GLENN, David L., Cpl., 2827 Park Ave., Cincinnati, Ohio.
GOODMAN, Donald W., Cpl., 1240 S. 21st St., Philadelphia, Pa.
GRAHAM, Moses L., Cpl., 1109 E. Madison, Ponca City Okla.

SIXTH ROW:
GREEN, James E., Jr., Cpl., 1201 15th Ave., Tuscaloosa, Ala.
GRICE, Isaiah, Jr., Cpl., 1179 Logan St., Jacksonville, Fla.
GRIGSBY, Ernest, Cpl., 4015 Cuney Dr., Houston, Tex.
HALL, Calvin H., Cpl., 315 Cottage Pl., Plainfield, N. J.
HAMMOND, William T., Cpl., 308 Highland Ave., Atlanta, Ga.
HARMON, John C., Cpl., 1706 Ninth St., N.W., Washington, D. C.

SEVENTH ROW:
HECTOR, Francis I., Cpl., 3 Claremont St., Boston, Mass.
HOLLAND, James W., Cpl., 808 Fifth Ave., Rock Island, Ill.
HOUSTON, George L., Cpl., 2190 West 27th St., Los Angeles, Calif.
JENKINS, Joseph, Cpl., 25 West 133rd St., New York, N. Y.
JOHNSON, Fred C., Cpl., 228 Burgess Pl., Passaic, N. J.
JOHNSON, Prather, Cpl., 818 19th St., Columbus, Ga.

EIGHTH ROW:
JOHNSON, Robert W., Cpl., Oswego, Kan.
KIMBROUGH, William E., Cpl., 2117 Eugenia St., St. Louis, Mo.
KING, Leo A., Cpl., 314 W. St., Chicago, Ill.
LANE, Clifford A., Cpl., 258 Starr St., New Haven, Conn.
LAWSON, Charles L., Cpl., 2607 E. St., N. E., Washington, D. C.
LAWSON, John D., Cpl., 623 E. Haussler St., Centralia, Ill.

NINTH ROW:
LISTENBEE, Wedelow, Cpl., Beloit, Wis.
McADORY, Howard C., Cpl., 1103 W. Mulberry St., Baltimore, Md.
McALLISTER, Norman L., Cpl., 167-10 108th Dr., Jamaica, N. Y.
McCALLUM, Robert, Cpl.
McKINNEY, Wade H., Jr., Cpl., 3410 East 137th St., Cleveland, Ohio.
MILLER, Garfield, Cpl., Rt. 1, Box 105, Lynchburg, S. C.

TENTH ROW:
MINOR, Edward L., Cpl., 917 O St., N.W., Washington, D. C.
MITCHELL, Waymon G., Cpl., 306 E. First Ave., Roselle, N. J.
MOORE, E. Nathaniel, Cpl., 720 S. Jackson St., Montgomery, Ala.
MORGAN, Edsol W., Cpl.

618TH BOMBARDMENT SQUADRON

FIRST ROW:
NORMAN, Sidney, Cpl., 724 14th St., Newport News, Va.
NORRIS, Howard B., Cpl., Ct. I, Apt. 5, Rosewood Cts., Austin, Tex.
OTEN, Henry J., Cpl., 279 Wendsor St., Hartford, Conn.
PITTS, Harold L., Cpl., 1118 Jackson Ave., Bronx, N. Y.
POOLE, Lloyd H., Cpl., 3708 Horne St., Ft. Worth, Tex.
POWELL, H. J., Cpl., Madison, W. Va.

SECOND ROW:
PROUDIE, Reuben, Cpl., 4308 Moffitt Court, Apt. 9, St. Louis, Mo.
ROBERSON, Nathaniel M., Cpl., 369 E. 53rd St., Chicago, Ill.
ROBERTS, Welton, Cpl., Box 177, Dekalb, Miss.
SMITH, Willie E., Cpl., Gatesville, Tex.
STOCKETT, Robert E., Cpl., 1718 Dean St., Brooklyn, N. Y.
SWEETING, Charles, Cpl., 327 Harmon, Detroit, Mich.

THIRD ROW:
TINCH, Robert J., Cpl., 77 Copeland St., Boston, Mass.
TOMKIES, Douglas, Cpl., 1638 Weinstock St., Shreveport, La.
TURNER, Thomas W., Cpl., 1261 Hinkley St., Detroit, Mich.
WALES, Louis W., Cpl., 73 West 128th St., New York, N. Y.
WALKER, John E., Cpl., 14 Beaver St., Ansonia, Conn.
WHEATON, Fred, Cpl., 920 N. Seventh St., Fredonia, Ky.

FOURTH ROW:
WILLIAMS, Albert, Cpl.
WILLIAMS, Albert, Cpl.
WILLIAMS, Leonard, Cpl.
WILLIAMS, Richard S., Cpl., 178 West Springfield St., Boston, Mass.
WILLIS, Samuel C., Cpl., 16 Irbing St., Wilson, Conn.
WRIGHT, A. V., Cpl., 5 Nelson Ave., Peekskill, N. Y.

FIFTH ROW:
YOUNG, John W., Cpl., 447 Park Ave., Clairton, Pa.
BAKER, Thomas, Pfc., Rt. I, Box 249, Arlington, Tenn.
BAXTER, Charles H., Pfc., Cerro Gordo, N. C.
BREWSTER, Walter A., Pfc., 51 Grove St., Hempstead, N. Y.
COLSTON, Fred, Pfc., Salisbury, N. C.
DUNLAP, Frank M., Pfc., 4461 Page Blvd., St. Louis, Mo.

SIXTH ROW:
FOSTER, Wilfred B., Pfc., 543 Medburry St., Detroit, Mich.
GROSS, Kenneth R., Pfc., 45 Olney St., Providence, R. I.
HULL, James S., Pfc., 1214 S. 23rd St., Philadelphia, Pa.
JACKSON, Andrew L., Jr., Pfc., 150 Prospect St., Providence, R. I.
JACKSON, John E., Pfc., 2022 Second St., N.W., Washington, D. C.
JACKSON, John H., Pfc., 1747 W. 13th St., Chicago, Ill.

SEVENTH ROW:
MALLORY, W. R., Pfc., 613 16th St., N.E., Washington, D. C.
MAYFIELD, John, Pfc., J 143 Bainkridge St., Philadelphia, Pa.
McGILL, Simuel D., Pfc., 4806 South Parkway, Chicago, Ill.
McRAE, John D., Pfc., South Orange Ave., Newark, N. J.
OWENS, Frank R., Pfc., 1159 Fulton Ave., Bronx, N. Y.
PEN RICE, Desoto, Pfc., 1208 Andrews St., Houston, Tex.

EIGHTH ROW:
PINKNEY, Louis, Pfc., Baton Rouge, La.
SAULSBURY, Curtis, Pfc., 91 Henry St., New Haven, Conn.
SMITH, Arnold A., Pfc.
STARKS, John E., Pfc., 1472 E. 103rd St., Los Angeles, Calif.
THOMPSON, Joseph F., Pfc., 1011 Steffens, Cincinnati, Ohio.
THOMAS, Wray, Pfc., 1410 Gennessee St., Houston, Tex.

NINTH ROW:
WELLS, Rufus D., Pfc., 944 Marshall Ave., Norfolk, Va.
WILSON, C. F., Pfc., 1862 S. Millard Ave., Chicago, Ill.
WINSTON, Elmer N., Pfc., 3922 N. Smedley St., Philadelphia, Pa.
WOODS, Neely E., Pfc., 530 Peachtree St., Gaffney, S. C.
YOUNG, Leo J., Pfc., 1011 16th St., Bakersfield, Calif.
SOUTHALL, James S., Pvt., 1328 Locust St., McKeesport, Pa.

TENTH ROW:
THOMAS, Gilbert, Pvt., Rt. 2, Box 124, Opelousas, La.
TODD, James E., Pvt., 801 W. Bowery St., Akron, Ohio.
BETHEL, Henry W., 205 Washington Dr., Miami, Fla.
KIRBY, Elmer D., 2641 Sherman St., Detroit, Mich.

99TH FIGHTER SQUADRON

WILLIAM A. CAMPBELL
Major
Commanding

CHARLES W. BROOKS, II
Captain
Flight Surgeon

MORRIS T. JOHNSON
Captain
Executive Officer

EDWARD L. TOPPINS
Captain
Senior Flight Leader

DUDLEY M. WATSON
Captain
Pilot

JOHN F. BRIGGS
First Lieutenant
Flight Leader

CHARLES W. DRYDEN
First Lieutenant
Assistant Operations Officer

WILLIAM W. GREEN
First Lieutenant
Flight Leader

WELDON K. GROVES
First Lieutenant
Flight Leader

JAMES J. JOHNS
First Lieutenant
Adjutant

FELIX J. KIRKPATRICK
First Lieutenant
Pilot

SPANN WATSON
First Lieutenant
Operations Officer

JAMES B. WILLIAMS
First Lieutenant
Engineering Officer

HALBERT L. ALEXANDER
Second Lieutenant
Pilot

ISHAM A. BURNS
Second Lieutenant
Pilot

McWHEELER CAMPBELL
Second Lieutenant
Pilot

EDWARD D. DORAM
Second Lieutenant
Wingman

THOMAS GLADDEN
Second Lieutenant
Pilot

ROBERT L. HARLLEE
Second Lieutenant
Intelligence Officer

JAMES E. HARRIS
Second Lieutenant
Pilot

RICHARD H. HARRIS, JR.
Second Lieutenant
Personal Equipment Officer

JAMES H. HARVEY
Second Lieutenant
Pilot

HENRY A. HUNTER
Second Lieutenant
Pilot

GARFIELD L. JENKINS
Second Lieutenant
Pilot

ALVIN J. JOHNSON
Second Lieutenant
Pilot

ANDREW JOHNSON
Second Lieutenant
Pilot

WILBERT H. JOHN
Second Lieutena
Assistant Maintena
Officer

LOUIS W. JOHNSON
Second Lieutenant
Pilot

THEODORE W. LANCASTER
Second Lieutenant
Pilot

CHARLES E. MILLER
Second Lieutenant
Pilot

JOE H. MILLETT
Second Lieutenant
Pilot

CHARLES P. MYERS
Second Lieutenant
Pilot

LINCOLN W. NELSON
Second Lieutenant
Pilot

FREDERICK D. PENDLETON
Second Lieutenant
Pilot

RICHARD G. STEVENS
Second Lieutenant
Pilot

CHARLES L. STOVALL
Second Lieutenant
Pilot

EUGENE G. THEODORE
Second Lieutenant
Pilot

ALLEN H. TURNER
Second Lieutenant
Pilot

LEONARD O. VAUGHN
Second Lieutenant
Pilot

WILLIAM M. WASHINGTON
Second Lieutenant
Pilot

JOHN J. BELL
Flight Officer
Pilot

LEROY BRYANT, JR.
Flight Officer
Pilot

JULIUS W. CALLOWAY
Flight Officer
Pilot

TAMEMUND DICKERSON, JR.
Flight Officer
Pilot

JAMES W. GREER
Flight Officer
Pilot

EUGENE L. GUYTON
Flight Officer
Pilot

VERNON HOPSON
Flight Officer
Pilot

EDWARD E. MANLEY
Flight Officer
Pilot

CALVIN G. MORET
Flight Officer
Pilot

MELVIN PARKER
Flight Officer
Pilot

REGINALD C. WADDELL, JR.
Flight Officer
Pilot

JAMES W. WARREN
Flight Officer
Pilot

99TH FIGHTER SQUADRON

★

FIRST ROW:

HENDERSON, Samuel W., 1/Sgt., 251 West 111th St., New York, N. Y.
ARCHER, Fred, M/Sgt., 32-41 108th St., Corona, N. Y.
DAWSON, Upsher, T/Sgt., 2911 E. 75th St., Cleveland, Ohio.
HILL, Franklin A., T/Sgt., Los Angeles, Calif.
MAHAN, Clifton W., T/Sgt., 5812 24th St., Detroit, Mich.

SECOND ROW:

BERRY, Harold E., S/Sgt., General Delivery, Fort Gibson, Okla.
BOWLES, Joseph H., S/Sgt., 1542 Lenn St., Cincinnati, Ohio.
BROWN, Sampson, S/Sgt., 1712 Brushton Ave., Pittsburgh, Pa.
CAPITI, J. K., S/Sgt., 1301 Laguna Ave., San Francisco, Calif.
CHANCE, Wallace H., S/Sgt., 492 North Fourth St., Newark, N. J.

THIRD ROW:

CONES, Robert A., S/Sgt., 254 Monroe St., Brooklyn, N. Y.
DOUGLAS, Virgil, S/Sgt., 924 Elm St., Quincy, Ill.
FIELDS, Andrew, Jr., S/Sgt., 7 Sorrell St., Asheville, N. C.
FOSTER, Patrick, S/Sgt., 809 N. Sixth St., Richmond, Va.
GRIFFITH, Otha E., S/Sgt., 67 Macombs Pl., New York, N. Y.

99TH FIGHTER SQUADRON

W:

Thomas L., S/Sgt., 2732-A Market St., St. Louis,

ON, George W., S/Sgt., 1042 Blackadore Ave.,
burgh, Pa.

, William M., S/Sgt., 774 N. Webb Ave., Al-
Ohio.

JENNINGS, Everrod T., S/Sgt., 6110 St. Lawrence Ave.,
Chicago, Ill.

MERRICK, Henry, Jr., S/Sgt., 1206 Turreganno St., Pal-
metto, La.

POWELL, William J., Jr., S/Sgt 6014 Michigan Ave.,
Chicago, Ill.

SECOND ROW:

SAUNDERS, Harris S., S/Sgt., 261 West 116th St., New
York, N. Y.

TERRELL, Hollis B., S/Sgt., Jones Store P. O., Spot-
sylvania Co., Va.

THOMAS, Christopher A., S/Sgt., Box 155, Lundale, W.
Va.

TUTT, Benjamin W., S/Sgt., 4338 Page Blvd., St. Louis,
Mo.

ABBOTT, Amos, Sgt., 500 Pyramid Court, Cairo, Ill.

ALEXANDER, Joseph, Sgt., 629 E. 50th St., Los Angeles, Calif.

THIRD ROW:

ANTHONY, Ernest W., Sgt., 201 Prospect Ave., Asbury
Park, N. J.

BAILEY, George O., Sgt., Pence Springs, W. Va.

BOYKIN, James E., Sgt., 2044½ N.W. Sixth Ct., Miami,
Fla.

BREEDLOVE, Charlie B., Sgt., 420 N. Hardford, Tulsa,
Okla.

CHAMBERS, Jesse, Sgt., 118 Binford, Ogden, Utah.

CLAYTON, George F., Sgt., 87 Bartram Ave., Lansdowne, Pa.

FOURTH ROW:

COFFEE, Bertrand W., Sgt., Rt. 2, Box 62, Frankfort,
Kan.

ELLIS, William R., Sgt., Springfield, Ohio.

FERRELL, Arthur, Sgt., 1390 Boston Rd., Bronx, N. Y.

FLORIDA, Perry, Sgt., Rt. 2, Hughes Spring, Tex.

FLETCHER, Nathan P., Jr., Sgt., 430 East Eighth St.,
Rushville, Ind.

GARRETT, Thirkield, Sgt., 6141 Indiana Ave., Chicago,
Ill.

FIFTH ROW:

GOODWIN, Charles H., Sgt., 148 Patchen Ave., Brooklyn, N. Y.

GREEN, Irving A., Sgt., 834 Vance St., Toledo, Ohio.

GRIFFIN, Lovell, Sgt., 5431 Owasco St., Cincinnati,
Ohio.

HALL, William F., Sgt., 132 N.S. Carolina Ave., Atlantic City, N. J.

HAYNES, Relfus J. Jr., Sgt., 10 Heminway Ave., New
Rochelle, N. Y.

HUCKABEE, James E., Sgt., 711 E. 50th St., Chicago,
Ill.

SIXTH ROW:

JOHNSON, James A., Sgt., P. O. Box 1377, Vanderbilt,
Pa.

KIMBROUGH, Ollie T., Sgt., 2101 Prospect Ave., Kansas City, Mo.

KINE, Moses L., Sgt., 3598 E. 143rd St., Cleveland,
Ohio.

LANE, Lowell H., Sgt., 40 West 136th St., New York,
N. Y..

LAWRENCE, Robert M., Jr., Sgt., 705 Second St., Warren, Ohio.

MASTERSON, Ralph H., Sgt., 2646 Lafayette St., Denver, Colo.

SEVENTH ROW:

McLEAN, Davis, Sgt., 6222 Desmond St., Cincinnati,
Ohio.

MEADE, Russell D., Sgt., 1704 Stockton St., Richmond,
Va.

POWELL, Robert M., Sgt., 535 Bergen St., Newark, N. J.

PRATOR, Julius N., Sgt., 283 W. 118th St., New York,
N. Y.

ROLLINS, Philip J., Sgt., Hustle, Va.

STEPHENS, Carl F., Sgt., 2219 E. 37th St., Cleveland,
Ohio.

EIGHTH ROW:

THOMAS, John W., Sgt., 3481 Howard Ave., Pennsau-
ken, N. J.

THOMPSON, Elmer, Sgt., Churchton, Md.

WARREN, Joseph F., Sgt., 5850 S. Michigan Ave., Chicago, Ill.

WESTON, Frederick L., Sgt., 845 Iglehartan, Saint Paul,
Minn.

WILLIAMS, Felix A., Sgt., P. O. Box 402, Winter Haven,
Fla.

WILLIAMS, Leroy E., Sgt., Rt. 1, Salem, N. J.

NINTH ROW:

WILSON, Roy, Sgt.

WINFREE, Saunders, Sgt.

YOUNG, William C., Sgt., Amonate, Va.

ABRAMS, Larry C., Cpl., 1707 Chicon St., Austin, Tex.

ALFRED, Edward R., Cpl., 3515 S. Kemper Dr., Arlington, Va.

BAGLEY, Samuel E., Cpl., 24 Montgomery Pl., Trenton,
N. J.

TENTH ROW:

BAKER, Clyde L., Cpl., 312-E Thompson St., Vidalia,
Ga.

Baker, Paul, Cpl., 121 Oakwood Pl., Orange, N. J.

BARBER, Chalmers, Cpl., 2903 Penn. Ave., Pittsburgh,
Pa.

BAYNES, Lucione, Cpl., 10 Heminway Ave., New Rochelle, N. Y.

BELL, Cleveland, Cpl., Box 2, Rt. 256., Tyler, Tex.

BILLUPS, Joseph, Cpl., 291 Winder St., Detroit, Mich.

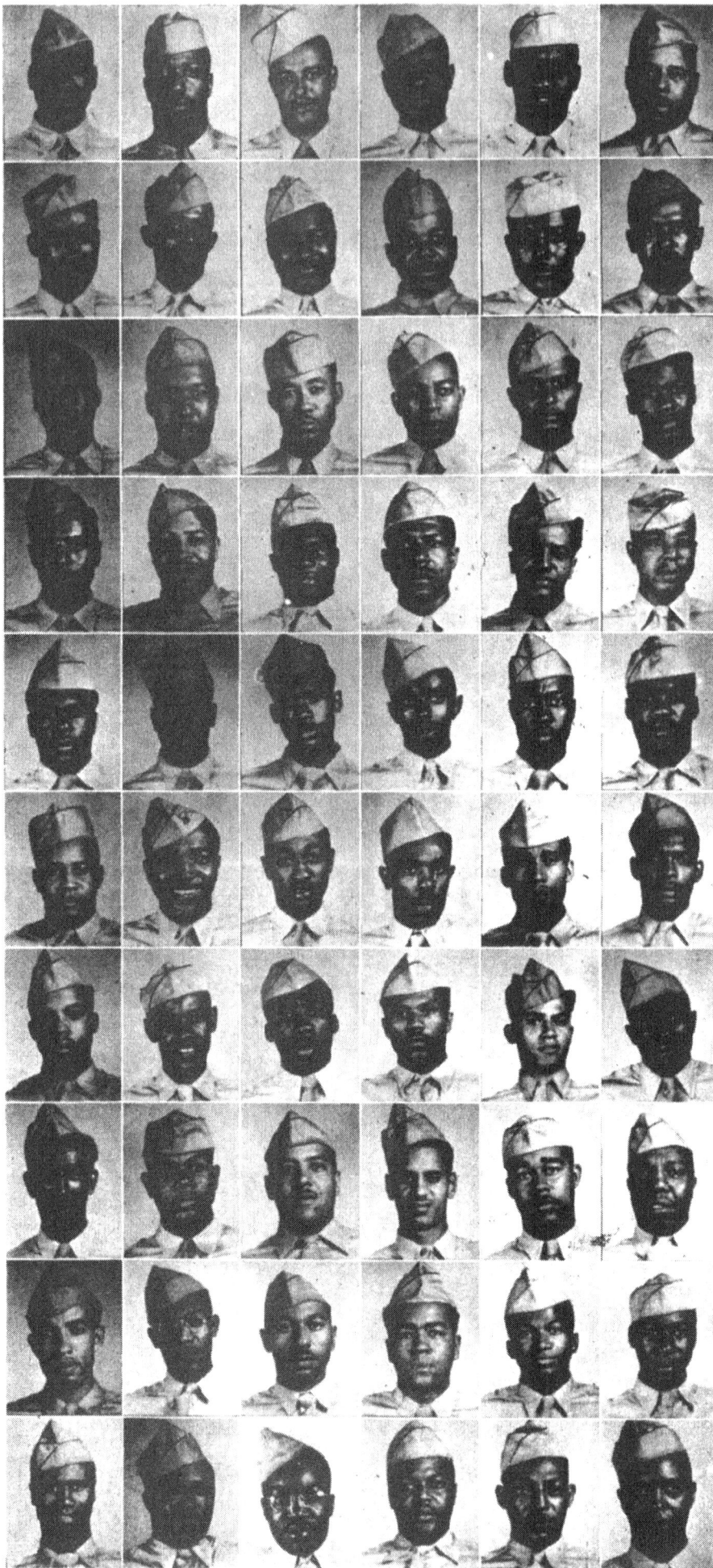

99TH FIGHTER SQUADRON

FIRST ROW:

BIRCH, A., Cpl., 63 Washington Terr., Cincinnati.
BROOKS, Wyoming, Cpl., 3251 108th St., Corona.
CARTER, Isaac, Cpl., 3209 Rhode Ave., Chicago.
CARTER, Jeru, Cpl., 2123 W. Nassau St., Phila.,
Pa.
CARUTHERS, Marion, Cpl., 310 Everett Ave., Kansas
City, Kan.
CHILDS, Thomas L., Cpl., 309 Maple Ave., Frankfort,
Ky.

SECOND ROW:

COLEMAN, Lemroy, Cpl., 27 Jones Bridge Rd., Chevy
Chase, Md.
COUCH, James C., Jr., Cpl., 1101 W. Second, Dayton,
Ohio.
DAVIS, Cornelius, Cpl., 6382 28th St., Detroit, Mich.
DIGGS, Homer C., Jr., Cpl., 2055 Prospect, Kansas
City, Mo.
FAISON, Fred, Cpl., 113 E. Hillsboro St., Mt. Olive,
N. C.
FLOWERS, Fletcher W., Cpl., 936 E. Ferry, Detroit,
Mich.

THIRD ROW:

FREEMAN, Harold L., Cpl., 5062 23rd St., Detroit,
Mich.
FUBLER, Arthur D., Cpl., 356 So. Seventh Ave., Mt.
Vernon, N. Y.
GAUER, John A., Cpl., 1505 Jefferson St., Buffalo,
N. Y.
GIPSON, Edward H., Cpl., 1502 N. Nevidro St., San
Antonio, Tex.
HAINES, Robert J., Cpl., 82 Winthrop Ave., New Ro-
chelle, N. Y.
HAMMOND, RUFUS F., Cpl., 4265 Cote Brilliante Ave.,
St. Louis, Mo.

FOURTH ROW:

HARRIS, Berry L., Cpl., 74 St. Felix St., Brooklyn, N. Y.
HENDERSON, Raymond, Cpl., 17 West 125th St., New
York, N. Y.
HENRY, Lewis, Cpl.
HILLEN, Leo E., Cpl., 707 W. Lanvale St., Baltimore,
Md.
HOLMES, Joseph W., Cpl., 1446 Madison St., Detroit,
Mich.
HOLMES, Zimri S., Cpl., Box 47, Cambria, Va.

FIFTH ROW:

JACKSON, Louis W., Cpl., 4409 Enright Ave., St. Louis,
Mo.
JAMES, Wilbur, Cpl., 79 East 119th St., New York,
N. Y.
JANUARY, Gilbert, Cpl.
JARRELL, Emanuel, Cpl., 2729 Desier St., New Orleans,
La.
JEFFERS, Glendower, Cpl., 132 Macon St., Brooklyn,
N. Y.
JENKINS, S. J., Cpl., 3428 Indiana Ave., Chicago, Ill.

SIXTH ROW:

KELLY, Grady, Cpl., 511 Revis St., LaGrange, Ga.
KENNEDY, John, Cpl., 1926 Lincoln Way, McKeesport,
Pa.
LARUE, Robert L., Cpl., 543 Douglas St., Indianapolis,
Ind.
LOGAN, Murry L., Cpl., 1220 So. 134th St., Baton
Rouge, La.
MASSEY, Wilbur E., Cpl., 1336 East 23rd St., Los Ange-
les, Calif.
McDANIELS, John C., Cpl., 211 West 146th St., Apt.
26, New York, N. Y.

SEVENTH ROW:

McDOWELL, Harry, Cpl., 6030 Brush St., Apt. 2, De-
troit, Mich.
MILLER, Hurlie C., Cpl., 387 Herkimer St., Brooklyn,
N. Y.
MOORE, Robert L., Cpl., P. O. Box 147, Hobart, Okla.
NOEL, James H., Cpl., Rt. 1, Westville, Ill.
NORMAN, Thurman T., Cpl., 936 Stebbins Ave., Bronx,
N. Y.
POPE, Nathan D., Cpl., Chattanooga, Tenn.

EIGHTH ROW:

POSEY, Raymond A., Cpl., 39 24th St., S.W., Barberton,
Ohio.
RAGLAND, M. David, Cpl., 7203 Milnor St., Philadel-
phia, Pa.
ROBERTSON, Leroy C., Cpl., 147 William St., Engle-
wood, N. J.
ROBINSON, Charles T., Cpl., P. O. Box 163, Kimball,
W. Va.
ROBINSON, Melvin A., Cpl., 314 Burrows St., Pitts-
burgh, Pa.
ROGERS, Hervey E., Cpl., 1582 East 23rd St., Los Ange-
les, Calif.

NINTH ROW:

SAUNDERS, Lionel C., Cpl., 218 Jefferson Ave., Brook-
lyn, N. Y.
SHAW, Harvey B., Cpl., 537 No. View St., Aurora, Ill.
SMITH, Fitz Herbert, Jr., Cpl., 63 Halsey St., Brook-
lyn, N. Y.
SMITH, Leonard T., Cpl., 3415-A Cook Ave., St. Louis,
Mo.
STANCIL, Thomas E., Cpl., 1613 Kramer St., N.E., Wash-
ington, D. C.
STEWART, Ralph B., Cpl., 3741 Indiana Ave., Chicago,
Ill.

TENTH ROW:

TAYLOR, Abram, Cpl., 1534 Linn St., Cincinnati, Ohio.
THOMPSON, Charles H., Cpl., 81 Burnet St., New
Brunswick, N. J.
TRAVERS, Clifton A., Cpl., 715-A N. Third St., Rich-
mond, Va.
WADLEY, E., Cpl., 628 Market, Richmond, Calif.
WARNER, Thomas H., Cpl., Box 72, Goldsboro, Md.
WEBBER, P. A., Cpl., 233 E. Maple Ave., Monrovia,
Calif.

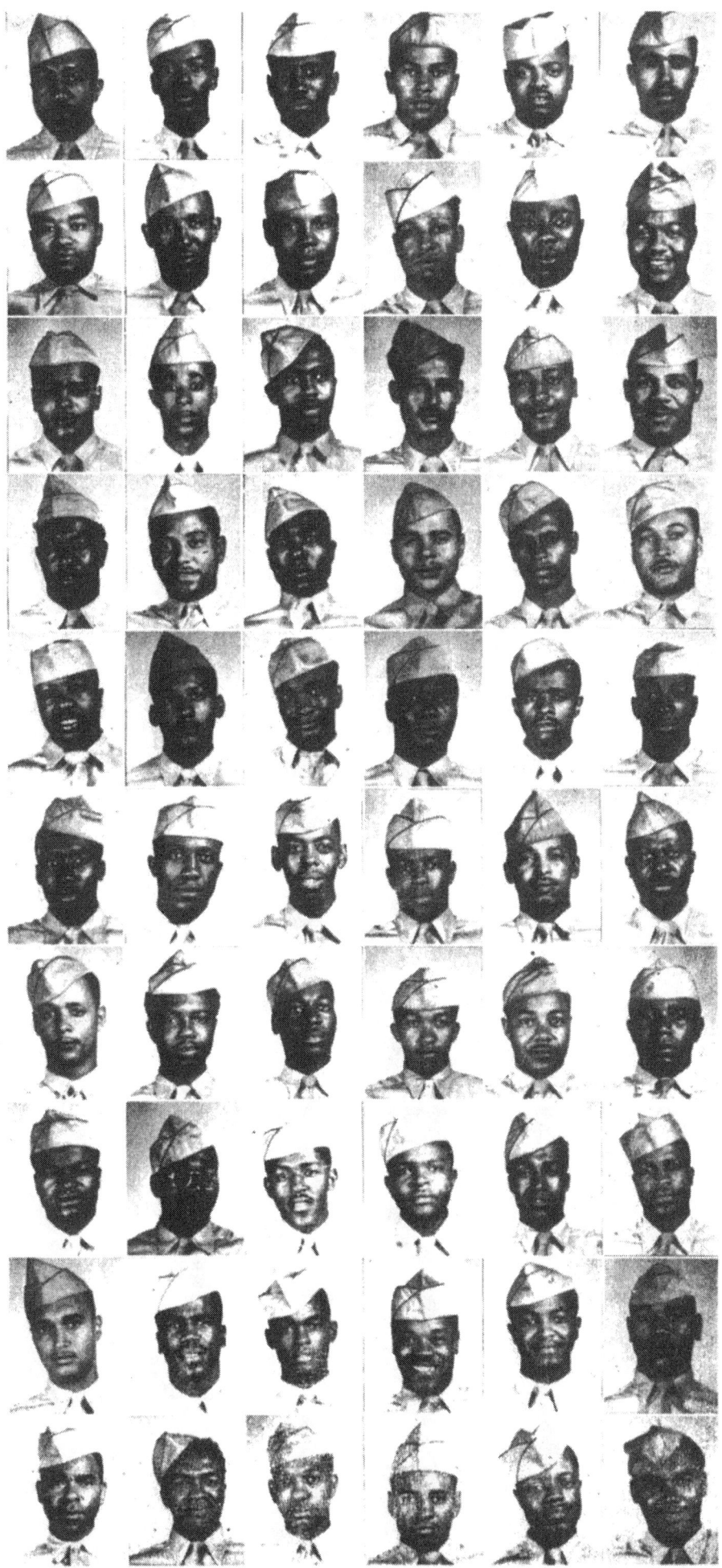

99TH FIGHTER
SQUADRON

FIRST ROW:
WELLS, Howard — 11 N. Ninth St., Philadelphia, Pa.
ALEXANDER, Ed— 1607 E. 27th St., Los Angeles, Calif.
BAILEY, Edward — 22 13th St., N.W., No. 1, Washington, D.
BA—— arry — 329 East Market St., Lebanon,
B—— obert, Pfc., — Stone St., Montgomery, Ala.
—— D., Raymond —. Pfc., 614 Leicester Ct., Detroit, Mich.

SECOND ROW:
—HOP, Louis, Pfc., 2328 Maypole Ave., Chicago, Ill.
BODDY, Homer H., Pfc., 618 Concord St., Havre De Grace, Md.
BRANCH, Rufus T., Pfc., 912 First St., S.W., Washington, D. C.
BREEDEN, Dock C., Pfc., 504 Lenox Ave., New York, N. Y.
BROOKS, Daniel, Pfc., Buffalo, N. Y.
BROWN, James, Pfc., 3005 Monfurt St., Cincinnati, Ohio.

THIRD ROW:
BURROUGHS, James, Pfc., 14 Jefferson St., Hot Springs, Ark.
BUTLER, Harold E., Pfc., 1064 N. Newstead, St. Louis, Mo.
BYRD, Edward L., Pfc., 2918 Southland Ave., Baltimore, Md.
CALDWELL, William, Pfc., 427 Hammond St., Kosciusko, Miss.
CALDWELL, Willie, Pfc., 15601 Elberta Ave., Cleveland, Ohio.
CHRISTIAN, Rudy, Pfc., 78 East 127th St., New York, N. Y.

FOURTH ROW:
COSEY, Joe, Pfc., 513 Cedar St., Chattanooga, Tenn.
DATCHER, Robert J., Pfc., 417 "A" St., N.E., Washington, D. C.
DAVIS, Ernest, Pfc., 1919 Melpomena St., New Orleans, La.
FENWICK, Raymond G., Pfc., 319 10th St., S.E., Washington, D. C.
FIELDS, Warner, Pfc., 539 Findlay St., Cincinnati, Ohio.
GILLON, Howard, Pfc., 9132 Cardon St., Detroit, Mich.

FIFTH ROW:
HAMMOND, Raymond, Pfc., 13 Clay St., Princeton, N. J.
HAYES, Primas, Pfc., 3379 E. Alabama St., Houston, Tex.
LITTLEJOHN, Cornelius, Pfc., 11 Horton St., Pittsburgh, Pa.
MADISON, Dee C., Pfc., 1204 Bob Harrison St., Austin, Tex.
MADISON, Otis H., Pfc., 14 Stewart St., Covington, Ky.
MAYE, Elisah, Pfc., 924 Fleming St., Greenville, N. C.

SIXTH ROW:
MAYLES, Nathan G., Pfc., Rt. 1, Sharpsburg, Ohio.
MITCHELL, Matthew P., Pfc., 508 Cherry Ave., S.E., Canton, Ohio.
PARRIS, George A., Pfc., 191 Quincy St., Boston, Mass.
PHILLIPS, Isaac, Pfc., 412 N.W. Fourth St., Fort Lauderdale, Fla.
RAINES, John H., Pfc., 2702 Lake St., Kansas City, Kan.
SOWELL, Robert E., Pfc., 448 East Wisconsin, Russell, Kan.

SEVENTH ROW:
STEEN, Walker, Pfc., 311 E. Valley St., Spartanburg, S. C.
TIBBS, Howard A., Pfc., 665 E. Pershing St., Salem, Ohio.
WALKER, Carl, Pfc., Box 172, Marlin, Tex.
WALLER, James C., Pfc., 3704 Haverford Ave., Philadelphia, Pa.
WARFIELD, Ernest, Pfc., 2612 Georgia Ave., Washington, D. C.
WATKINS, Thomas S., Pfc., 506 Mary St., Atlanta, Ga.

EIGHTH ROW:
WEAVER, H. Willie, Pfc., 91 Lucy St., Atlanta, Ga.
WRIGHT, Freemann, Pfc., 31 Humboldt Ave., Roxbury, Mass.
BAILEY, Booker T., Pvt., 3800 Olive St., Philadelphia, Pa.
BOSTIE, Robert O., Pvt., 66 Eye St., N.E., Washington, D. C.
BRANCH, Roy, Pfc., 4429 Nth 44th Ct., Portland, Ore.
BROOKS, William, Pvt., 1420 Eighth St., Alexandria, La.

NINTH ROW:
BYRON, Cyril O., 281 West 119th St., New York, N. Y.
GARDNER, Joseph, Pvt., 529 Auburn Ave., Swedesboro, N. J.
GAUL, Sidney J., Pvt., 42 Olney St., Providence, R. I.
JOHNSTON, Perry S., Jr., 316 MacDonough St., Brooklyn, N. Y.
JONES, Edward T., Pvt., 15-E Palm Terr., Galveston, Tex.
LONG, Thomas, Pvt., 6217 So. Wabash Ave., Chicago, Ill.

TENTH ROW:
NOFFLET, Albert J., Pvt., 1538 Layman Pl., Bronx, N. Y.
OTTRIX, Johnny, Pvt., 2366 East 85th St., Cleveland, Ohio.
SELLMAN, Edward D., Pvt., 6520 Beechwood Ave., Detroit, Mich.
—————————————

GEORGE W. WEBB
Major
Commanding

LOTT S. CARTER
Captain
Plans and Training Officer

CLINTON C. CANADY
First Lieutenant
Dental Surgeon

JOHN L. S. HOLLOMAN, JR.
First Lieutenant
Surgeon

EDWIN M. JOHNSON
First Lieutenant
Communications Officer

ROBERT S. LOWERY
First Lieutenant
Adjutant

MARION MANN
First Lieutenant
Medical Administrative Officer

WILLIAM J. PARKS, JR.
First Lieutenant
Provost Marshal

EMMETT J. RICE
First Lieutenant
Statistical Officer

CHARLES O. SOUTHERN
First Lieutenant
Communications Officer

FREDERICK E. WHITE, JR.
First Lieutenant
Radio Officer

THERNELL R. ANDERSON
First Lieutenant
Transportation Officer

CLAUDE D. CLAPP
Second Lieutenant
Adjutant

ABISHIC CUNNINGHAM
First Lieutenant
Legal Officer

WILLIAM R. DASH
Second Lieutenant
Utilities and Construction
Officer

HERMAN A. JOHNSON
Second Lieutenant
Assistant Finance Officer

FRANCIS A. RAMSEUR
Second Lieutenant
Finance Officer

387TH HEADQUARTERS AND SERVICE SQUADRON

FIRST ROW:
LOMBARD, Russell J., M/Sgt., 1211 E. 11th St., Austin, Tex.
HILTON, Harold A., T/Sgt., 438 Pleasant St., Mononga-hela, Pa.
LEWIS, Donald T., T/Sgt., 6128 Prairie Ave., Chicago, Ill.
ROBINSON, Scrappie, T/Sgt.
BELL, David W., S/Sgt., 84 Walnut St., Framingham, Mass.
BRAXTON, Elijah, S/Sgt., 8 North St., Ambler, Pa.
SECOND ROW:
COLEMAN, Mitchell, Jr., S/Sgt., 345 Middle St., New Bedford, Mass.
DAVISON, Walter G., Jr.
DUNNING, Robert L., S/Sgt., P. O. Box 83, Van Buren, Ark.
EVANS, Cecil, S/Sgt., 2307 Elydia St., Kansas City, Mo.
HOLSTON, Hugh, S/Sgt., Chicago, Ill.
JANUARY, Joseph A., S/Sgt., 724 Pottawatomie St. Leavenworth, Kan.

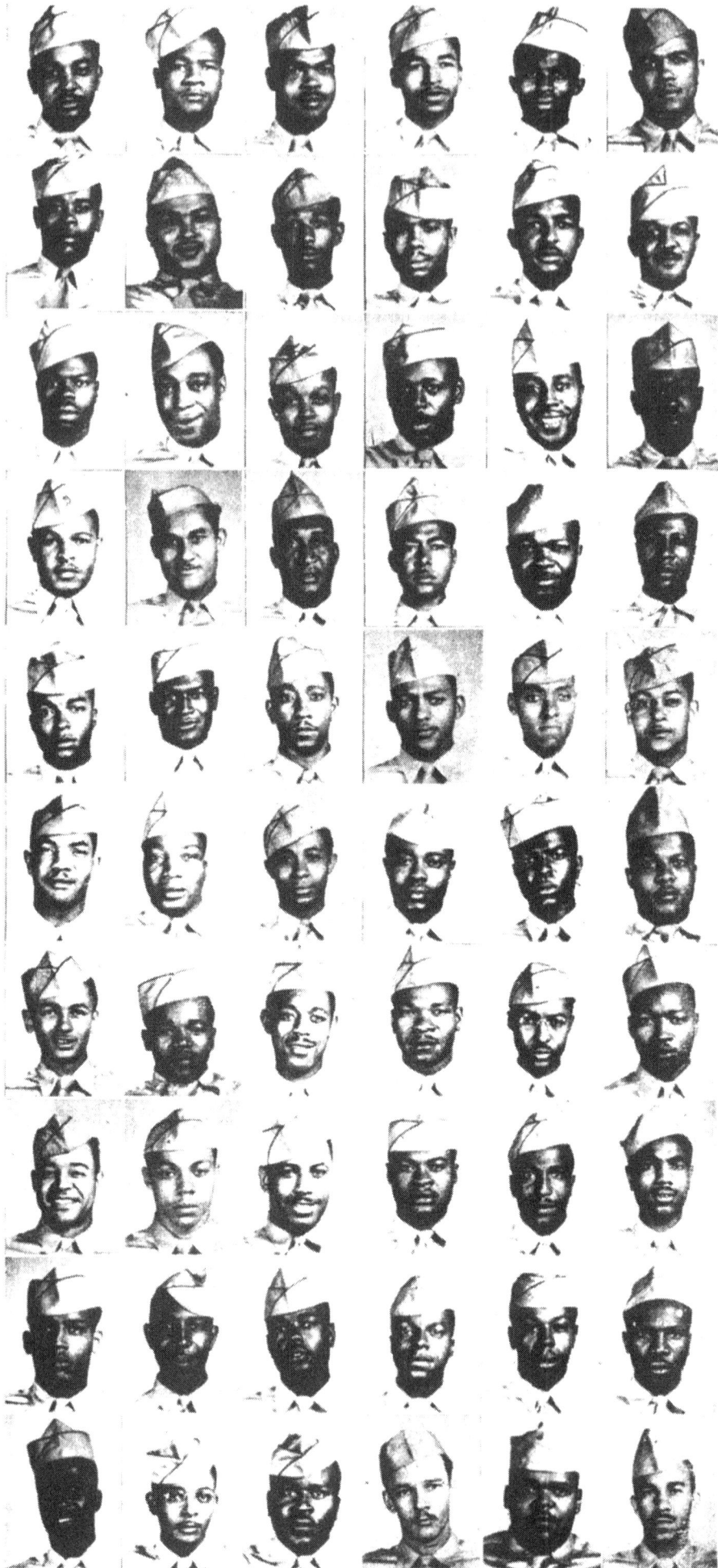

387TH HEADQUARTERS AND SERVICE SQUADRON

FIRST ROW:

ROBINSON, Edward A., S/Sgt., 850 East 49th Pl., Los Angeles, Calif.

SIMS, James R., S/Sgt., 1040 E. 21st St., Los Angeles, Calif.

WALKER, Melvin L., S/Sgt., Rt. 1 Trenton, N. J.

WALTON, John J., S/Sgt., 850 Stebbins Ave., Bronx, N. Y.

ARTIS, Isaac, Sgt., Bath, N. C.

BETHEL, Beverly V., Sgt., 45 Ripley Ave., Covington, Tenn.

SECOND ROW:

GRAY, Artil, Sgt., 1125 E. Summit St., Alliance, Ohio.

JONES, Lillard G., Sgt., 507 E. Sycamore St., Evansville, Ind.

MARTIN, Robert B., Sgt., 1327 N. Sarah St., St. Louis, Mo.

McDOWELL, Herman, Sgt., 1231 Desiard St., Monroe, La.

MILLER, Whitt Jr., Sgt., 124 Flavel St., Pittsburgh, Pa.

ORENDORFF, Alfred R., Sgt., 312 Ninth St., Lincoln, Ill.

THIRD ROW:

SNODGRASS, Harvey W., Sgt., 2257 Antietam St., Detroit, Mich.

WALKER, Benjamin M., Sgt., 521 So. Underhill St., Peoria, Ill.

WILSON, Manuel, Sgt., 2178 E. 79th St., Cleveland, Ohio.

ARMOUR, Jim, Cpl., Scots Dale, Ga.

AXAM, Frederick, Cpl., 407 King St., Beaufort, S. C.

BANKS, Hobart M., Cpl., 719 S. Seventh St., Muskogee, Okla.

FOURTH ROW:

BOUDREAUX, Alex A., Cpl., 1335 Webster St., San Francisco, Calif.

BOWERS, Edward I., Cpl., 220 Clyde St., Bakersfield, Calif.

BROWN, Floyd H., Cpl., 2349 Washington, Gary, Ind.

BROWN, M., Cpl., 217 Third St., Chillicothe, Mo.

BYRD, John L., Cpl., 4829 Fairmount Ave., Philadelphia, Pa.

CARD, Edward J., Cpl., 1006 Adams St., Knoxville, Tenn.

FIFTH ROW:

CHRISTIAN, Houston, Cpl., P. O. Box 132, Rockford, Ala.

DARWIN, Leroy, Cpl., 2511 N. Quincy, Tulsa, Okla.

DOWDY, Clayton, Cpl., 474 West 158th St., Apt. 34, New York, N. Y.

DRISDALE, Edward O., Cpl., 2831 Park St., Berkeley, Calif.

DURANT, John H., Cpl., 106 West Bond St., Marion, S. C.

ELLINGTON, Chas. S., Cpl., 1915 Harrison, Topeka, Kan.

SIXTH ROW:

FIELDS, Clyde E., Cpl., 202 Ashwood Pl., Orange, N. J.

FINLEY, Bossie, Cpl., 2816 Avenue G., Galveston, Tex.

FLOWERS, William P., Cpl., Rt. 1, Honey Brook, Pa.

GIST, Fred, Cpl., 837 N. 13th St., Philadelphia, Pa.

GREEN, Dee W., Cpl., Rt. 1, Box 205, Tylertown, Miss.

HANKERSON, Earl, Cpl., 704 Park Drive, Daytona Beach, Fla.

SEVENTH ROW:

HARRIS, Vernon J., Jr., Cpl., 1105 N. 29th St., Richmond, Va.

HARRISON, Edward L., Sr., Cpl., 3 Township Line, Penllyn, Pa.

HOUSE, James L., Cpl., 243 N. Arlington Ave., Baltimore, Md.

HUBBARD, Jessie D., Cpl., 1801 Hall St., Dallas, Tex.

HUNTER, Hensen F., Cpl., 5206 25th St., Detroit, Mich.

JACOBS, Fairfax C., Cpl., 2673 Pine St., Apt. 1, San Francisco, Calif.

EIGHTH ROW:

JAMES, Joe, Cpl., 202 New St., Greenville, N. C.

JAMIESON, W. Z., Cpl., 6392 Hartford Ave., Detroit, Mich.

JENNINGS, Louis J., Cpl., 61 Nunan St., Charleston, S. C.

JOHNSON, J. C., Cpl., 3124 Refugio St., Ft. Worth, Tex.

JONES, John L., Cpl., 216 W. 133rd St., New York, N. Y.

JONES, Charles E., Cpl., Rt. 1, Frankfort, Ohio.

NINTH ROW:

JONES, Wilberforce C., Cpl., 1011 Villa Pl., Nashville, Tenn.

LAIRD, Lace H., Cpl., 4514 McKinley St., Detroit, Mich.

LEWIS, Edwin B., Cpl., 2209 Davis, Houston, Tex.

LIDDELL, Leon D., Cpl., 1503 Cruft Ave., Terre Haute, Ind.

LINTON, Harry, Cpl., 68 So. Second St., Elizabeth, N. J.

MACE, William O., Cpl., 1315 N. Warnock St., Philadelphia, Pa.

TENTH ROW:

MACKEY, Joseph J., Cpl., 6529 N. U. 13 Pl., Miami, Fla.

MEDLEY, Henry I., Cpl., 8 McDonough St., Brooklyn, N. Y.

MINGO, Curley, Cpl.

PAIGE, Huey J., Cpl., 600 N. 19th St., Palatka, Fla.

SATTERFIELD, Joe, Cpl., Rt. 5, Box 35-A, Mt. Airy, N. C.

SMOTHERS, Henderson M., Jr., 4121 St. Aubin, Detroit, Mich.

387TH HEADQUARTERS AND SERVICE SQUADRON

FIRST ROW:

STARKEY, Jessie B., Cpl., 311 Longworth St., Cincinnati, Ohio.

STITH, James D., Cpl., Rt. 1, Box 25, Crewe, Va.

THOMPSON, William B., Cpl., 521 St. Nicholas Ave., Apt. 201, New York, N. Y.

WALKER, Winthrop, Cpl.

WELLS, Herman T., Cpl., 111 Lippitt St., Providence, R. I.

WHITE, James, Cpl., 1729 South St., Philadelphia, Pa.

SECOND ROW:

WILSON, Ernest, Cpl., 1034 Europe St., Baton Rouge, La.

WILSON, Michael R., Cpl., 1308 Pearl St., Sandusky, Ohio.

WILSON, Robert A., Cpl., 4066 Rookwood Ave., Indianapolis, Ind.

WILSON, William, Cpl., Fordoche, La.

WOODS, Joseph L., Cpl., Mars, Pa.

ASHLEY, Wiley L., Pfc.

THIRD ROW:

BARKER, Twiley W., Pfc., P. O. Box 99, Franklinton, La.

BLAIR, Robert E., Pfc., Rt. 1, Box 58, Angus, Tex.

BOLDEN, Eddie, Pfc., Rt. 1, Box 22, Fountain Inn, S. C.

BROWN, Harry H., Pfc., 63 Chauncey St., Brooklyn, N. Y.

COOK, John B. G., Pfc., Cape Charles, Va.

DAVIS, Clinton B., Pfc., 613 Hancock St., Brooklyn, N. Y.

FOURTH ROW:

DAVIS, I., Pfc., 146-42 106th Ave., Jamaica, N. Y.

DAVIS, Steve, Pfc., 1160 Eighth St., Oakland, Calif.

ELLIS, Albert W., Sr., Pfc., 2313 Soniat St., New Orleans, La.

ETLEN, James S., Pfc., 4111 Spring Garden St., Philadelphia, Pa.

FLETCHER, Phelix, Pfc., Brooksville, Fla.

GREEN, Charlie, Pfc., 1210 West St., Vicksburg, Miss.

FIFTH ROW:

HALL, Greeley W., Pfc., 520 E. 20th St., Little Rock, Ark.

HATTON, Melvin H., Pfc., 422 Canal St., S.E., Washington, D. C.

JOHNSON, Marvin A., Pfc., 3400 Lafayett Pl., Dallas, Tex.

JONES, Paul A., Pfc., 48 West 98th St., Apt. 4-E, New York, N. Y.

KERR, Herman J., Pfc., 642 N. Seventh St., Oxford, Miss.

LAWSON, Leon B., Pfc., 2620 E. Glenwood Dr., Philadelphia, Pa.

SIXTH ROW:

LILLY, Warren D., Pfc., 630 Richmond St., Painesville, Ohio.

MAYO, Joseph R., Pfc., 3766 Milford Ave., Detroit, Mich.

McCLAIN, John W., Pfc., 1015 Trinity Ave., Bronx, N. Y.

McKEE, Mizell, Pfc., 125 E. Division St., Biloxi, Miss.

MOODY, Allen, Pfc., 1109 South Wallcott, Chicago, Ill.

MORTON, Moses W., Pfc., 13 Third St., Winchester, Ky.

SEVENTH ROW:

OWENS, Frank J., Pfc., 1205 Walnut Ave., East St. Louis, Ill.

PULLIN, Rufus, Pfc., Hogansville, Ga.

ROSS, Robert L., Pfc., Rt. 4, York, S. C.

SAMPLE, Thomas L., Pfc., 153 Baldwin St., New Brunswick, N. J.

SMITH, Zephro, Pfc., 417 42nd Pl., Chicago, Ill.

WALLACE, Archie L., Pfc., 608 Cedar St., Beaufort, N. C.

EIGHTH ROW:

WILSON, Marvin, Pfc., 1814 28th Ave., Tuscaloosa, Ala.

ANDERSON, David W., Pvt., 1035 W. Jefferson St., Orlando, Fla.

BARKER, Francis, Pvt., 25 So. Terry St., Albany, N. Y.

BLAKLEY, John, Pvt.

CAMPBELL, Walter E., Pvt., Rt. 1, Mullins, S. C.

DOYAL, Clarence O., Pvt., Lincoln Ct., Apt. 20, Paducah, Ky.

NINTH ROW:

HEYWARD, Nathaniel P., Pvt., 39 Elizabeth St., Charleston, S. C.

HILL, George V., Pvt., 438 Montea Ave., Woodbury, N. J.

JENKINS, Samuel J., Pvt., 64 East 129th St., New York, N. Y.

JOHNSON, Robert L., Pvt., Rt. 1, Box 146, Midland, Ga.

LOGAN, John O., Pvt., Rt. 1, Box 99, Uree, N. C.

TENTH ROW:

MILLER, Walter, Pvt., 832 Hampgreen St., Greenville, Miss.

MORBHEAD, Jeremiah, Pvt., Reedsville, N. C.

PENDLETON, Isaac H., Pvt.

ROBERTS, Robert, Pvt., 5858 Indiana Ave., Chicago, Ill.

ROY, Floyd O., Pvt., 27 Bedford St., E. Orange, N. J.

SMITH, James, Pvt., Edisto Island, S. C.

OMAR D. BLAIR
Captain
Commanding Officer

JESS W. AINSWORTH
First Lieutenant
Assistant Group Materiel
Officer

HENRY D. McCULLOUGH
First Lieutenant
Sq. Adj., Mess and Supply
Officer

ARTHUR B. POLITE
First Lieutenant
Post Signal P&J
Officer

VERNON V. RANDALL
First Lieutenant
Squadron Ordnance Officer

ROBERT K. SHOECR
First Lieutenant
Accountable Office

590TH MATERIEL SQUADRON

FIRST ROW:

WALKER, Edward J., 1/Sgt., 2215 Monroe St., Yazoo City. Miss.
NICKENS, Malvin, T/Sgt., 30 N. Yewdell St., Philadelphia, Pa.
HARGROVE, John S., S/Sgt., Tuscaloosa, Ala.
SMOOT, James S., S/Sgt., Madison, W. Va.
WEST, Floyd N., S/Sgt., 1108 N. Ninth St., Fort Smith, Ark.
BOHANNON, L. C., Sgt.

SECOND ROW:

GILBERT, Bertram R., Sgt., 2497 East 84th St., Cleveland, Ohio.
GRIMES, James W., Sgt., 71 Washington Courts, Utica, N. Y.
HILL, Leonard J., Sgt., 505 E. State, Enid, Okla.
HUNTER, Alvin F., Sgt., 1402 Short Bloir St., Jackson, Miss.
JONES, Howard, Sgt., 442 Gates Ave., Brooklyn, N. Y.
LEE, James D., Sgt., 3317 110th St., Corona, N. Y.

THIRD ROW:

MACKEY, William H., Sgt., 626 Rowe St., Dublin, Ga.
MARTIN, Frederick L., Sgt., 1149 N.W. First Pl., Miami, Fla.
McDAVIS, Joe, Sgt.
OVERTON, Leonard, Sgt., 465 Putnam Ave., Brooklyn, N. Y.
OWENS, Dwight L., Sgt., Eudora, Ark.
POE, Thomas E., Sgt., 1102 E. Jones St., Raleigh, N. C.

FOURTH ROW:

SLATER, Arthur J., Sgt., 141 Bartram Ave., Lansdowne, Pa.
THOMAS, Edward J., Sgt., 2220 12th St., N.W., Washington, D. C.
WATKINS, Claudius A., Sgt., 3002 Scovill Ave., Cleveland, Ohio.
BANKS, Junious T., Cpl., 105 Braxton Court, Williamsburg, Va.
BURNETT, Willie, Cpl., Prescott, Ark.
DRAPER, William C., Cpl., 34 Hayden Ave., Bryn Mawr, Pa.

FIFTH ROW:

EDWARDS, Marcus, Cpl., 135 Monroe St., Campbell, Ohio.
FESTUS, Chancetine W., Cpl., 238 N. Horton St., Philadelphia, Pa.
FREEMAN, Mac D., Cpl., 5 Chestnut St., Oil City, Pa.
GARRISON, Homer F., Cpl., 4113 Powelton Ave., Philadelphia, Pa.
GRAY, John F., Cpl., Big Sandy, W. Va.
JARVIS, Orville J., Cpl., Sutton, W. Va.

SIXTH ROW:

JOHNSON, James O., Cpl., 71 Henry St., Staten Island, N. Y.
LAWS, George A., Cpl., 128 S. Queen St., Dover, Del.
MARSHALL, Frederick C., Cpl., 516 Price St., Savannah, Ga.
McBRIDE, Leroy, Cpl.
McCABE, Wynne H., Cpl., 320 Broadway, Buffalo, N. Y.
McCLENDON, Robert, Jr., Cpl., 2919 Avenue "L", Galveston, Tex.

SEVENTH ROW:

MILES, Humphrey, Cpl., 60 Hancock St., Brooklyn, N. Y.
MISKEDINI, John, Cpl., Summit, Miss.
MONTGOMERY, Elige, Cpl.
PETTIFORD, Arthur W., Cpl., 401 Rondo St., St. Paul, Minn.

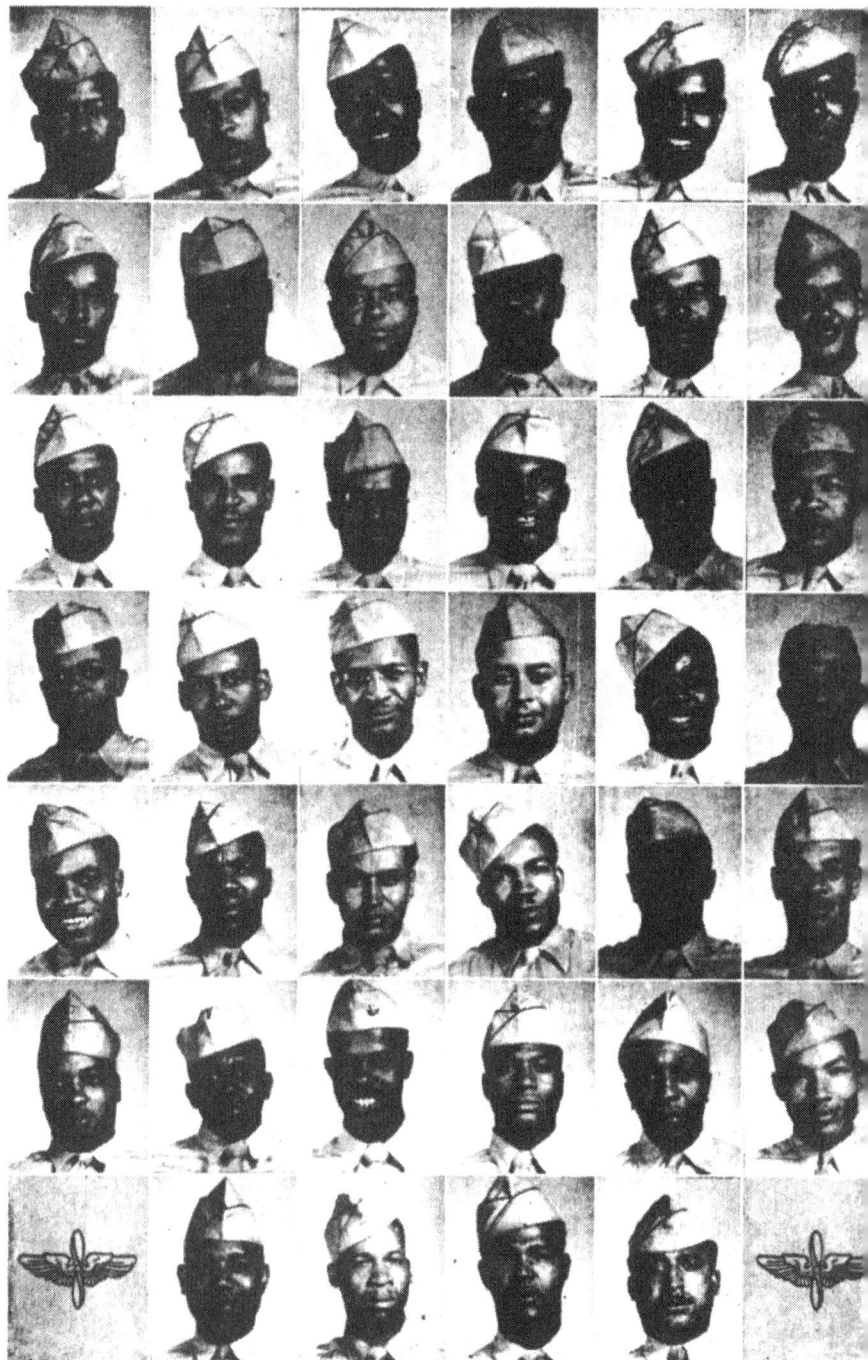

590TH MATERIEL SQUADRON

FIRST ROW:
PURIFIE, Jesse A., Cpl., 1033½ Oakdale Ave., Toledo, Ohio.
RANDOLPH, Harry N., Cpl., 88 Herzl St., Brooklyn, N. Y.
RICHARDSON, Simon R., Cpl., 610 Latimer Pl., Tulsa, Okla.
RILEY, Theodore R., Cpl., 547 W. 158th St., New York, N. Y.
SEALE, Samuel L., Cpl., 609 Second St., Birmingham, Ala.
SIMMONS, Clarence D., Cpl., 1812 W. Diamond St., Philadelphia, Pa.

SECOND ROW:
SMITH, Andrew, Cpl., 2224 Calliope St., New Orleans, La.
THOMAS, Love P., Cpl., 5450 S. State St., Chicago, Ill.
WILLIAMS, Samuel B., Cpl., 728 W. Walker St., Denison, Tex.
WILSON, Kenneth, Cpl., 6021 Calumet Ave., Chicago, Ill.
ADKISSON, Robert D., Pfc., 8 Murrell St., Nashville, Tenn.
BOYD, Thomas, Pfc., 1649 N. Wornock St., Philadelphia, Pa.

THIRD ROW:
CLINCY, Cleveland, Pfc., Flora, Miss.
CROSS, Otis W., Pfc., Renfroe, Ala.
CRUTCHFIELD, Edwin C., Pfc., 770 Coates St., Coatesville, Pa.
DENNIS, Elbert A., Pfc., 1704 Gratz St., Philadelphia, Pa.
DOZIER, Willie F., Pfc., 190 Merrittis Ave., Atlanta, Ga.
DUPREE, Neal, Pfc.

FOURTH ROW:
FAISON, John, Pfc., Brunswick, N. C.
FEATHERSON, Herbert L., Pfc., 414 N. Greenwood Ave., Winston-Salem, N. C.
FOSTER, Isiah, Pfc., Rt. B, Griffin, Ga.
FRANKLIN, Lonnie, Pfc., 820 E. 32½ St., Houston, Tex.
GARRED, Norman L., Pfc., 2641 Greenup Ave., Ashland, Ky.
GARY, Walter, Pfc., 2532 W. Dakota St., Philadelphia, Pa.

FIFTH ROW:
GREEN, Leslie, Pfc., 5336 Beaubier, Detroit, Mich.
HAWKINS, Ralph, Pfc., 622 Jasper, Baltimore, Md.
HENRY, Steve, Pfc., 149 E. Iowa Ave., Memphis, Tenn.
JEFFERIES, Zeman, Pfc., 796 S. Lugan St., Gaffney, S. C.
KELLY, Herbert, Pfc., 93 Jensen Dr., Houston, Tex.
LATHAN, Joseph A., Pfc., 384 Bellevue St., Hartford, Conn.

SIXTH ROW:
MILTON, Operice, Pfc., 3437 Prairie Ave., Chicago, Ill.
MINOR, Tommie, Pfc., Eighth Ave., Birmingham, Ala.
MITCHELL, Richard B., Pfc., 518 W. Pine St., Lexington, Ky.
MONTGOMERY, John A., Pfc., Menlo, Ga.
MURPHY, William E., Pfc., 33 West 128th St., New York, N. Y.
NELSON, Samuel, Pfc., Rt. I, Box 79, Summerton, S. C.

SEVENTH ROW:
NUNN, Willie, Pfc., 203 S. Ripple St., Samson, Ala.
PICKENS, Elias, Pfc., Bluefield, W. Va.
PREWITT, James C., Pfc., 476 High St., Memphis, Tenn.
RUTLEDGE, Jesse P., Pfc., 340 56th St., Fairfield Sta., Birmingham, Ala.
SHAVIS, Flanders, Pfc., 525 Glodis St., Los Angeles, Calif.
SHELTON, Bill, Pfc., 304 Ivanhoe St., Perry, Okla.

EIGHTH ROW:
SIMMONS, Otis, Pfc., Summerville, S. C.
SMITH, Earsley W., Pfc., 19 Sixth Ave., Birmingham, Ala.
SMITH, Maceo L., Pfc., 698 Larkin St., Apt. 473, Atlanta, Ga.
STALLINGS, T. J., Pfc., 351 Taylor St., Augusta, Ga.
TERRELL, Alex, Jr., Pfc., 1713 Eighth Ave., Birmingham, Ala.
THOMAS, Roosevelt, Pfc., 812 Manginal St., Port Gibson, Miss.

NINTH ROW:
WALL, Jasper C., Pfc., 1409 S. Galvez St., New Orleans, La.
WALLACE, Warren H., Pfc., 816 Scot St., Talladega, Ala.
WILSON, David R., Pfc., 1142 Mary St., Akron, Ohio.
BILLUPS, Printess S., Pfc., 2104 Dumaine St., New Orleans, La.
CASS, James N., Pfc., 4216 Brush St., Detroit, Mich.
DIXON, Marion, Pvt., 103 S. Griffen St., Florence, S. C.

TENTH ROW:
MOORE, John, Pvt., 314 E. Bellmont St., Pensacola, Fla.
THOMAS, Revo, Pvt., 352 W. 117th St. New York, N. Y.
WASHINGTON, Sheffield S., Pvt., 922 Evans St., Tallahassee, Fla.
WINLEY, Arthur C., Pvt., 28 Hawkin St., Georgetown, S. C.

251

JOHN H. WILLIAMS
Captain
Engineering Officer

ERBBIE L. CROOM
First Lieutenant
Adjutant

MATTHEW W. MERIWEATHER
First Lieutenant
Engineering Officer

MAURICE R. PAGE
First Lieutenant
Test Pilot

DUDLEY V. SIMMS
First Lieutenant
Communications Maintenance
Officer

ARTHUR L. WARD
First Lieutenant
Supply Officer

GASTON A. JOSEPH, JR.
Second Lieutenant
Motor Repair Officer

602ND AIR ENGINEERING SQUADRON

FIRST ROW:
DOUGHTY, Otis C., M/Sgt., 851 Napier Courts, Nashville, Tenn.
HANCOCK, McNeal, M/Sgt.
BLUE, Harold G., T/Sgt., 400-W 128th St., New York, N. Y.
BUTLER, Thomas A., T/Sgt., 1510 Teras St., Pine Bluff, Ark.
HUBERT, Alvin W., T/Sgt., 3018 Calhoun Ave., Houston, Tex.
SUMMERS, Joseph, T/Sgt., 315½ East Easton Ave., Tulsa, Okla.

SECOND ROW:
WILSON, Walter D., T/Sgt., 554 Decatur St., Brooklyn, N. Y.
AILSTER, J. W., S/Sgt., 2408 Greenup Ave., Ashland, Ky.
ALLEN, George T., S/Sgt., 301-W 150th St., New York, N. Y.
BLAND, A. J., S/Sgt., 1331 W. Clay St., Richmond, Va.
CHAFFIN, Walter H., S/Sgt.
CHARLES, Leonard, S/Sgt., 2105 Bell Ave., Houston, Tex.

THIRD ROW:
CLARK, Lonice L., S/Sgt., 3616 Ruskin St., Dallas, Tex.
CUTCHLOW, James S., S/Sgt., 1102 Lincoln Ave., Pasadena, Calif.
EDMONDSON, James H., S/Sgt., 914 Delaware, Coffeyville, Kan.
HEARD, Thomas L., S/Sgt., 485 Foundry St., Atlanta, Ga.
HILLIARD, Stratford S., S/Sgt.
McBRIDE, Evine, S/Sgt., 434 Liberty St., Jackson, Tenn.

FOURTH ROW:
REID, Victor D., S/Sgt., 36 Ado Place, Buffalo, N. Y.
SIMMONS, Arthur, S/Sgt., 474 Central Park West, New York, N. Y.
TAYLOR, Samuel, S/Sgt., 514 E. North, Charlestown, W. Va.
BRADLEY, James M., Sgt., 523 Seaton St., Ft. Worth, Tex.
BYOUS, Charles, Sgt., 9544 Cameron Ave., Detroit, Mich.
CALLOWAY, E. E., Sgt., 701 Third St., N.E., Washington, D. C.

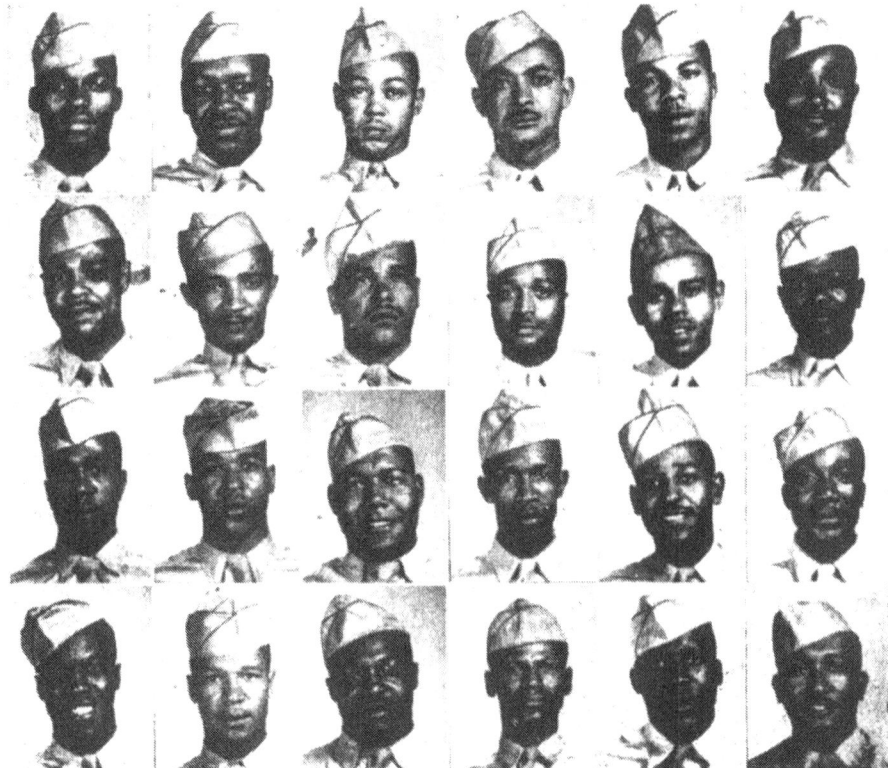

602ND AIR ENGINEERING SQUADRON

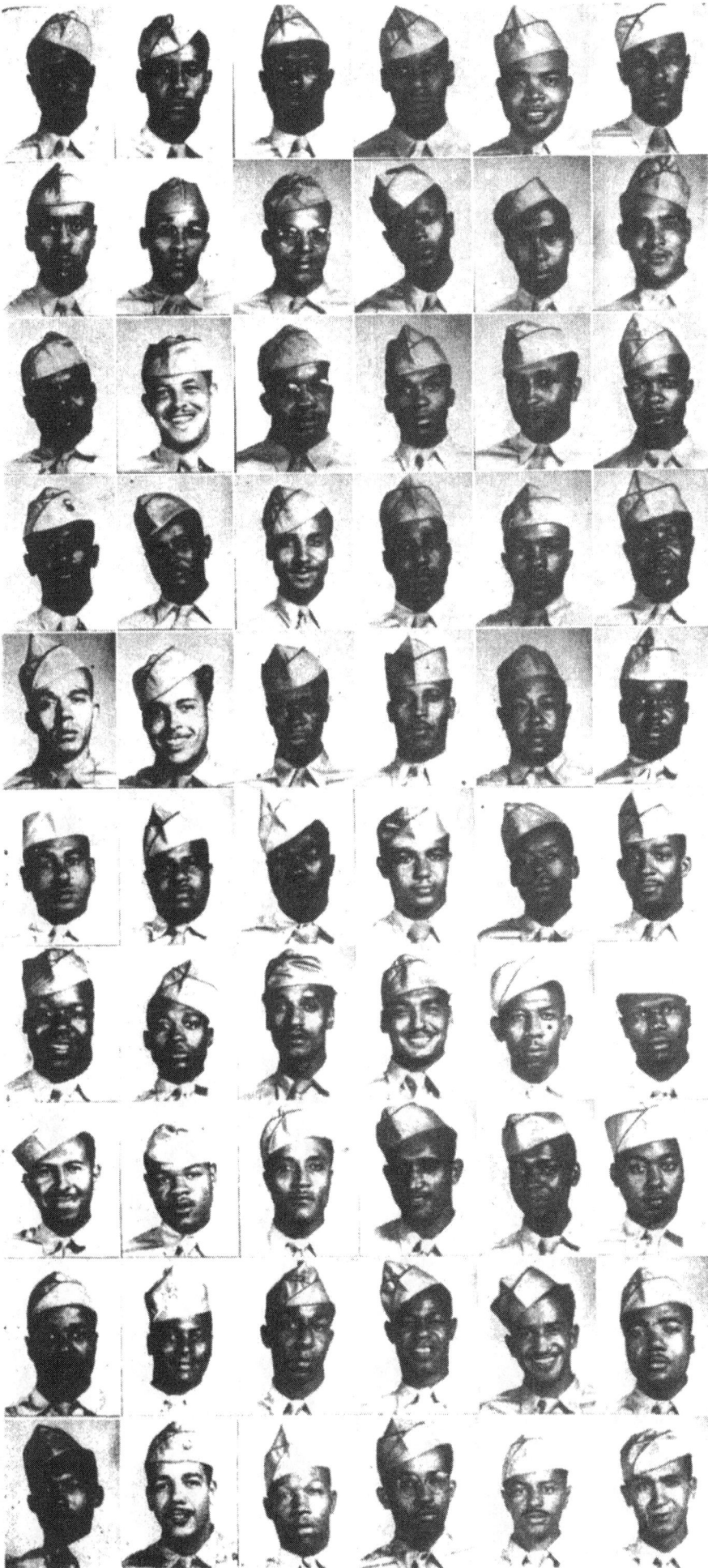

FIRST ROW:
CLARK, James R., Sgt., Wilkesburg, N. C.
CLAY, George W., Sgt., 600 William St., Paus, Ky.
DEAN, Charles A., Sgt., 2441 Seventh Ave., New York, N. Y.
FISHER, Robert J., Sgt., 4718 Forestville Ave., Chicago, Ill.
GARY, Frank, Jr., Sgt., 1805 Oak St., Columbia, S. C.
GOODMAN, Howard, Cpl., 120 Winter St., New Haven, Conn.

SECOND ROW:
HACKETT, Charles B., Sgt., 513 Herkimer St., Brooklyn, N. Y.
HOLITHCO, Wm. H., Sgt., 2275 Wilson, Saginaw, Mich.
HAMPTON, Clifford E., Sgt., 939 Dayton St., Cincinnati, Ohio.
JOHNSON, Albert, Jr., Sgt., 119 S. 27th St., Omaha, Neb.
KING, Clifford S., Sgt., 190 Prospect St., Johnstown, Pa.
KING, Henry, Sgt., 1467 Ninth Ave., Huntington, W. Va.

THIRD ROW:
MARKS, James M., Sgt., 1832 Chapel St., Norfolk, Va.
MOORE, Charles E., Sgt., 938 Butler St., Richmond, Ind.
NELSON, Johnnie F., Sgt., 2516 Thomas Ave., Dallas, Tex.
NESBITT, Morton C., Sgt., 1916 N. Camac St., Philadelphia, Pa.
OSBORNE, Edward K., Sgt., 1138 N. 14th St., Paducah, Ky.
PARKER, Jesse E., Sgt., 1498 W. 35th St., Los Angeles, Calif.

FOURTH ROW:
PATTERSON, Willie B., Sgt., 409 S. 19th St., East St. Louis, Ill.
RAY, John L., Sgt., 600 McWhorter St., Mineola, Tex.
ROBINSON, Douglass M., Sgt., 606 N. 57th St., Philadelphia, Pa.
SAMPSON, Charles M., Sgt., 7970 Richmond Ave., Detroit, Mich.
TURNER, Orville L., Sgt., No. 1 Rose Alley, Springfield, Ohio.
WASHINGTON, Samuel, Sgt., 1902 Packard St., Springfield, Tenn.

FIFTH ROW:
WHITE, George A., Sgt., 62 East 114th St., New York, N. Y.
WHITE, Herbert L., Sgt., 109 22nd North, Seattle, Wash.
WILLIAMS, Howard J., Sgt., 136 Lexington Ave., Brooklyn, N. Y.
WIMBUSH, Wedon, Sgt., Rt. 2, Box 68-A, Danville, Va.
ASBURY, Eddie, Cpl., 843 So. 13th St., Baton Rouge, La.
BELLE, H. O., Cpl., 425 Putnam Ave., Brooklyn, N. Y.

SIXTH ROW:
BETHEA, Floyd H., Cpl., P. O. Box 234, Lotta, S. C.
BOWMAN, Howard S., Cpl., 532 Doe St., Danville, Va.
BREWER, Lovejoy, Cpl., 305 Crescent St., Hopkinsville, Ky.
BROWN, George R., Cpl., 1427 William St., Harrisburg, Pa.
CARR, Timothy D., Cpl., 1306 S. Ninth St., Paducah, Ky.
CAVITT, Earl H., Cpl., 97 Adams St., Buffalo, N. Y.

SEVENTH ROW:
COGER, Wallace E., Cpl., 1018 West Brown St., Milwaukee, Wis.
COKELAY, Hubert J., Cpl., 4518 Jamaica St., Dallas, Tex.
COLEMAN, Wayne A., Cpl., 523 Lincoln Park Dr., Cincinnati, Ohio.
CUMMINGS, Sidney J., Cpl., 605 W. Central Ave., St. Paul, Minn.
DAVIS, Charlie H. J., Cpl., Windsor St., Atlanta, Ga.
DEAS, Dan, Cpl., 8 Moultrie Court, Charleston, S. C.

EIGHTH ROW:
DOUGLAS, Carl F., Cpl., 4232 St. Ferdinand, St. Louis, Mo.
FISHER, Harrison E., Cpl., Washington, D. C.
FULMER, Ira, Cpl., 6235 St. Lawrence Ave., Chicago, Ill.
GARNES, Paul, Cpl., 665 Delaware Ave., Columbus, Ohio.
GOODING, Edward, Cpl., 517 W. Wright St., Pensacola, Fla.
GORDON, Cornelious, Cpl., Barnabus, W. Va.

NINTH ROW:
GRANGER, Edward, Cpl., 419 W. Earlham Terr., Philadelphia, Pa.
GREEN, Clifford, Cpl., Rt. 1, Box 107-B, Franklin, La.
GREEN, Clifford S., Cpl., 5020 Brown St., Philadelphia, Pa.
HAUGHTON, Henry D., Cpl., 1914 N. Mervine St., Philadelphia, Pa.
HENDERSON, Shields A., Cpl., 1110 Baker St., Frisco, Calif.
HENDERSON, Wellington, Cpl.

TENTH ROW:
HINTON, David M., Cpl., 1308 E. Fourth St., Winston-Salem, N. C.
HUTCHESON, James A., Cpl., 825 University Pl., Chattanooga, Tenn.
ISON, John H., Cpl., 374 Henry St., S.W., Atlanta, Ga.
JACKSON, Claude D., Cpl., 218 Rondo Ave., St. Paul, Minn.
JONES, Leslie L., Cpl., 538 Oklahoma Ave., N.E., Washington, D. C.
KELKER, Alfred, Cpl., 1212 W. Eads St., Urbana, Ill.

602ND AIR ENGINEERING SQUADRON

FIRST ROW:
KENDRICKS, James W., Cpl., 1349 Chestnut St., Tampa, Fla.
KILGORE, Alphus A., Cpl., 1448½ Shilby St., Louisville, Ky.
KING, James B., Cpl., 127 N. Cherry St., Forrest City, Ark.
KOGER, Herman E., Cpl., 4631 Indiana Ave., Chicago, Ill.
LEFTWICH, Nathaniel B., Cpl., Box 385, White Sulphur Springs, W. Va.
LEWIS, Booker, Cpl., 124 Dunbeith Ave., Winston-Salem, N. C.

SECOND ROW:
MALONE, Edward, Cpl., 92 Walnut St., Buffalo, N. Y.
MANNING, Arthur F., Cpl., 55-W 129th St., New York, N. Y.
MORGAN, Leon M., Cpl., Box 100, Camden, S. C.
PARROTT, James, Cpl., 716 Gresham Pl., N.W., Washington, D. C.
PETERSON, Thomas H., Cpl., 258 Visger Rd., River Rouge, Mich.
PINKETT, William H., Cpl., 2650 Gilpin St., Denver, Colo.

THIRD ROW:
QUINTON, Harry A., Cpl., 506 Ward St., Salisbury, Md.
SAMUELS, Harold O., Cpl.
SIMMONS, Henry L., Cpl., 3121 Giles Ave., Chicago, Ill.
STERRETT, Wendell J., Cpl., 533 East Marion St., Princeton, Ill.
STROUD, William E., Cpl., 2529 Olive St., Kansas City, Mo.
TANKSLEY, Frank E., Cpl., 1225 Florence St., Augusta, Ga.

FOURTH ROW:
TATE, Robert H., Jr., Cpl., 1127 North Dakota Ave., Soux Falls, S. D.
TAYLOR, Paul, Cpl., 9904 People St., Memphis, Tenn.
THOMAS, J. E., Cpl., 1803 Granger St., Houston, Tex.
WADE, Willie, Cpl., 634 W. 41st St., Savannah, Ga.
WALKER, Aaron L., Cpl., 4634 Hasting St., Detroit, Mich.
WALKER, James, Cpl., Durham, N. C.

FIFTH ROW:
WARD, George H., Cpl., 789 East 166th St., Bronx, N. Y.
WATSON, Matthew R., Cpl., 102 North Michigan Ave., Atlantic City, N. J.
WELTON, George F., Cpl., 1710 Rodmen St., Philadelphia, Pa.
WHETSTONE, Levarn C., Cpl., 520 N. Holly St., Philadelphia, Pa.
WILLIAMS, Clarence, Cpl., 106 High St., S.W., Atlanta, Ga.
WILLIAMS, Martin C., Cpl., 2506 East 33rd St., Cleveland, Ohio.

SIXTH ROW:
WILSON, Charles E., Cpl., Rt. 7, Cleveland Rd., Lexington, Ky.
YOUNG, John T., Cpl., 1719 W. Franklin St., Baltimore, Md.
BETTS, Charles D., Pfc., 2492 Washington St., Boston, Mass.
BROWN, Christopher, Pfc., 458 Monterey Ave., Washington, D. C.
CHENIER, Charles C., Pfc., Oakland, Calif.
DOLEMAN, Foster, Pfc., R. R., Box 7, Berryville, Va.

SEVENTH ROW:
DUFFY, Henry, Pfc., 10919 Compton Ave., Los Angeles, Calif.
EDMONDSON, Robert, Pfc., 1139 E. Long St., Columbus, Ohio.
FIELDS, Ernest, Pfc., 3838 Brush St., Detroit, Mich.
FOSTER, Oliver T., Pfc., 1603 Chicon St., Austin, Tex.
FRAZIER, Albert L., Pfc., 1605 N. Howard St., Philadelphia, Pa.
HOLLEY, Earl H., Pfc., 6506 Winslow St., Pittsburgh, Pa.

EIGHTH ROW:
HOWARD, Newton, Pfc., Rt. 5, Box 306, Rock Hill, S. C.
HUTCHINSON, Frank D., Pfc., 111 Ozone St., Atlanta, Ga.
KEYS, James H., Pfc., 296 10th St., No., St. Petersburg, Fla.
LEWIS, Matthew H., Pfc., 1431 Lead St., Norfolk, Va.
LONG, Gordon R., Pfc., 100 Honeysuckle Ct., Day Village, Dundalk, Mo.
MERRIWETHER, George H., Pfc., 4135-A Finney Ave., St. Louis, Mo.

NINTH ROW:
PARHAM, Pat O., Pfc., Sunrise Ave., Bridgehampton, N. Y.
PHARR, Maurice, Pfc., 240 W. Black St., Rock Hill, S. C.
RILEY, Owen V., Pfc., 1619 N. Alcaning St., Pensacola, Fla.
SAILES, Oscar, Pfc., Birmingham, Ala.
WILKINSON, Hercules, Pfc., 833 Beckwith St., S.W., Atlanta, Ga.
BURNELL, James A., Pvt., 1419 10th St., N.W., Washington, D. C.

TENTH ROW:
LEAKE, Dillard A., Pvt., 376 Bainbridge St., Brooklyn, N. Y.
MURRAY, Dickson C., Pvt., New Gulf, Tex.
REYNOLDS, H., Pvt., 3879 Seventh Ave., Sacramento, Calif.
HARRISON, F. J., Jr., 5348 Long Beach Ave., Los Angeles, Calif.
McLEOD, Odell, Rt. 2, Box 5, Union Springs, Ala.

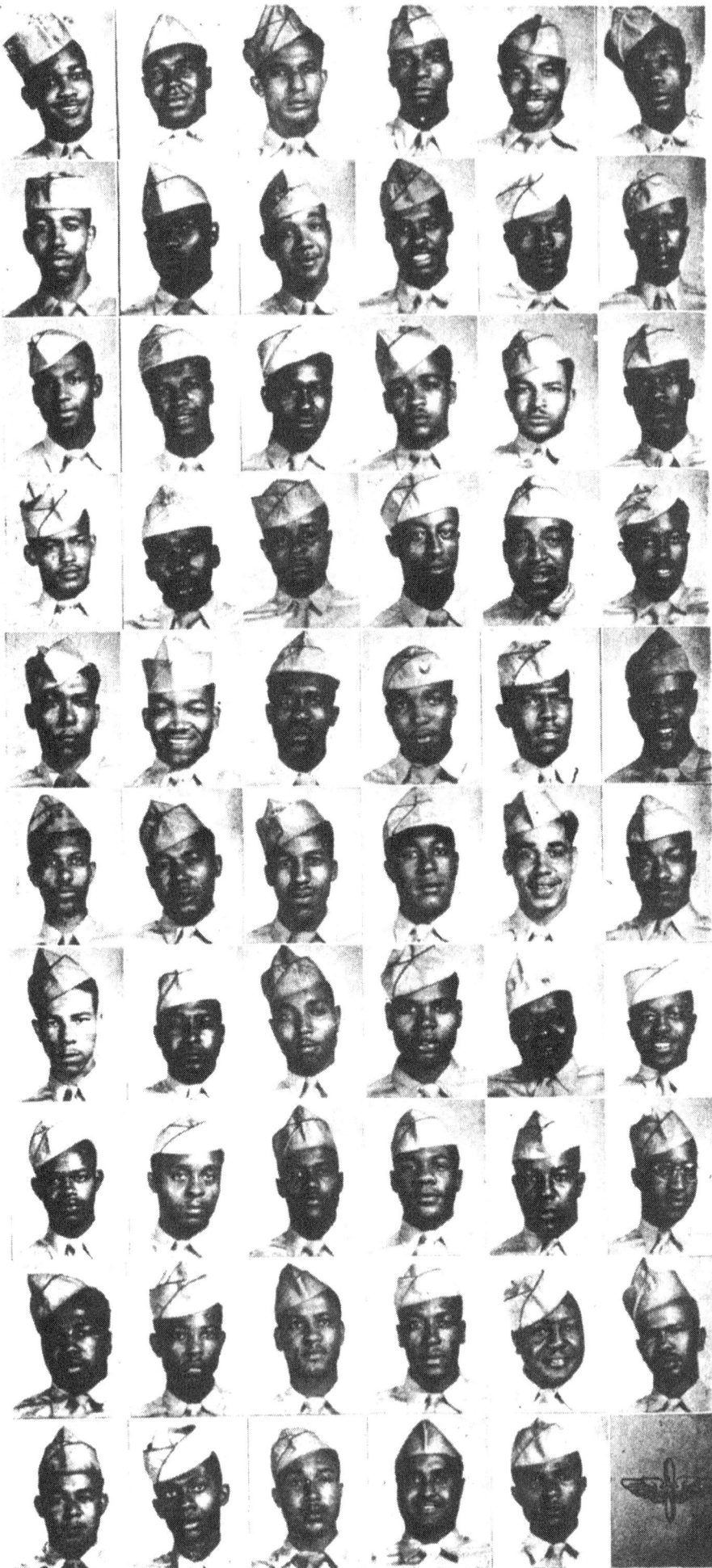

DAVID L. WARD
Warrant Officer (jg)
Bandleader

766TH ARMY AIR FORCES BAND

FIRST ROW:

ELLIS, James L., S/Sgt., 708 Seventh St., Crossett, Ark.
CARSON, Eddie, Sgt., 1314 So. Edith St., Albuquerque, N. Mex.
JOHNSON, Walter, Sgt., 146 Sylvan Ave., Asbury Park, N. J.
LEGGETT, Laurence L., Sgt., 503 W. Shattuck St., Brazil, Ind.

SECOND ROW:

NORMAN, Lamarr, Sgt., 31 Walnut St., Buffalo, N. Y.
BEES, Walter, Cpl., 1170 Dean St., Brooklyn, N. Y.
CARTER, Emmett A., Cpl., 3029 Lambdin Ave., St. Louis, Mo.
FITZGERALD, Alphonso, Cpl., 4014 St. Ferdinand St., St. Louis, Mo.
LAWRENCE, Howard, Jr., Cpl., 7826 Forshey St., New Orleans, La.
WOODSON, Albert, Cpl., 1122 Kerr Ave., Memphis, Tenn.

THIRD ROW:

COBBS, George E., T/5, 1604 Avenue T., Birmingham, Ala.
COLBERT, James L., Pfc., 3432 Webster Ave., Pittsburgh, Pa.
HARRIS, Matthew, Pfc., 148 Adams St., Buffalo, N. Y.
PALMER, Raymond M., Pfc., 5840 Hazlett Ave., Detroit, Mich.
SAUNDERS, Vertna L., Pfc., 3817-A Windsor Pl., St. Louis, Mo.
SMITH, Charles, Pfc., 42 Wanser Ave., Inwood, L. I., N. Y.

FOURTH ROW:

VAN BURAEN, George I., Pfc., 607 Washington St., Hampton, Va.
ALEXIS, Joseph E., Pvt., 1531 W. 111th St., Chicago, Ill.
CURRY, Carleton, Pvt., 3817-A Windsor Pl., St. Louis, Mo.
GREEN, Jerome G., Sr., Pvt., 320 N. Rocheblave St., New Orleans, La.
JOHNSON, Daniel, Pvt., 173 Monroe St., Aliquippa, Pa.
LEONARD, Walter W., Pvt., 2009 E. 24th St. Terr., Kansas City, Mo.

FIFTH ROW:

LOCKHART, Earl, Pvt., 659 Hancock St., Brooklyn, N. Y.
SIMMS, Arthur W., Pvt., 10 N. State St., Painesville, Ohio.
TAYLOR, Samuel B., Pvt., 39 Elmwood Ave., Montclair, N. J.
WOODS, Irvin L., Pvt., 1816 Cora Ave., St. Louis, Mo.

MARGARET G. ALLEN
Second Lieutenant
Adjutant

SQUADRON A

118TH ARMY AIR FORCES BASE UNIT

FIRST ROW:

GAY, Minnie B., I/Sgt., 2328 Catherine St., Philadelphia, Pa.
WARD, Rebecca, S/Sgt., 10-12 West 98th St., New York, N. Y.
WILSON, Amelia R., Sgt., 536½ East Park Ave., Savannah, Ga.
GRAY, Jessie M., Cpl.
LITTLE, Sara B., Cpl., Rt. 1, Box 55, Mill Spring, N. C.
ROGERS, Estella, Cpl., 5 K. P. Moore's Lane, Macon, Ga.

SECOND ROW:

VAIDEN, Katie F., Cpl., 184 Court St., Welch, W. Va.
WILSON, Sandy A., Cpl., 347 Dison Ave., Memphis, Tenn.
BLAKEY, Mary G., Pfc., 101 N. Yewdall St., Philadelphia, Pa.
BROOKS, Laura A., Pfc., 533 North Church St., Moorestown, N. J.
CHEATHAM, Grace E., Pfc., 2307 Carrington St., Richmond, Va.
COOPER, Mae D., Pfc., 343 E. Garfield Blvd., Chicago, Ill.

THIRD ROW:

HEARD, Willina I., Pfc., 3410 Rhodes Ave., Chicago, Ill.
JOHNSON, Jeannette T., Pfc., 4756 Langley Ave., Chicago, Ill.
NEALY, Edna O., Pfc., 3721 South Parkway, Chicago, Ill.
WILLIAMS, Frances H., Pfc., 845 Ella Ave., Kansas City, Kan.
WYNN, Clara K., Pfc., 106 E. Gale St., Edenton, N. C.
ALFORD, Theresa F., Pvt., 6662 Frankstown Ave., Pittsburgh, Pa.

FOURTH ROW:

ANDERSON, Ora L., Pvt., 4001 Mainer St., Flint, Mich.
ASKEW, Gloria W., Pvt., 204-38 45th Rd., Bayside, New York, N. Y.
BAILEY, Bettie, Pvt., 24 W. 135th St., New York, N. Y.
BARNES, Louise N., Pvt., 306 St. James Pl., Brooklyn, N. Y.
BARRETT, Romine E., Pvt., 217 Macon St., Brooklyn, N. Y.
BONNER, Lois, Pvt., 135 Albany Ave., Brooklyn, N. Y.

FIFTH ROW:

BOOKER, Lula M., Pvt.
BURKE, Eloise F., Pvt., Rt. 1, Lowell, Ohio.
CAROTHERS, Jacqueline L., Pvt., 1429 Frendley Ave., East St. Louis, Ill.
CARTER, Virginia B., Pvt., 966 W. Eighth St., Jacksonville, Fla.
CLARK, Doris E., Pvt., 380 Halsey St., Brooklyn, N. Y.
CLAY, Tena J., Pvt., 933 48th Ave., Meridian, Miss.

SIXTH ROW:

DANIELS, Thelma, Pvt., 2926 Sheridan, St. Louis, Mo.
DAVIS, Estella N., Pvt., Rt. 1, Box 3, Morgan, Ga.
DESSAU, Annabelle, Pvt., 633 Clifford St., Portsmouth, Va.
DRAPER, Saralie, Pvt., East Lake St., Middletown, Del.

SQUADRON A

FIRST ROW:
DURHAM, Mabei, Pvt., Rt. 3, Box 355, Kingston, N. Y.
EDWARDS, Katherine B., Pvt., 714 E. 48th St., Chicago, Ill.
FORD, Elnora E., Pvt., 177 N. Champion Ave., Apt. A., Columbus, Ohio.
CARTER, Merle Jean, Pvt., 3830 Victory Blvd., Portland, Ore.
GAY, June S., Pvt., 5844 So. Michigan Ave., Chicago, Ill.
GEARY, Naomi S., Pvt., 1511 N. Eighth St., Philadelphia, Pa.

SECOND ROW:
GORE, Una Mae, Pvt., 55 Bristol St., Cambridge, Mass.
GRACE, Jackie L., Pvt., 418th E. 40th St., Chicago, Ill.
GRAY, Ada C., Pvt., 684 N. 34th St., Philadelphia, Pa.
GREENE, Mable J., Pvt., 734 South 22nd St., Philadelphia, Pa.
HALL, Tharon C., Pvt., 613 So. Campbell St., Daytona Beach, Fla.
HARRISON, Bertha M., Pvt., 80 Chilton St., Montgomery, Ala.

THIRD ROW:
HARRIS, Ruth M., Pvt., 1440 Brady Ave., East St. Louis, Ill.
HENDERSON, Elizabeth, Pvt., 1017 Foraker Ave., Cincinnati, Ohio.
HIGGINS, Johnnie D., Pvt., 1029 W. Broad St., Albany, Ga.
HODGE, Imogene C., Pvt., 2019-E Third Ave., Denver, Colo.
HARGROVES, Eve S., Pvt., 231 N. 21st St., New York, N. Y.
JACKSON, Esther H., Pvt., 89 Bell St., 71 S.E., Atlanta, Ga.

FOURTH ROW:
JEFFRIES, Ruth, Pvt.
JOHNSON, Ella Marie, Pvt., 635 Greenwood St., Decatur, Ill.
JOHNSON, Helen W., Pvt., 1230 Second St., S.E., Canton, Ohio.
JOHNSON, Henrietta, Pvt., 519 S. Linwood Ave., Evansville, Ind.
JOHNSON, Rosie F., Pvt., 1706 Bulover Pl., Indianapolis, Ind.
JONES, Lillie M., Pvt., 2418 N. Alder St., Philadelphia, Pa.

FIFTH ROW:
KING, Eva, Pvt., 1031 Camden Ave., Columbus, Ohio.
KING, Marion E., Pvt., 11 Market St., Palmyra, N. J.
LANIER, Thelma, Pvt., 3905 Guthrie St., East Chicago, Ind.
LAWRENCE, Dorothy E., Pvt., 92 St. Nicholas Ave., Apt. B, New York, N. Y.
McBRIDE, Helen V., Pvt., 440 S. Christian St., Lancaster, Pa.
McDUDLEY, Rosetta, Pvt., 109 E. 49th St., Chicago, Ill.

SIXTH ROW:
MEDLOCK, Sarah F., Pvt.
MERRIWEATHER, Aldora, Pvt., 986 Farnsworth, Detroit, Mich.
MOORE, Jacqueline B., Pvt., 1901 15th St., Washington, D. C.
OWENS, Elaine G., Pvt.
PARKS, Doris, Pvt., 1118 E. Hill St., Charlotte, N. C.
POWERS, Daisy L., Pvt., 403-485 Western Ave., Atlanta, Ga.

SEVENTH ROW:
PRIDE, Jacqueline, Pvt., 2939 Michigan Ave., Chicago, Ill.
REY, Lucinda C., Pvt., 656 Monroe St., Brooklyn, N. Y.
ROBERTS, Fredrica V., Pvt., 724 So. 19th St., Philadelphia, Pa.
SCOTT, Mary A., Pvt., 6038 Epworth Blvd., Detroit, Mich.
SEAY, Rosa Lee, Pvt., 418 N. Sennee Ave., Indianapolis, Ind.
SHARPE, Rosabelle, Pvt., 2256 N. Camac St., Philadelphia, Pa.

EIGHTH ROW:
SHORT, Dorothy M., Pvt.
SMITH, Francis, Pvt., 10964 Graps, St., Los Angeles, Calif.
STANLEY, Muriel W., Pvt., 11 Irvin St., Montclair, N. Y.
STYLES, Ella J., Pvt., 110 Moore St., Lexington, Va.
THOMAS, Dora E., Pvt., 8 St., Altavista, Va.
TUCKER, Ailine A., Pvt.

NINTH ROW:
CHASE, Vernell R., Pvt.
WALKER, Beatrice C., Pvt., 311 N. 10th St., Darby, Pa.
WATKINS, Helen E., Pvt., 2120 East 30th St., Cleveland, Ohio.
WATSON, Louella E., Pvt., 248 No. Broadway, Aurora, Ill.
WATSON, Sadie C., Pvt., 1425 Linden St., Augusta, Ga.
WELLS, Julia E., Pvt., 511 S. Church St., Decatur, Ill.

TENTH ROW:
WHITE, Mary, Pvt., 126 Newton St., Newark, N. J.
WILLIAMS, Elvira, Pvt., 3714 So. Lake Park, Chicago, Ill.
WILLIAMS, Franceis, Pvt., 2773 Eighth Ave., New York, N. Y.
YOUNTZ, Marie L., Pvt., 3721 N. Bouvier St., Philadelphia, Pa.

THOMAS J. BUSTER, JR.
First Lieutenant
Commanding

HARRY B. ANDERSON
Captain
Flight Surgeon

GEORGE P. SCHANCK, JR.
Captain
Neuropsychiatrist

ALFRED E. THOMAS, JR.
Captain
Flight Surgeon

JAMES A. WALKER
Captain
Assistant Base Chaplain

KARL W. CARTER
First Lieutenant
Dental Officer

JAMES F. DEAL
First Lieutenant
Dental Officer

JAMES C. FLOWERS
First Lieutenant
Intelligence Officer

HARRISON C. JOHNSON
First Lieutenant
Chief of Dental Clinic

CHARLES A. NEWSOME
First Lieutenant
Dental Surgeon

S Q U A D R O N B

FIRST ROW:
ARNETT, Jordan E., S/Sgt., 781 Bayard Ave., St. Louis, Mo.
FARMER, Lawrence C., S/Sgt., 1715 E. Colfax Ave., Denver. Colo.
GARRISON, Marshall, S/Sgt., 1001 Howard St., Vicksburg, Miss.
HALL, Kinslow W., S/Sgt., 721½ Poland Ave., Youngstown, Ohio.
O'BERRY, Benny L., S/Sgt., 1474 N.W. Fifth Pl., Miami, Fla.
PUGH, George B., S/Sgt., 1415 Webster Ave., Pittsburgh, Pa.

SECOND ROW:
BIRNEL, Zoroastro A., Sgt., 246 Manhattan Ave., New York, N. Y.
BOWERS, Joseph P., Sgt, 199 Oakwood Pl., Orange, N. J.
BRANCH, Albert, Jr., Sgt., 963-B Stalkesway, Alameda, Calif.
CHEATHAM, Melvin P., Sgt., Pittsburgh, Pa.
LETSON, Edward, Sgt., 97 Chestnut St., Atlanta, Ga.
MYLES, James T., Sgt., 1121 Fairmont St., N.W., Washington, D. C.

THIRD ROW:
ALLEN, Lloyd E., Cpl., Box 434, Linden, Ala.
ANDREWS, James C., Cpl., 1247 E. 25th St., Los Angeles, Calif.
ELLINGTON, William D., Cpl., 1332 Ellis St., San Francisco, Calif.
HEWITT, Rufus I., Cpl., Rt. 1, Covin, Ala.
JOHNSON, Tom, Jr., Cpl., 565 Henrietta St., Macon, Ga.
MACK, General G., Cpl., 1529 W. 25th Ave., Gary, Ind.

FOURTH ROW:
McSWAIN, Erven, Cpl., 2221 Seward Plaza, Omaha, Neb.
MITCHELL, Ellis E., Cpl., 103 Seventh St., Beckley, W. Va.
MOSLEY, Norris, Cpl., 1343 Jonesboro Rd., Atlanta, Ga.
NANCE, Charles T. M., Cpl., 228 Dakota St., Dayton, Ohio.
NEWBY, George P., Cpl., 1008 Park St., Elizabeth City, N. C.
WALKER, Henry, Cpl., 1224 Young St., Middletown, Ohio.

FIFTH ROW:
BROWN, Irvin E., Pfc., 114 E. 107th St., New York, N. Y.
COKELY, Clarence, Pfc., 732 Pulliam St., Talladega, Ala.
DABNEY, James T., Pfc., 942 Ivy Ave., Newport News, Va.
DAVIS, Albert K., Pfc., 6222 Eberhart Ave., Chicago, Ill.
FARLEY, Matthew, Pfc., 1032 Grove Pl., Chattanooga, Tenn.
SMITH, William B., Pfc., 320 W. 115th St., New York, N. Y.

THOMAS HAUGABROOKS
Second Lieutenant
Adjutant

ROLAND M. BROWN
Second Lieutenant

★

S Q U A D R O N   C

★

FIRST ROW:

GREEN, William A., 1/Sgt., 634 So. Prairie St.,, Jacksonville, Ill.
BUTLER, Washington, Sgt., 937 26th St., Washington, D. C.
COUNCIL, Grover C., Sgt., 128 W. 117th St., New York, N. Y.
PARKER, Joseph J., Sgt., 510 Bloomfield Ave., Newark, N. J.
GILLYARD, Richard, Sgt., 3001 Sounder St., Camden, N. J.

SECOND ROW:

ARMSTEAD, Jesse, Cpl., 1105 Allison Ave., Chandler, Okla.
EVERETT, George H., Cpl., 300 Railroad Ave., Hackensack, N. J.
QUANDER, Edward, Cpl., 761 19th St., N.E., Washington, D. C.
GRAY, John P., Pfc., 128 Atkins Ave., Asbury Park, N. J.
HODGE, Samuel K., Pfc., 123 Kinilworth Ave., Detroit, Mich.

THIRD ROW:

LEE, Parker, S., Pfc. 325 Ridgewood Ave., Newark, N. J.
McCLINTON, Fred C., Pfc., 522 S. Wahsotch Ave., Colorado
    Springs, Colo.
MITCHELL, Eddie, Pfc., 310 Harding Ave., Lake Wales, Fla.
SHEPHERD, Joseph E., Pfc., 2370 E. 79th St., Cleveland, Ohio.
KIZZEE, Ozziee C., Pvt.

FOURTH ROW:

McVEY, Franklin G., Pvt., 813 Olive St., Concordia, Kan.
REELS, Chester A., Pvt., 16 Noyes St., Apponaug, R. I.
WALTON, William H., Pvt., 624 Shelby St., Sanesville, Ohio.
WILLIAMS, John, Pvt., 147 Eagle St., Buffalo, N. Y.

SQUADRON D

★

EDWARD K. NICHOLS
First Lieutenant
Commanding

WILLIAM R. MING, JR.
Captain
Base Legal Officer

FIRST ROW:

NICKERSON, Daniels, I/Sgt., 499 West 158th St., New York, N. Y.
MATHIS, Charles E., S/Sgt., 323 Walnut St., Rockford, Ill.
NEALY, Johnson A., S/Sgt., 3721 S. Parkway, Apt. 41 First, Chicago, Ill.
GIBBS, Harold P., Sgt., 109-44 143rd St., Jamaica, N. Y.
JACKSON, Charles E., Sgt., 2716 Stoddard St., St. Louis, Mo.

SECOND ROW:

JEFFERSON, William A., Sgt., 4637 West Minister Ave., Philadelphia, Pa.
JENKINS, William M., Sgt., 837 W. 28th St., Indianapolis, Ind.
JOHNSON, Benjamin T., Sgt., 46 Mayflower St., Pittsburgh, Pa.
McCOWAN, Howard P., Sgt., 211 Mt. Vernon St., Detroit, Mich.
OLIVER, Edgar, Sgt.

THIRD ROW:

PERKINS, Wentz S., III, Sgt., 4488 24th St., Detroit, Mich.
RICHARDSON, Frederick T., Sgt., West Woodward Ave., Big Rapids, Mich.
ROBERSON, Ray M., Sgt., 612 E. Fifth St., Coffeyville, Kan.
ROBINSON, Clinton E., Sgt., 2131 St. Albans St., Philadelphia, Pa.
ROBINSON, Jeff, Jr., Sgt., 823 East 166th St., Apt. 3-B, Bronx, N. Y.

FOURTH ROW:

VAUGHAN, Simon, Sgt., 1108 St. Peter St., Richmond, Va.
ATHEY, Elliott W., Cpl., 702 N. Preston St., Philadelphia, Pa.
BARNES, Lowry C., Cpl., 1226 Irving St., N.W., Washington, D. C.
BARRETT, Albert W., Cpl., 2101 Denison St., Muskogee, Okla.
BRECKENRIDGE, Walter L., Cpl., 509 21st St., New Orleans, La.

FIFTH ROW:

DAVIS, Lonnie, Cpl., 2411 N. Mississippi Ave., Portland, Ore.
DEW, John E., Cpl., 4549-A McMillian, St. Louis, Mo.
FULTON, Edward J., Cpl., 1057 E. Long St., Columbus, Ohio.
HERRING, D. E., Jr., Cpl., Rt. 2, Box 59, Lucy, Tenn.
JOHNSON, Silas, Jr., Cpl., 618 E. 38th St., Los Angeles, Calif.

SIXTH ROW:

LIVINGSTON, William A., Cpl., 909 East 102nd St., Cleveland, Ohio.
LONGUS, Ralph, Cpl., 110 N. 11th Ave., Marshalltown, Iowa.
MATTHIS, Robert J., Cpl., Box 329, Jefferson, Tex.
McKNIGHT, James, Cpl., 138 Winter St., New Britian, Conn.
MOORE, Marion N., Cpl., 723 Sixth Ave., Nebraska City, Neb.

SEVENTH ROW:

MUSE, Forrest R., Cpl., 1305 S. Lee St., Quitman, Ga.
NOBLE, Ray A., Cpl., 1848 Third St., N.W., Washington, D. C.
WIDGENS, Ulysses, Jr., Cpl., 2118 Fitzwater St., Philadelphia, Pa.
WILKINSON, Leonard R., Sr., Cpl., 192 Oxford St., Orange, N. J.
JONES, John H., Pfc., 186 Prall St., Lexington, Ky.

EIGHTH ROW:

SIMMS, Joseph H., Pfc., 1879 Clinton Ave., Bronx, N. Y.
SMITH, Elwood, Pfc., 1007 South 16th St., Springfield, Ill.
STANLEY, R. C., Pfc., 6337 Langley Ave., Chicago, Ill.
THOMPSON, Timothy M., Pfc., 114 S. Williams, El Reno, Okla.
WILSON, Lloyd H., Pfc., 1910 N. 19th St., Philadelphia, Pa.

NINTH ROW:

WING, Wilbert G., Jr., Pfc., 135 N. 53rd St., Philadelphia, Pa.
CRAWFORD, Billy, Jr., Pvt., 608 W. 138th St., New York, N. Y.
HAMILTON, Herschell L., Pvt., 2012 N. Sixth Ave., Pensacola, Fla.
HOLTS, Robert D., Pvt., 2507 Indiana Ave., Omaha, Neb.

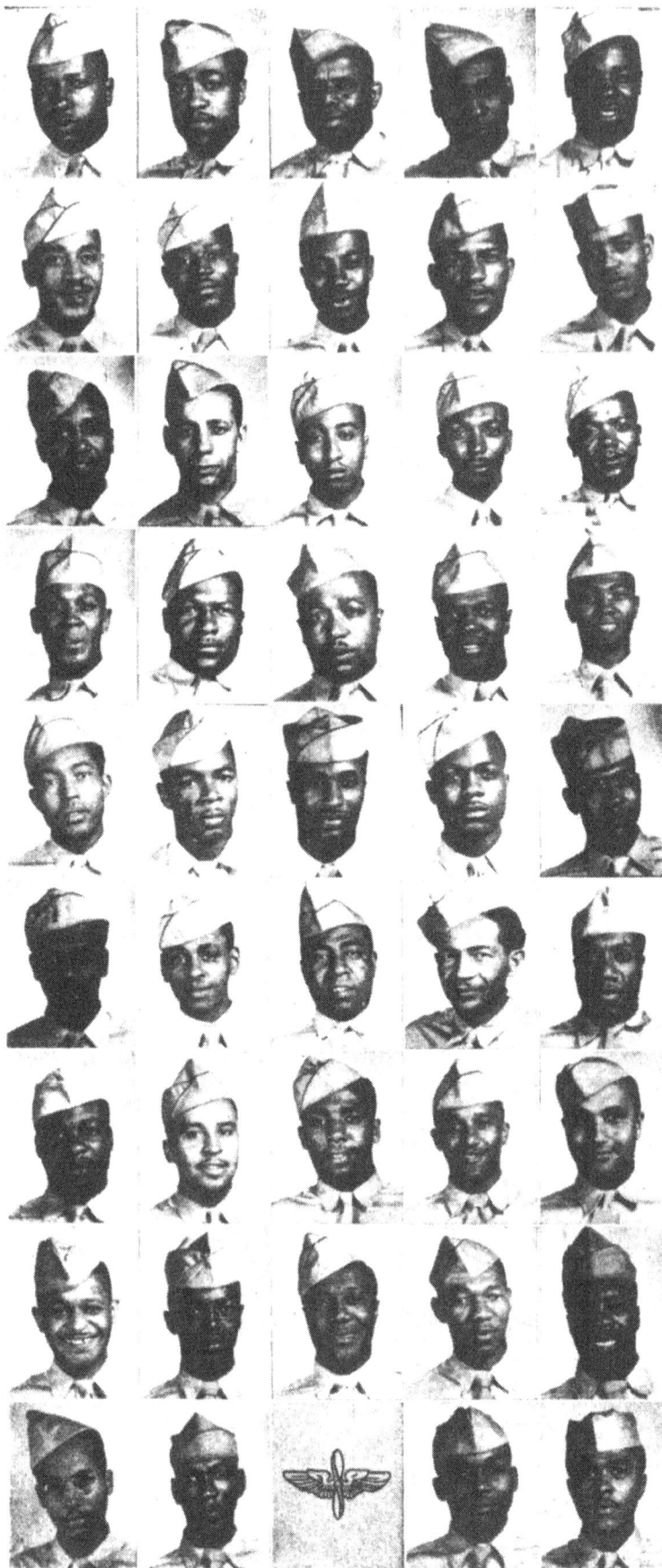

SQUADRON F

★

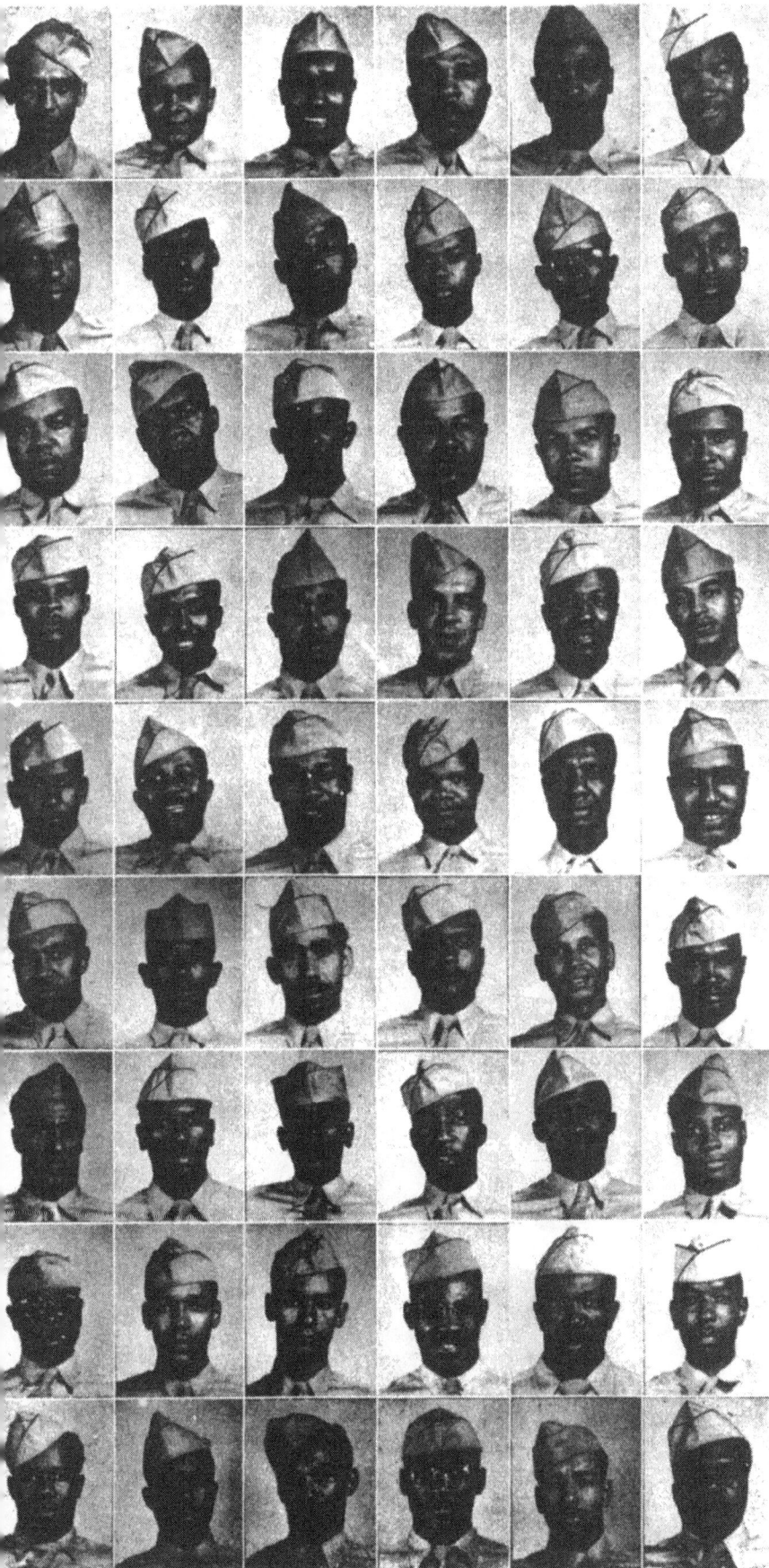

JACK D. HOLSCLAW
Captain
Assistant Base Operations
Officer

JOHN H. DUREN
Captain
Director of Supply and
Maintenance

FIRST ROW:
HATCHETT, Stokes, Jr., T/Sgt., 427 E. 43rd St., Los Angeles, Calif.
WALKER, Raymond, T/Sgt., 1424 Crusado Lane, Apt, 169, Los Angeles, Calif.
COY, Lorraine, S/Sgt., 1206 S. 21st, Muskogee, Okla.
ALLEN, Mack W., Sgt., 607 E. 62nd St., Chicago, Ill.
FORD, Clyde, Sgt., 116 Church St., Birmingham, Ala.
HECKERD, Charles, Sgt., 1217 Crofton St., Shreveport, La.

SECOND ROW:
HUNTE, William K., Sgt., 333 Tompkins Ave., Brooklyn, N. Y.
LEGGETTE, Jaymes, Sgt., 11 Torrence St., Pittsburgh, Pa.
LOFTON, Edward J., Sgt., 1114 Paseo Blvd., Kansas City, Mo.
SCIPIO, Thomas, Sgt., 37 N. Redfield St., Philadelphia, Pa.
WATTS, Fred, Sgt., 3415 Stonewall, Houston, Tex.
ANTHONY, E. E., Cpl., 3683 Charleviox St., Detroit, Mich.

THIRD ROW:
BENNETT, George, Cpl., 711 Illinois Ave., Jeffersonville, Ind.
CASEY, Charles F., Cpl., 5039 Prairie Ave., Chicago, Ill.
EXBY, Albert, Cpl., 213 Buboro St., Lafayette, La.
GAULDEN, Reuben L., Cpl., 514 Jenkins St., Mansfield, La.
HOLLOWAY, Winston, Cpl., Vancouver, Wash.
HOLLOWELL, James R., Cpl., Princeton, Ky.

FOURTH ROW:
JACKSON, James, Cpl., 525 Ninth St., Birmingham, Ala.
JOYNER, Clyde P., Cpl., 2358 Progress St., Memphis, Tenn.
LANDRUM, Howard, Cpl., 600 Jonesboro Ave., Russellville, Ark.
NORSWEATHER, Emmet, Cpl., 1248 W. 18th Ave., Gary, Ind.
PARRAN, Samuel L., Cpl., Colp, Ill.
STROTHERS, Carl O., Cpl., 3510 10th St., Washington, D. C.

FIFTH ROW:
TURNER, Peter R., Cpl., 253 Governor St., Paterson, N. J.
WATERS, James P., Cpl., 330 Decatur St., Brooklyn, N. Y.
WILSON, John I., Cpl., 5525 Jay St., N.E., Washington, D. C.
BARNES, Wardell, Pfc., 4546 S. State St., Chicago, Ill.
BOLES, Clarence, Pfc., 1605 Vine St., Savannah, Ga.
CARSON, John H., Pfc., 2229 E. 49th St., Cleveland, Ohio.

SIXTH ROW:
CHRISTIAN, Kermit A., Pfc., 626 21st St., N.E., Washington, D. C.
DAVIS, C. L., Pfc., 521 N. New York Ave., Atlantic City, N. J.
DeLOACH, Tom Pfc., 917 Elliott Ave., Savannah, Ga.
GORE, Wilbert C., Pfc., 721 Maupin St., Portsmouth, Va.
GREEN, Ernest, Pfc., Rt. 1, Box 64, Ocala, Fla.
GRIFFIN, George B., Pfc., 84 Monroe St., Buffalo, N. Y.

SEVENTH ROW:
MITCHELL, Lewis F., Pfc., 2652 E. 67th St., Cleveland, Ohio.
MOSS, Calvin, Pfc., 5 Butler Court, Stratford, Conn.
NAPPER, Herman R., Pfc., 157 Harrison Ave., Brooklyn, N. Y.
NESBIT, Oliver, Pfc., 613 N. Perth St., Philadelphia, Pa.
PILLOW, C., Pfc., Halls, Tenn.
ROBISON, Cleve, Pfc., Box 47, Ruston, La.

EIGHTH ROW:
RUTLEDGE, Norman W., Pfc., 267 Tajor St., N.W., Atlanta, Ga.
BABCOCK, George T., Pvt., 2946 Merrick St., Detroit, Mich.
BANKS, J. Drexel, Pvt.
BELLE, Louis E., Pvt., 4716 S. Michigan Ave., Chicago, Ill.
BROOKS, George W., Pvt., 9343 S. State St., Chicago, Ill.
BURDINE, Roy, Pvt., 626 Coke St., Louisville, Ky.

NINTH ROW:
COCHRAN, Isom C., Pvt., 4713 Tyre St., Houston, Tex.
ELMORE, Benjamin, Pvt., 1005 N. Frankfait, Tulsa, Okla.
FREEMAN, Kermit C., Pvt., 913 Sixth St., Rock Island, Ill.
HALLOWAY, Frank, Pvt., 2262 N. Capitol Ave., Indianapolis, Ind.
HUNTER, James W., Pvt., Rt. 4, Lima, Ohio.
PRUITT, Charles B., Pvt., 241 Vollintine Ave., Memphis, Tenn.

OWEN E. HAGUE
First Lieutenant
Commanding

LEE RAYFORD
Major
Base Operations Officer

DON V. ESTILL
Captain
Assistant Base Surgeon

CLARENCE C. JAMISON
Captain
Assistant Operations Officer

DANIEL J. BAILEY
First Lieutenant
Adjutant

ALEXANDER B. ROSE
First Lieutenant
Executive and Mess Officer

DAVID J. BROWN
Second Lieutenant
Base Communications Officer

ROBERT L. CLARK
Second Lieutenant
Combat Intelligence Officer

CRAWFORD B. DOWDELL
Second Lieutenant
Aerial Gunnery Officer

WILLIAM C. PERKINS, JR.
Second Lieutenant
Gunnery Officer

F. MOORE   3830 Lincoln Lane   Robbins

★

S Q U A D R O N   G

FIRST ROW:

HARRIS, Otha B., S/Sgt., 1722 W. Walnut St., Louisville, Ky.
HOUSTON, John A., M/Sgt., 2917 Conti St., Houston, Tex.
OLIVER, Amsden C., T/Sgt., 386 S. Kilmer St., Dayton, Ohio.
GOODLOW, Albert E., S/Sgt., 1285 Hasting St., Chicago, Ill.
BERRY, Joseph, Sgt., Rt. 40, Box 59, Triadelphia, W. Va.

SECOND ROW:

BUCHANAN, David, Sgt., 1311 Avenue K, Birmingham, Ala.
GREEN, John E., Sgt., 544 Herron Ave., Pittsburgh, Pa.
JUST, C. E., Sgt., 641 So. Ninth Ave., Mt. Vernon, N. Y.
LUCK, Thomas, Sgt., Box 317, Freeman, W. Va.
McDOWELL, Elmer H., Sgt., 48 Admiral St., New Haven, Conn.

THIRD ROW:

ODUMS, Richard H., Sgt., 1814 Live Oak St., Houston, Tex.
SCOTT, William J., Jr., Sgt., 705 Oakland Ave., Kansas City, Kan.
RECTOR, Elmer R., Sgt., 140 Chalfont St., Pittsburgh, Pa.
ADAMS, Russell, Cpl., 7509 Calumet St., Swissvale, Pa.
BANKS, Robert G., Cpl., 405 Cliff St., Fairmont, W. Va.

FOURTH ROW:

BERTRAND, Arthur J., Cpl., 2508 St. Anthony St., New Orleans, La.
BRITTINGHAM, Joseph, Cpl., 76th Wesley Ave., Atlantic Highlands, N. J.
BROWN, Edmund H., Cpl., 852 Dawson St., Bronx, N. Y.
BROWN, Marion L., Cpl.
BURT, W. L., Cpl., 2575 E. 40th St., Cleveland, Ohio.

SQUADRON G

FIRST ROW:
BURTON, Wilmotte A., Cpl., 2340 Seventh Ave., New York, N. Y.
CALHOUN, Alonzo C., Cpl., 531 E. Jasper St., Tulsa, Okla.
COLLINS, Louis H., Cpl., 21 Stanger Ave., Glassboro, N. J.
DIXON, Allen H., Cpl., 2014 Annin St., Philadelphia, Pa.
FRAZIER, Roman, Jr., Cpl., 1202 McElderry Court, E. Baltimore, Md.
GARDENER, Winston, Cpl., 17357 Charest St., Detroit, Mich.

SECOND ROW:
HAWKINS, David E., Cpl., 912 N. Mount St., Baltimore, Md.
HENRY, Walter, Cpl., 321 N. Howard St., Akron, Ohio.
KENDRICK, Claborn L., Cpl., 5 Washington Terr., Cincinnati, Ohio.
MOORE, Arthur W., Cpl., 769 Jennings St., New York, N. Y.
PAXTON, Welborn, Cpl., 63 Walter Ave., Inwood, L. I., N. Y.
PEURIFOY, Otis, Cpl.

THIRD ROW:
SCHOOLER, James C., Cpl., 201 Summer St., New Albany, Miss.
SHUMATE, William M., Cpl., Boston Heights, Hudson, Ohio.
STEWART, Malcom, Cpl., 210-Q West 153rd St., New York, N. Y.
TURNER, George C., Cpl., 109 Hazel St., McGehee, Ark.
WELCH, Arthur W., Cpl., 4160-A Aldine Ave., St. Louis, Mo.
WILLIAMS, Henry E., Cpl., 924 Belle Fontaine St., Indianapolis, Ind.

FOURTH ROW:
WILLIAMS, Jesse E., Cpl., 411 N. Carey St., Baltimore, Md.
BAILEY, Herman A., Pfc.
BARNES, Matthew, Pfc., 438 Melbourne, Detroit, Mich.
BENNETT, David T., Pfc., 19 Auburn St., Boxbury, Mass.
BERRY, Varian L., Pfc., 39 Walnut Ave., Trenton, N. J.
BLACKMON, John L., Pfc., Chicago, Ill.

FIFTH ROW:
DAGINS, James H., Pfc., 441 Codorus St., York, Pa.
DIXSON, Theodore J., Pfc., 13833 Reynolds, Detroit, Mich.
DOUGHERTY, Robert C., Pfc., 119 S. Chicago St., Joliet, Ill.
EUELL, Otis, Pfc., 5645 Calumet, Chicago, Ill.
GHOLSTON, Theodore E., Pfc., 2535 537th St., Cleveland, Ohio.
GREEN, W. D., Pfc., 6120 Beechwood St., Philadelphia, Pa.

SIXTH ROW:
GREEN, James W., Pfc., 213 Lincoln St., Hampton, Va.
HAMMOND, John, Pfc., 22 W. 128th St., New York, N. Y.
KELLY, Henry C., Pfc., 733 W. Clay St., Marianna, Fla.
PICKETT, Lawrence, Pfc., 901 Walton St., St. Louis, Mo.
PIPER, George J., Pfc., 720 St. Joe St., South Haven, Mich.
RUFFIN, Kirby, Pfc., 600½ N. Main St., Wichita, Kan.

SEVENTH ROW:
SIMPSON, Melvin R., Pfc., 1540 Wilson Rd., Norfolk, Va.
SNOWDEN, W. E., Pfc., 3400 Camp St., Pittsburgh, Pa.
WARREN, Lemuel S., Pfc., 2733 E. 79th St., Cleveland, Ohio.
WILLIAMS, Frank, Pfc., Leary, Ga.
WILLIAMS, Joseph C., Pfc., 430 N. California St., Indianapolis, Ind.
YOUNG, Ervin, Pfc., 457 Theta St., Birmingham, Ala.

EIGHTH ROW:
BARNHILL, William H., Pvt., Washington, D. C.
BROWN, Gwynn, Pvt., 1824 S St., N.W., Washington, D. C.
BUCHANAN, R. J., Pvt., 1728 W. Madison St., Louisville, Ky.
DRAYTON, Galway O., Pvt.
FLETCHER, Orlando T., Pvt., 2192 Seventh Ave., New York, N. Y.
GLADDEN, Samuel, Pvt., 924 Brevard St., Baltimore, Md.

NINTH ROW:
GOLDIE, Frank C., Pvt., 42 Grand Whitlock Homes, Toledo, Ohio.
GRIFFIN, Nelson, Pvt., 5227 Westminster Ave., Philadelphia, Pa.
LEE, Ulysses S., Pvt., 9904 Natural Bridge, Bridgeton, Mo.
POULSON, Robert T., Pvt., 647 N. 33rd St., Philadelphia, Pa.
ROBERTS, James W., Pvt., 315 W. Washington St., Ocala, Fla.
ROBINSON, George T., Pvt., 2230 Scovill Ave., Cleveland, Ohio.

TENTH ROW:
SHAW, Willis S., Pvt., 1002 N. Boyce St., Gastonia, N. C.
SIMS, Stanford L., Pvt., 1351 N. Lansing Tulsa, Okla.
WILLIAMS, Branch, Pvt., 4640 Paschall Ave., Philadelphia, Pa.
WILLIAMS, John E., Pvt., 1084 William St., Elizabeth, N. J.
WILLIAMS, J. E., Pvt., 5807 Grand Ave., Cleveland, Ohio.

AERIAL VIEW OF GODMAN FIELD

477th
COMPOSITE
GROUP

Lineage: Constituted as 477th Bombardment Group (Medium) on 13 May 1943. Activated on 1 June 1943. Assigned to Third Air Force. Trained with B-26 aircraft. Inactivated on 25 August 1943. Activated on 15 June 1944. Assigned to First Air Force. Trained with B-25's. Redesignated 477th Composite Group in June 1945. Equipped with B-25's and P-47's. Inactivated on 1 July 1947.

Squadrons: 99th Fighter, 1945-1947; 616th Bombardment, 1943, 1944 - 1945; 617th Bombardment, 1943, 1944 - 1947; 618th Bombardment, 1943, 1944 - 1945; 619th Bombardment, 1943, 1944 - 1945.

Stations: MacDill Field, Florida, 1 June - 25 August 1943; Selfridge Field, Michigan, 15 January 1944; Godman Field, Kentucky, 6 May 1944; Lockbourne Army Air Base, Ohio, 13 March 1946 - 1 July 1947.

Commanders: Lieutenant Colonel Andrew O. Lerche, 1943; Colonel Robert R. Selway, Jr., 21 January 1944; Colonel Benjamin O. Davis, Jr., 21 June 1945 - 1 July 1947.

Campaigns: American Theater

Decorations: None.

Insigne: None.

616th
BOMBARDMENT
SQUADRON

Lineage: Constituted 616th Bombardment Squadron (Medium) on 13 May 1943. Activated on 1 June 1943. Inactivated on 25 August 1943. Activated on 15 January 1944. Inactivated on 22 June 1945.

Assignments: 477th Bombardment Group, 1 June - 25 August 1943. 477th Bombardment Group, 15 January 1944 - 22 June 1945.

Stations: MacDill Field, Florida, 1 June - 25 August 1943; Selfridge Field, Michigan, 15 January 1944; Godman Field, Kentucky, 6 May 1944; Sturgis Army Air Field, Kentucky, 19 June 1944; Godman Field, Kentucky, 20 July 1944; Freeman Field, Indiana, 5 March 1945; Godman Field, Kentucky, 27 April - 22 June 1945.

Aircraft: B-26, 1943. B-25, 1944 - 1945.

Operations: Training, June - August 1943, and January 1944 - June 1945.

Service Streamers: American Theater.

Campaigns: None

Decorations: None.

Emblem: On a light turquoise blue diamond, bordered dark blue, a caricatured wolf in red flight suit and helmet, seated in cockpit of dark blue caricatured aircraft, with wings, tail fin, from open bomb bay doors, all emitting white speed lines to rear (Approved 14 August 1944)

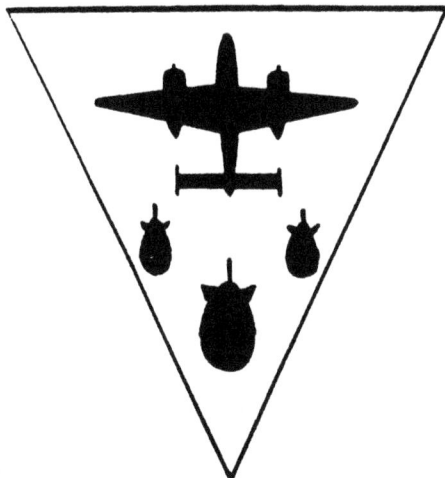

617th
BOMBARDMENT
SQUADRON

Lineage: Constituted 617th Bombardment Squadron (Medium) on 13 May 1943. Activated on 1 June 1943. Inactivated on 25 August 1943. Activated on 15 April 1944. Inactivated on 1 July 1947.

Assignments: 477th Bombardment Group, 1 June - 25 August 1943. 477th Bombard (later Composite) Group, 15 April 1944 - 1 July 1945.

Stations: MacDill Field, Florida, 1 June - 25 August 1943; Selfridge Field, Michigan, 15 April 1944; Godman Field, Kentucky, 6 May 1944; Sturgis Army Air Field, Kentucky, 22 July 1944; Godman Field, Kentucky, 23 August 1944; Freeman Field, Indiana, 26 April 1945; Lockbourne Army Air Base, Ohio, 13 March 1946 - 1 July 1947.

Aircraft: B-26, 1943. B-25, 1944 - 1947.

Operations: Training, June - August 1943, and April 1944 - July 1947.

Service Streamers: American Theater.

Campaigns: None.

Decorations: None.

Emblem: On a light turquoise blue triangle, point to base, bordered dark blue on base leg, and on sides terminating in apex triparted red, white, and blue, a dark blue plan view, silhouette, B-25 aircraft in center chief point, over three red aerial bombs, trimmed in dark blue, falling toward base point, in perspective (Approved 14 August 1944)

618th
BOMBARDMENT
SQUADRON

Lineage: Constituted 618th Bombardment Squadron (Medium) on 13 May 1943. Activated on 1 June 1943. Inactivated on 25 August 1943. Activated on 15 May 1944. Inactivated on 8 October 1945.

Assignments: 477th Bombardment Group, 1 June - 25 August 1943. 477th Bombard (later Composite) Group, 15 May 1944 - 8 October 1945.

Stations: MacDill Field, Florida, 1 June - 25 August 1943; Godman Field, Kentucky, 15 May 1944; Atterbury Army Air Field, Indiana, 2 March 1945; Godman Field, Kentucky, 27 April - 8 October 1945.

Aircraft: B-26, 1943. B-25, 1944 - 1945.

Operations: Training, June - August 1943, and May 1944 - August 1947.

Service Streamers: American Theater.

Campaigns: None.

Decorations: None.

Emblem: On a light turquoise blue rectangle, long axis horizontal, corners rounded, bordered dark blue, a caricatured yellow orange "swoose" in flight, trimmed brown, blowing a blue cannon shell from the beak, encircled by white smoke ring, and having a plexiglass turret on the back with two guns firing, proper, while dropoping a large dark blue aerialbomb with nose and tail fins dark red. All in front of a large white cloud formation; like cloud formations to dexter and sinister base. (Approved 18 August 1944)

619th
BOMBARDMENT
SQUADRON

Lineage: Constituted 619th Bombardment Squadron (Medium) on 13 May 1943. Activated on 1 June 1943. Inactivated on 25 August 1943. Activated on 27 May 1944. Inactivated on 22 June 1945.

Assignments: 477th Bombardment Group, 1 June - 25 August 1943. 477th Bombardment Group, 27 May 1944 - 22 June 1945.

Stations: MacDill Field, Florida, 1 June - 25 August 1943; Godman Field, Kentucky, 27 May 1944; Atterbury Army Air Field, Indiana, 29 August 1944; Godman Field, Kentucky, 3 January 1945; Freeman Field, Indiana, 7 March 1945; Godman Field, Kentucky, 26 April - 22 June 1945.

Aircraft: B-26, 1943. B-25, 1944 - 1945.

Operations: Training, June - August 1943, and May 1944 - June 1945.

Service Streamers: American Theater.

Campaigns: None.

Decorations: None.

Emblem: On a light turquoise blue figure in the shape of an aircraft cannon shell, bordered dark blue, a large yellow orange aerial bomb palewise, surmounted by a jagged red lightning bolt striking from a white cloud formation, edged black, in chief (Approved 18 August 1944)

Sammy Rayner (Upper Left) and his B-25 Crew

Top (left to right); Middleton, Navigator; Henderson, Co-Pilot; Hervey, Pilot.
Bottom (left to right); Jones, Tail Gunner; Hector, Radio Gunner; Starks, Engineer.

CLASS 43-K — TWIN ENGINE
TUSKEGEE ARMY AIR FIELD
DECEMBER, 1943

Left to Right Rear: Sam Lynn, Capt. Elmore Kennedy, Wendell Wells,* Willie Byrd,* Harold Brazil
Middle: Harold Hillery, Richard Highbaugh, Joseph Whiten,* Eugene Cheatham, Henry Hervey
Bottom: Lt. Fitzroy Newsom, Stewart Fulbright, Sam Black,* Amos Rogers, John Harrison

* Deceased

271

4413 WAF Squadron

1st. Lt. O. L. Crain

Lockbourne Air Force Base

Columbus

1st. Lt. V. M. Hickambottom

Ohio

M/Sgt. A. L. Bates

S/Sgt. G. Clark

S/Sgt. E. B. Dover

S/Sgt. M. E. Neal

S/Sgt. H. P. Pettigrue

S/Sgt. E. M. Phifer

S/Sgt. M. T. Sublett

S/Sgt. L. Y. Turpin

Sgt. O. M. Caver

Sgt. S. M. Dorsey (wac)

Sgt. V. L. Ford

Sgt. R. B. Gilbert

Sgt. H. N. Guy

Sgt. W. Heard

Sgt. J. T. Hynson

Sgt. D. E. Lounds

Sgt. I. Morse

Sgt. E. Rivers

Sgt. L. M. West

Cpl. M. L. Banks

Cpl. A. E. Donnie

Cpl. A. L. Ellis

Cpl. L. Wheat

Pfc. A. C Gray

Pfc. T. V. Green

Pfc. V. Hill

Pfc. M. Z. Hogan

Pfc. H. M. Jenkins

Pfc. L. M. Mitchell

Lt. Herky Perry briefs the group prior to take off. Members of the 477th shown here are: seated L to R: Lt. Toler, Capt. C. Jamison, Lt. Wm. Ellis, Lt. John Briggs, Capt. Joe Ellsberry. Standing L to R: Lt. Bynum, Lt. Blue, and Lt. Weldon Groves, seated rear. Photo taken maneuvers at Blythe, Calif., 1946.

B-25s of the 477th over the Pacific Ocean during war games held in Southern California during 1946. Group was stationed at Blythe, Calif.

L to R: Lts. R. Highbaugh, Sam Lynn, Daniel "Chappie" James, Harvey Pinkney, and Capt. Fitzroy Newsum.

Waist Gunner, shown here in B-3 Cold Weather Flight Gear.

North American B-25J Mitchell, of the 618 Bomb Squadron Godman, Field, Kentucky.

Cadets LeRoy Gillead, Everett Richardson, and Reginald Freeman at Hondo Field, Texas for navigation training.

www.ingramcontent.com/pod-product-compliance
Lightning Source LLC
Chambersburg PA
CBHW050410110426
42812CB00006BA/1850